LAO FOR BEGINNERS

LAO FOR BEGINNERS

An Introduction to the Spoken and Written Language of Laos

by Tatsuo Hoshino and Russell Marcus

Charles E. Tuttle Company: Publishers
Rutland, Vermont & Tokyo, Japan

Some of the material in this book was first published
in 1973 by Siam Communications Ltd., Bangkok,
under the title *Basic Lao*

Published by the Charles E. Tuttle Company, Inc.
of Rutland, Vermont & Tokyo, Japan
with editorial offices at
2-6 Suido 1-chome, Bunkyo-ku, Tokyo 112

First edition, 1981
First paperback edition, 1989
Fifth printing, 1997

LCC Card No. 81-50487
ISBN 0-8048-1629-8
PRINTED IN SINGAPORE

TABLE OF CONTENTS

HOW TO USE THIS BOOK

Lao for Beginners is for the person who is beginning to learn Lao, be he businessman, student, refugee worker, tourist or simply a person with Lao friends. Lao for Beginners is primarily a workbook full of exercises to help beginners practice and acquire the ability to communicate with Lao people in Lao. It is not a phrase book to scratch the surface of the Lao language. The book has been tested in classrooms and by individuals who have used it successfully to learn Lao.

Lao for Beginners was designed for people who want to learn Lao fast and communicate with Lao people in the Lao language. The book mainly teaches speaking (PART 1), although there is also a section which teaches reading (PART 3). The vocabulary in the whole text is limited to the 1,000 most frequently used words in everyday speech based on one of the author's own research in Vientiane.

The Lao words are listed in a special glossary for beginners (PART 4) which is arranged in English alphabetical order. (An English-Lao glossary is not included since the English-Lao, Lao-English Dictionary (Tuttle, 1970) is intended as a companion book to this one.)

To make the going easier, all exercises are written in phonetics which are English letters for Lao sounds. (Lao phonetics are explained in the introduction to PART 1.) As an additional aid, a review of the major features of Lao grammar is condensed into only 16 pages (including very useful tables) and is located in one place (PART 2) so that it can be read quickly and used as a reference frequently.

Everyone who already knows one language has proven his language ability. This book permits people to exercise this ability and successfully learn the Lao language.

Acknowledgements

We wish to express our sincere appreciation to the following people for their cooperation, assistance and patience in preparing this book.

To Thao Nene and Nang Chanob Pathammavong whose comments were valuable assistance in the research to analyze and record the Lao language as it is actually spoken in the Vientiane area, on which this book is based.

To Mr. Shigeo Hatsushiba who provided facilities and guidance in the techniques of manuscript preparation, to Miss Hitomi Komiya who did most of the typing and to Miss Tamami Watanabe who performed most of the mechanical work.

And finally, we wish to pay tribute to our wives and to the concept of mutual encouragement which was an essential catalyst for the realization of this work.

October, 1980

Tatsuo Hoshino
Russell Marcus

PART 1: HOW TO SPEAK LAO

PART 1: HOW TO SPEAK LAO

Introduction on Phonetics

The Lao script is a very ingenious invention; it communicates not only the sounds of words, but also the tones or pitch on which they should be spoken. Thus for example, the Lao script for the word "house" not only indicates the sound of the Lao word ("ban"), but also that this word should be spoken with a high falling tone.

Furthermore, the Lao script is a phonetic script which means that words are usually spelled the way they sound. English is not phonetic since there are many ways to spell one sound (such as "write," "right" and "rite") and also different sounds for the same letter (as for example the letter "c" in the words "cake," "church" and "cease").

Nonetheless, this ingeniousness of the Lao alphabet has its limitations since the alphabet is a modified ancient Indian script, and it cannot be read by English speakers who have not studied a course on how to read the Lao alphabet (see PART 3 of this book).

To surmount this difficulty, this book uses the phonetic system from the English-Lao: Lao-English Dictionary (Tuttle, 1970) which converts the phonetic Lao letters systematically into English character equivalents (a "phonetic" system using English letters) along with a number to indicate the tone of each syllable. The resulting phonetics for consonants and vowels together with a tone pitch chart are presented for reference in the tables on the following pages. A summary of the main features of Lao consonants, vowels and tones is given below.

1. <u>CONSONANTS</u>
   There are 33 Lao consonants (as shown on the next page) which fall into 3 groups which are distinguished by tone: namely, low, high and rising. With one exception, all the consonants in the high and rising groups have the same sound excluding tone; thus for example, there are two letters "s": a high-tone "s" and a rising-tone "s". Since their sounds are the same, this means that the number of different sounds in Lao is only 20. All of these 20 sounds exist in English,

	PHONETICS FOR CONSONANTS			
	Phonetic	Similar English sound	Tone Number	Lao Consonants
1	b	band	1	ບ
2	bp	rabbit	1	ປ
3	ch	joke	1	ຈ
4	d	deck	1	ດ
5	dt	model	1	ຕ
6	f	fish	3, 4	ຟ ຝ
7	g	girl	1	ກ
8	h	house	3, 4	ຮ ຫ
9	k	king	3, 4	ຄ ຂ
10	l(r)	list	3	ຣ
11	l	"	3, 4	ລ ຫຼ
12	m	man	3, 4	ມ ໝ
13	n	new	3, 4	ນ ໜ
14	ng	sing	3, 4	ງ ຫງ
15	ny	canyon	3, 4	ຍ ຫຍ
16	p	pen	3, 4	ພ ຜ
17	s	sail	3, 4	ຊ ສ
18	t	time	3, 4	ທ ຖ
19	w	win	3, 4	ວ ຫວ
20	y	yes	1	ຢ
21	-	-	1	ອ
	Total	20	3	33

but it may take a little practice to say some of them as initial letters (ng for example, since in English this sound is only used at the ends of words). Additionally, there is one Lao consonant letter which has no sound. It is used to start syllables which begin with a vowel sound since it is a rule for writing to begin all syllables with a consonant letter.

2. VOWELS

There are 28 Lao vowel sounds (as shown on the next page) which can be divided into 2 types: short and long vowel sounds which differ from each other only in terms of the duration over which they are pronounced. A close equivalent exists for most Lao vowel sounds. The written form of vowels depends on whether they are written as open syllables (ie, initial consonant plus vowel without a final consonant) or closed syllables (ie, initial consonant plus vowel plus final consonant); however, this feature need not concern the beginner since the phonetic is the same for a vowel in an open syllable and a closed one.

3. TONES

There are six tones in Lao: namely 3 level tones (low, mid and high), 1 rising tone and 2 falling tones (high falling and low falling). The tones are relative pitches for each speaker (as shown in the tone pitch chart below) in order to accommodate for different tonal qualities between people's voices. The six tone numbers are written together with every phonetic syllable in this book so that the syllables may be correctly sung.

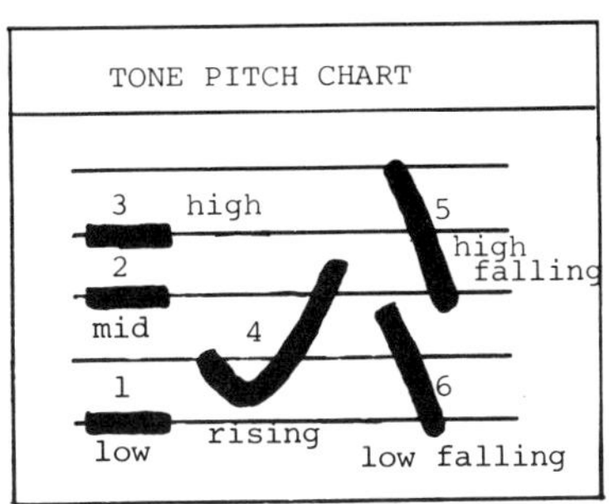

PHONETICS FOR VOWELS

	Phonetic	Similar English sound	No. of spelling variations	Lao Vowels (short and long)		
				short	short + final	
1	a:	back	2	xະ	xັx	BASIC VOWELS
2	i:	easy	1	xິ	-	
3	eu:	few *	1	xຶ	-	
4	u:	school	1	xຸ	-	
5	e:	less	2	ເxະ	ເxັx	
6	ae:	bake	2	ແxະ	ແxັx	
7	o:	flow	2	ໂxະ	xົx	
8	oh:	flaw	2	ເxາະ	xັອx	
9	er:	her	1	ເxິ		
10	ia:	asia	2	ເxັຍະ	xັຽx	DIPHTHONGS
11	ua:	fuel	2	xົວະ	xັວx	
12	eua:	fewer*	1	ເxຶອ	-	
13	ai:	life	2		ໄx | ໃx	SPECIAL VOWELS
14	ao:	out	1		ເxົາ	
15	a:m	hum	1		xໍາ	
				long	long + final	
16	a	Same as above only longer duration	1	xາ	-	BASIC VOWELS
17	i		1	xີ	-	
18	eu		1	xື	-	
19	u		1	xູ	-	
20	e		1	ເx	-	
21	ae		1	ແx	-	
22	o		1	ໂx	-	
23	oh		2	xໍ	xອx	
24	er		1	ເxີ	-	
25	ia		2	ເxັຍ	xຽx	DIPHTHONGS
26	ua		2	xົວ	xວx	
27	eua		1	ເxືອ	-	
28	oy		1		xອຍ	
	Total	28	39	24	15	

* Note: smile to approximate the Lao sound more closely.

HOW TO USE PART 1

Each of the 12 lessons in PART 1 consists of substitution exercises, vocabulary exercises and a text. The elements of these exercises are explained below. The phonetics in each exercise are the essence of this book for beginners. The Lao is presented for teachers and for students who have completed PART 3 and have learned to read Lao.

Substitution Exercises introduce Lao vocabulary in the context of sentences, one sentence pattern at a time. Box frames are used so that a sentence pattern can be varied and practiced with alternative verbs, subjects, adjectives, objects, etc. The position of words is identical in the Lao, phonetic and English blocks to permit easy comparisons.

Example:

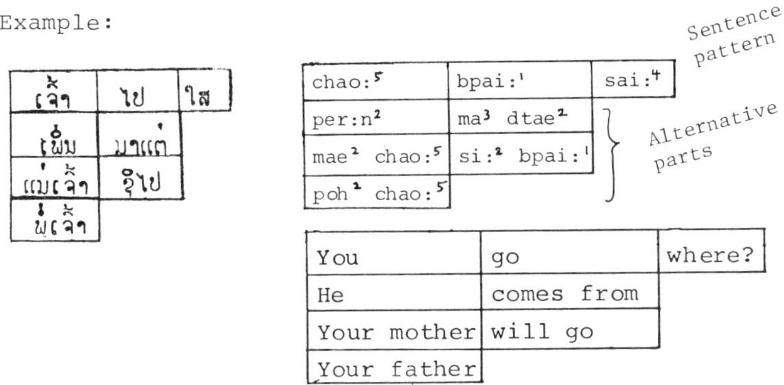

Vocabulary Exercises define the 160 most frequently used words by listing common sentences for each key word, one at a time. The position of the Lao, phonetic and English sentences is identical in each column to permit easy comparisons.

Example:

ໄປ	bpai:^{1} *Key word shown in the sentences below.*	To go
ເຈົ້າໄປໃສ	chao:^{5} bpai:^{1} sai:^{4}	Where are you going?
ແມ່ຊິໄປຕລາດ	mae^{2} si:^{2} bpai:^{1} dta:^{3} lat^{6}	Mother will go to market.
ພໍ່ໄປນາ ດຽວນີ້	poh^{2} bpai:^{1} na^{3} diaw^{1} ni^{5}	Father is going to the rice-field now.

Texts present common situations and conversations using the vocabulary and sentence patterns introduced in the exercises. Each sentence on speech is numbered the same in all 3 texts (Lao, phonetic and English) to permit easy comparisons.

Example:

1. ຄຳ ສບາຍດີ

2. ຈິດ ສບາຍດີ

3. ຄຳ ເຈົ້າຊິໄປໃສ

4. ຈິດ ຊິໄປນາ ເຈົ້າມາແຕ່ໃສ

reference number

1. Ka:m^{3}: Sa:^{3} bai^{4} di^{1}.

2. Chi:t^{3}: Sa:^{3} bai^{4} di^{1}.

3. Ka:m^{3}: Chao:^{5} si^{2} bpai:^{1} sai:^{4}?

4. Chi:t^{3}: Si^{2} bpai:^{1} na^{3}.
   Chao:^{5} ma^{3} dtae^{2} sai:^{4} ?

1. Kham: Hello.

2. Chit: Hello.

3. Kham: Where are you going?

4. Chit: I'm going to the rice-field.
   Where are you coming from?

Additional Learning Aids:

PART 1: Introduction on Phonetics is a 4-page summary of the phonetic system used to transcribe Lao words into English letters.

PART 2: Grammar Review is a 16-page summary of the major features of the Lao language. However, if you really want to learn Lao, you should rely on the exercises in PART 1 to learn how to speak Lao and on the exercises in PART 3 to learn how to read Lao.

LESSON 1: COMING AND GOING

Substitution Exercise

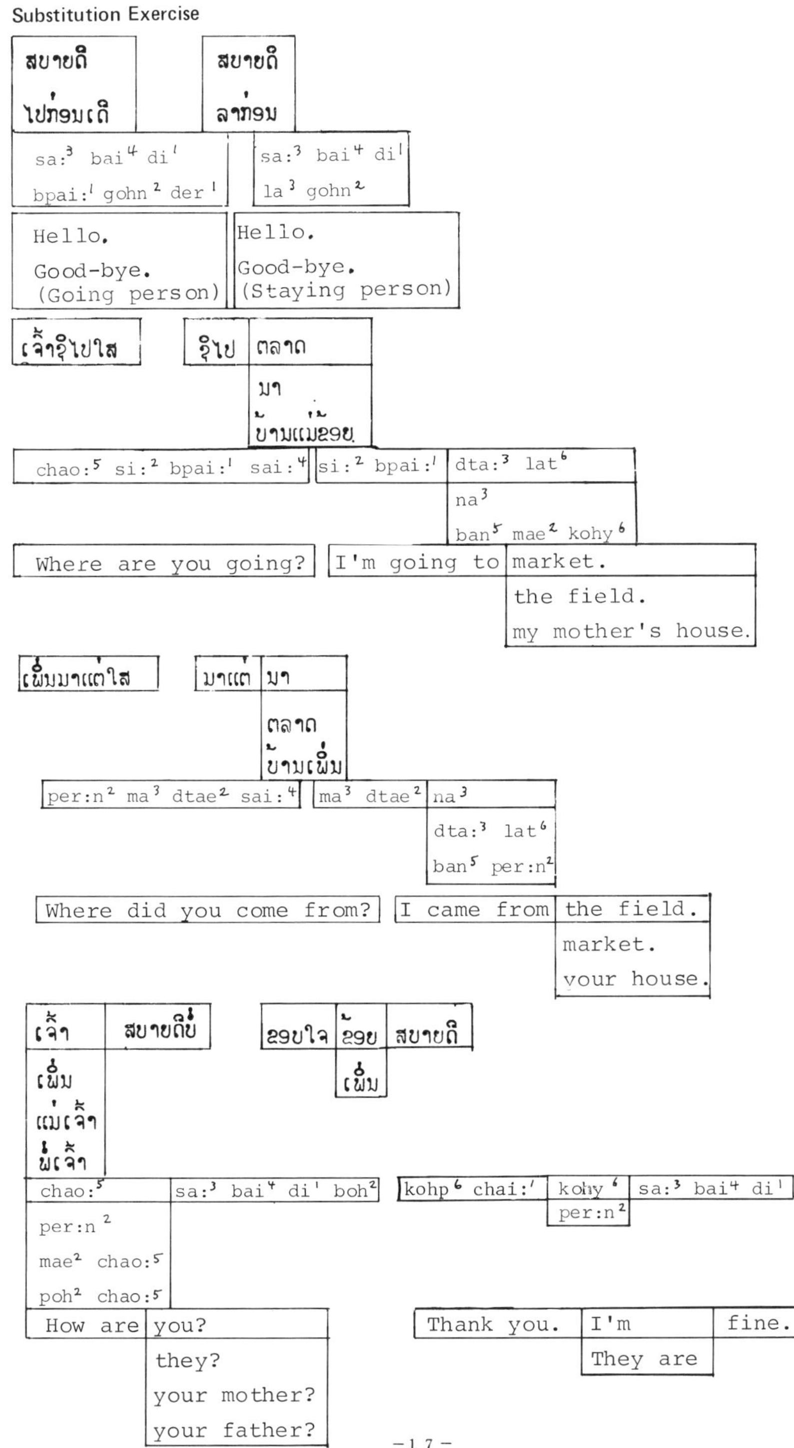

ສບາຍດີ ໄປກ່ອນເດີ	ສບາຍດີ ລາກ່ອນ
sa:3 bai4 di1 bpai:1 gohn2 der1	sa:3 bai4 di1 la3 gohn2
Hello. Good-bye. (Going person)	Hello. Good-bye. (Staying person)

ເຈົ້າຊິໄປໃສ	ຊິໄປ	ຕລາດ ນາ ບ້ານແມ່ຂ້ອຍ
chao:5 si:2 bpai:1 sai:4	si:2 bpai:1	dta:3 lat6 na3 ban5 mae2 kohy6
Where are you going?	I'm going to	market. the field. my mother's house.

ເພິ່ນມາແຕ່ໃສ	ມາແຕ່	ນາ ຕລາດ ບ້ານເພິ່ນ
per:n2 ma3 dtae2 sai:4	ma3 dtae2	na3 dta:3 lat6 ban5 per:n2
Where did you come from?	I came from	the field. market. your house.

ເຈົ້າ ເພິ່ນ ແມ່ເຈົ້າ ພໍ່ເຈົ້າ	ສບາຍດີບໍ່	ຂອບໃຈ	ຂ້ອຍ ເພິ່ນ	ສບາຍດີ
chao:5 per:n2 mae2 chao:5 poh2 chao:5	sa:3 bai4 di1 boh2	kohp6 chai:1	kohy6 per:n2	sa:3 bai4 di1
How are	you? they? your mother? your father?	Thank you.	I'm They are	fine.

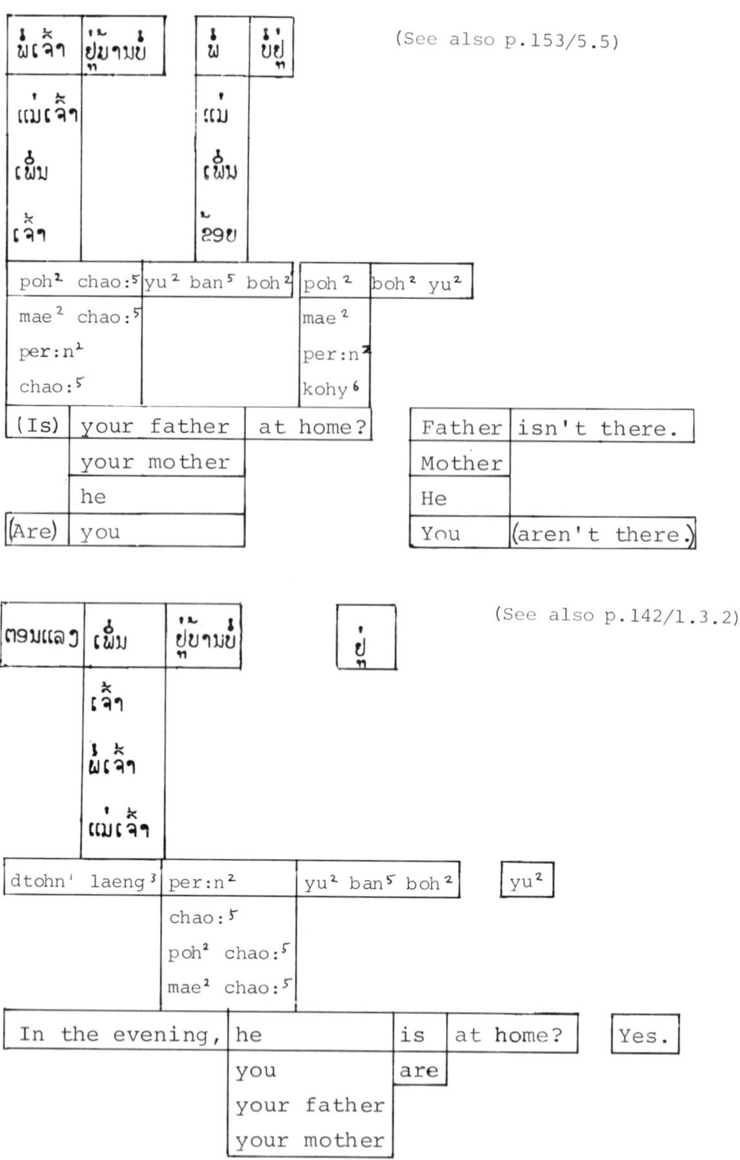

(See also p.153/5.5)

ພໍ່ເຈົ້າ	ຢູ່ບ້ານບໍ່
ແມ່ເຈົ້າ	
ເພິ່ນ	
ເຈົ້າ	

ພໍ່	ບໍ່ຢູ່
ແມ່	
ເພິ່ນ	
ຂ້ອຍ	

poh² chao:⁵	yu² ban⁵ boh²
mae² chao:⁵	
per:n²	
chao:⁵	

poh²	boh² yu²
mae²	
per:n²	
kohy⁶	

(Is)	your father	at home?
	your mother	
	he	
(Are)	you	

Father	isn't there.
Mother	
He	
You	(aren't there.)

(See also p.142/1.3.2)

ຕອນແລງ	ເພິ່ນ	ຢູ່ບ້ານບໍ່
	ເຈົ້າ	
	ພໍ່ເຈົ້າ	
	ແມ່ເຈົ້າ	

ຢູ່

dtohn¹ laeng³	per:n²	yu² ban⁵ boh²
	chao:⁵	
	poh² chao:⁵	
	mae² chao:⁵	

yu²

In the evening,	he	is	at home?
	you	are	
	your father		
	your mother		

Yes.

ເຈົ້າ	ມາແຕ່	ຕລາດ	ບໍ່
ເພິ່ນ	ໄປ	ນາ	
ແມ່ເຈົ້າ	ຢູ່	ບ້ານ	
ພໍ່ເຈົ້າ			

chao:^{5}	ma^{3} dtae^{2}	dta:^{3} lat^{6}	boh^{2}
per:n^{2}	bpai:^{1}	na^{3}	
mae^{2} chao:^{5}	yu^{2}	ban^{5}	
poh^{2} chao:^{5}			

You	come from	market	?
He	goes to	the field	
Your mother	is at	home	
Your father			

ລາວ	ໄປ	ຕລາດ
ແມ່ຂ້ອຍ	ໄປ	ນາ
ຂ້ອຍ	ມາແຕ່	ນາ
ພໍ່ຂ້ອຍ	ຢູ່	ບ້ານ

lao^{3}	bpai:^{1}	dta:^{3} lat^{6}
mae^{2} kohy^{6}	bpai:^{1}	na^{3}
kohy^{6}	ma^{3} dtae^{2}	na^{3}
poh^{2} kohy^{6}	yu^{2}	ban^{5}

They	go to	market.
My mother	goes to	the field.
I	come from	the field.
My father	is at	home.

ແມ່ຂ້ອຍ	ມາຫາ	ເຈົ້າ
ຂ້ອຍ	ໄປຫາ	ພໍ່ລາວ
ພໍ່ຂ້ອຍ		

mae^{2} kohy^{6}	ma^{3} ha^{4}	chao:^{5}
kohy^{6}	bpai^{1} ha^{4}	poh^{2} lao^{3}
poh^{2} kohy^{6}		

My mother	comes to see	you.
I	go to see	his father.
My father		

ເຈົ້າ	ໄປ	ໃສ
ເພິ່ນ	ມາແຕ່	
ແມ່ເຈົ້າ	ຊິໄປ	
ພໍ່ເຈົ້າ		

chao:^{5}	bpai:^{1}	sai:^{4}
per:n^{2}	ma^{3} dtae^{2}	
mae^{2} chao:^{5}	si:^{2} bpai:^{1}	
poh^{2} chao:^{5}		

You	go	where?
He	comes from	
Your mother	will go	
Your father		

Vocabulary Exercise

1-1	<u>ໄປ</u> (See also p.154/5.7)	<u>bpai:^{1}</u>	<u>To go</u>
	ເຈົ້າໄປໃສ	chao:^{5} bpai:^{1} sai:^{4}	Where are you going?
	ແມ່ຊິໄປຕລາດ	mae^{2} si:^{2} bpai:^{1} dta:^{3} lat^{6}	Mother will go to market.
	ພໍ່ໄປນາ ດຽວນີ້	poh^{2} bpai:^{1} na^{3} diaw^{1} ni^{5}	Father is going to the rice-field now.
	ຂ້ອຍຊິໄປບ້ານລາວ	kohy^{6} si:^{2} bpai:^{1} ban^{5} lao^{3}	I will go to his house.
	ເຈົ້າໄປບ້ານບໍ່	chao:^{5} bpai:^{1} ban^{5} boh^{2}	Are you going home?
1-2	<u>ມາແຕ່</u>	<u>ma^{3} dtae^{2}</u>	<u>To come from</u>
	ລາວມາແຕ່ໃສ	lao^{3} ma^{3} dtae^{2} sai:^{4}	Where does he come from?
	ຂ້ອຍມາແຕ່ຕລາດ	kohy^{6} ma^{3} dtae^{2} dta:^{3} lat^{6}	I'm coming from the market.
	ພໍ່ແມ່ຂ້ອຍມາແຕ່ນາ	poh^{2} mae^{2} kohy^{6} ma^{3} dtae^{2} na^{3}	My father and mother are coming from the rice-field.
	ເຈົ້າມາແຕ່ບ້ານເຈົ້າບໍ່	chao:^{5} ma^{3} dtae^{2} ban^{5}	Do you come from your home?
	ເພິ່ນມາແຕ່ນາ	per:n^{2} ma^{3} dtae^{2} na^{3}	They come from the rice-field.
1-3	<u>ຢູ່</u> (See also p.153/5.5)	<u>yu^{2}</u>	<u>To be at (in, etc.)</u>
	ພໍ່ເຈົ້າຢູ່ໃສ	poh^{2} chao:^{5} yu^{2} sai:^{4}	Where is your father?
	ຂ້ອຍຢູ່ບ້ານ	kohy^{6} yu^{2} ban^{5}	I am at home.

	ເຈົ້າຢູ່ບ້ານບໍ່	chao:^{5} yu^{2} ban^{5} boh^{2}	Are you at home?
	ຕອນແລງ ລາວຢູ່ບ້ານ	dtohn^{1} laeng^{3} lao^{3} yu^{2} ban^{5}	In the evening he is at home.
1-4	ຫາ	ha^{4}	(Go, come) to see
	ຂ້ອຍຊິໄປຫາເຈົ້າ	kohy^{6} si:^{2} bpai:^{1} ha^{4} chao:^{5}	I'll go to see you.
	ລາວມາຫາຂ້ອຍ	lao^{3} ma^{3} ha^{4} kohy^{6}	He comes to see me.
	ຕອນແລງ ຊິໄປຫາພໍ່	dtohn^{1} laeng^{3} si:^{2} bpai:^{1} ha^{4} poh^{2}	In the evening (I) will go to see (my) father.
	ເພິ່ນມາຫາແມ່ຂ້ອຍ	per:n^{2} ma^{3} ha^{4} mae^{2} kohy^{6}	He came to see my mother.
1-5	ກໍໄດ້	goh^{1} dai:^{5}	Can, It's all right to..., will do, okay
	ເຈົ້າມາດຽວນີ້ກໍໄດ້	chao:^{5} ma^{3} diaw^{1} ni^{5} goh^{1} dai:^{5}	You can come now.
	ຕອນແລງກໍໄດ້ ດຽວນີ້ກໍໄດ້	dtohn^{1} laeng^{3} goh^{1} dai:^{5} diaw^{1} ni^{5} goh^{1} dai:^{5}	Evening is okay; now is okay too.
	ຂ້ອຍຊິໄປກໍໄດ້	kohy^{6} si:^{2} bpai:^{1} goh^{1} dai:^{5}	It's all right for me to go.
	ລາວໄປຫາເພິ່ນກໍໄດ້	lao^{3} bpai:^{1} ha^{4} per:n^{2} goh^{1} dai:^{5}	He can go and see him.

Text

ບົດ ຮຽນ ທີ່ ໜຶ່ງ

1. ຄຳ ສບາຍດີ

2. ຈິດ ສບາຍດີ

3. ຄຳ ເຈົ້າຊິໄປໃສ

4. ຈິດ ຊິໄປນາ ເຈົ້າມາແຕ່ໃສ

5. ຄຳ ມາແຕ່ຕລາດ

6. ຈິດ ແມ່ເຈົ້າສບາຍດີ ບໍ່

7. ຄຳ ຂອບໃຈ ແມ່ຂ້ອຍສບາຍດີ ດຽວນີ້ພໍ່ເຈົ້າຢູ່ບ້ານ ບໍ່

8. ຈິດ ພໍ່ບໍ່ຢູ່ ເພິ່ນໄປນາແລ້ວ

9. ຄຳ ຕອນແລງ ເພິ່ນຢູ່ບ້ານ ບໍ່

10. ຈິດ ຢູ່ ຕອນແລງເຈົ້າມາຫາເພິ່ນ ກໍໄດ້

11. ຄຳ ເອີ ຂ້ອຍຊິໄປຫາເພິ່ນ

12. ຈິດ ໄປກ່ອນເດີ ຂ້ອຍຊິໄປນາ

13. ຄຳ ລາກ່ອນ

BO:T^{3} HIAN^{3} TI^{2} NEU:NG^{2}

1. Ka:m^{3}: Sa:^{3} bai^{4} di^{1}!
2. Chi:t^{3}: Sa:^{3} bai^{4} di^{1}!
3. Ka:m^{3}: Chao:^{5} si^{2} bpai:^{1} sai:^{4}?
4. Chi:t^{3}: Si^{2} bpai:^{1}na^{3}. Chao:^{5} ma^{3} dtae^{2} sai:^{4} ?
5. Ka:m^{3}: Ma^{3} dtae^{2} dta:^{3} lat^{6}.
6. Chi:t^{3}: Mae^{2} chao:^{5} sa:^{3} bai^{4} di^{1} boh^{2}.
7. Ka:m^{3}: Kohp^{6} chai:^{1}. Mae^{2} kohy^{6} sa:^{3} bai^{4} di^{1}! Diaw^{1} ni^{5} poh^{2} chao:^{5} yu^{2} ban^{5} boh^{2} ?
8. Chi:t^{3}: Poh^{2} boh^{2} yu^{2}. Per:n^{2} bpai:^{1} na^{3} laew^{5}.
9. Ka:m^{3}: Dtohn^{1} laeng^{3} per:n^{2} yu^{2} ban^{5} boh^{2}?
10. Chi:t^{3}: Yu^{2}dtohn^{1} laeng^{3} chao:^{5} ma^{3} ha^{4} per:n^{2} goh^{1} dai:^{5}.
11. Ka:m^{3}: Er^{1} kohy^{6} si:^{2} bpai:^{1} ha^{4} per:n^{2}.
12. Chi:t^{3}: Bpai:^{1} gohn^{2} der^{1}. Kohy^{6} si:^{2} bpai:^{1} na^{3}.
13. Ka:m^{3}: La^{3} gohn^{2}.

LESSON 1: COMING AND GOING

1. Kham: Hello.
2. Chit: Hello.
3. Kham: Where are you going?
4. Chit: I'm going to the rice-field. Where are you coming from?
5. Kham: From the market.
6. Chit: How is your mother?
7. Kham: Thank you. My mother is fine. Is your father at home now?
8. Chit: He's not there. He went to the rice-field already.
9. Kham: This evening will he be at home?
10. Chit: Yes. Tonight you can come to see him.
11. Kham: Okay. I will go to see him.
12. Chit: Good-bye. I will go to the rice-field.
13. Kham: Good-bye.

LESSON 2: INTRODUCTIONS

Substitution Exercise

(See also p.145/2.2.4a)

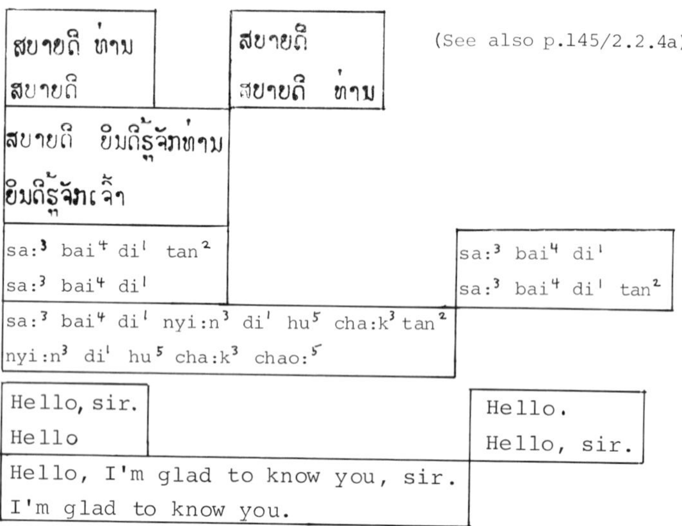

ສບາຍດີ ທ່ານ ສບາຍດີ	ສບາຍດີ ສບາຍດີ ທ່ານ
ສບາຍດີ ຍິນດີຮູ້ຈັກທ່ານ ຍິນດີຮູ້ຈັກເຈົ້າ	
sa:^{3} bai^{4} di^{1} tan^{2} sa:^{3} bai^{4} di^{1}	sa:^{3} bai^{4} di^{1} sa:^{3} bai^{4} di^{1} tan^{2}
sa:^{3} bai^{4} di^{1} nyi:n^{3} di^{1} hu^{5} cha:k^{3} tan^{2} nyi:n^{3} di^{1} hu^{5} cha:k^{3} chao:^{5}	
Hello, sir. Hello	Hello. Hello, sir.
Hello, I'm glad to know you, sir. I'm glad to know you.	

(See also p.153/5.6)

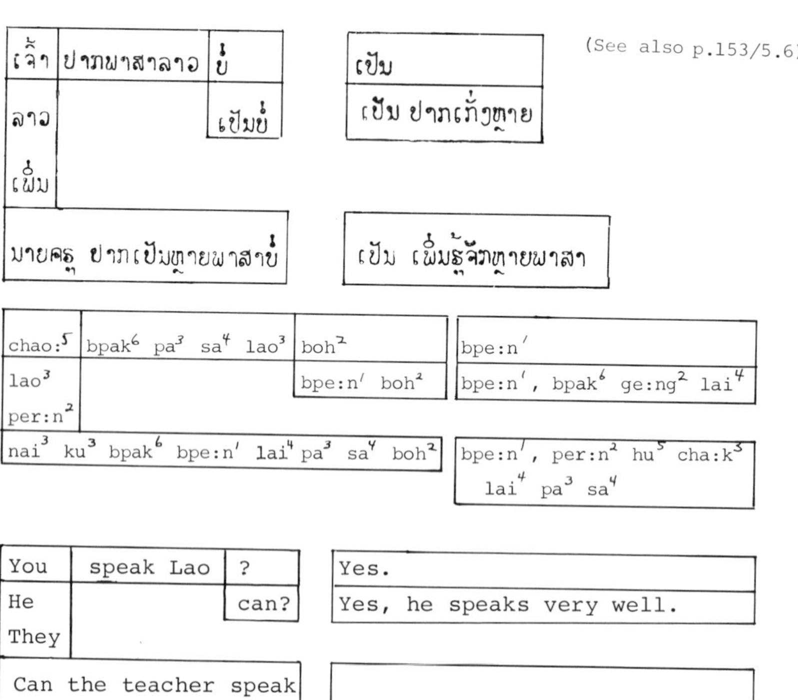

ເຈົ້າ ລາວ ເພິ່ນ	ປາກພາສາລາວ	ບໍ່ ເປັນບໍ່	ເປັນ ເປັນ ປາກເກັ່ງຫຼາຍ
ນາຍຄູ ປາກເປັນຫຼາຍພາສາບໍ່			ເປັນ ເພິ່ນຮູ້ຈັກຫຼາຍພາສາ
chao:^{5} lao^{3} per:n^{2}	bpak^{6} pa^{3} sa^{4} lao^{3}	boh^{2} bpe:n^{1} boh^{2}	bpe:n^{1} bpe:n^{1}, bpak^{6} ge:ng^{2} lai^{4}
nai^{3} ku^{3} bpak^{6} bpe:n^{1} lai^{4} pa^{3} sa^{4} boh^{2}			bpe:n^{1}, per:n^{2} hu^{5} cha:k^{3} lai^{4} pa^{3} sa^{4}
You He They	speak Lao	? can?	Yes. Yes, he speaks very well.
Can the teacher speak many languages?			Yes, he knows many languages.

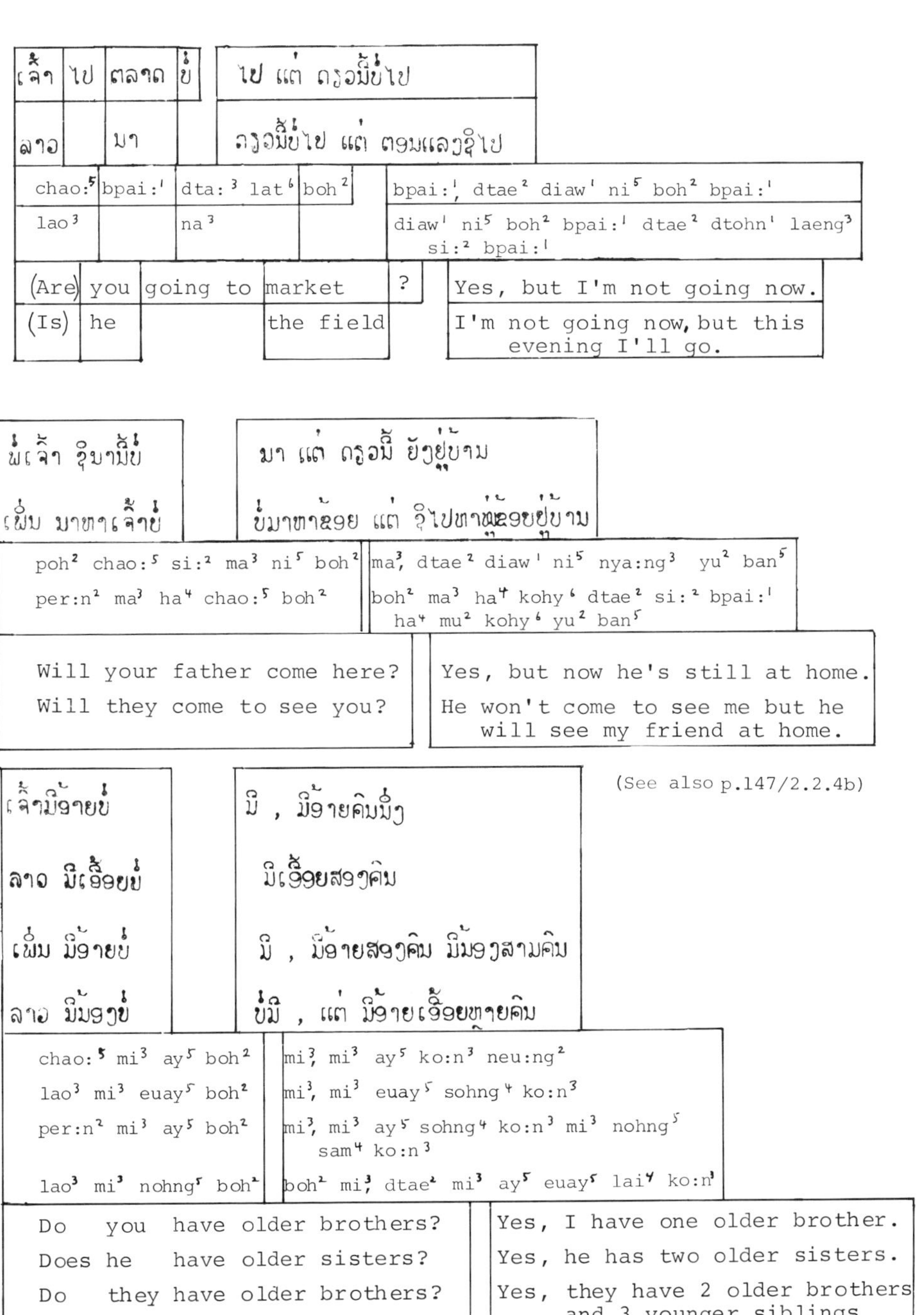

ເຈົ້າ	ໄປ	ຕລາດ	ບໍ່
ລາວ		ນາ	
chao:5	bpai:1	dta:3 lat6	boh2
lao3		na3	
(Are) you	going to	market	?
(Is) he		the field	

ໄປ ແຕ່ ດຽວນີ້ບໍ່ໄປ
ດຽວນີ້ບໍ່ໄປ ແຕ່ ຕອນແລງຊິໄປ
bpai:1, dtae2 diaw1 ni5 boh2 bpai:1
diaw1 ni5 boh2 bpai:1 dtae2 dtohn1 laeng3 si:2 bpai:1
Yes, but I'm not going now.
I'm not going now, but this evening I'll go.

ພໍ່ເຈົ້າ ຊິມານີ້ບໍ່	ມາ ແຕ່ ດຽວນີ້ ຍັງຢູ່ບ້ານ
ເພິ່ນ ມາຫາເຈົ້າບໍ່	ບໍ່ມາຫາຂ້ອຍ ແຕ່ ຊິໄປຫາໝູ່ຂ້ອຍຢູ່ບ້ານ
poh2 chao:5 si:2 ma3 ni5 boh2	ma3, dtae2 diaw1 ni5 nya:ng3 yu2 ban5
per:n2 ma3 ha4 chao:5 boh2	boh2 ma3 ha4 kohy6 dtae2 si:2 bpai:1 ha4 mu2 kohy6 yu2 ban5
Will your father come here?	Yes, but now he's still at home.
Will they come to see you?	He won't come to see me but he will see my friend at home.

(See also p.147/2.2.4b)

ເຈົ້າມີອ້າຍບໍ່	ມີ, ມີອ້າຍຄົນນຶ່ງ
ລາວ ມີເອື້ອຍບໍ່	ມີເອື້ອຍສອງຄົນ
ເພິ່ນ ມີອ້າຍບໍ່	ມີ, ມີອ້າຍສອງຄົນ ມີນ້ອງສາມຄົນ
ລາວ ມີນ້ອງບໍ່	ບໍ່ມີ, ແຕ່ ມີອ້າຍເອື້ອຍຫຼາຍຄົນ
chao:5 mi3 ay5 boh2	mi3, mi3 ay5 ko:n3 neu:ng2
lao3 mi3 euay5 boh2	mi3, mi3 euay5 sohng4 ko:n3
per:n2 mi3 ay5 boh2	mi3, mi3 ay5 sohng4 ko:n3 mi3 nohng5 sam4 ko:n3
lao3 mi3 nohng5 boh2	boh2 mi3, dtae2 mi3 ay5 euay5 lai4 ko:n3
Do you have older brothers?	Yes, I have one older brother.
Does he have older sisters?	Yes, he has two older sisters.
Do they have older brothers?	Yes, they have 2 older brothers and 3 younger siblings.
Does he have younger siblings?	No, but he has many older brothers and sisters.

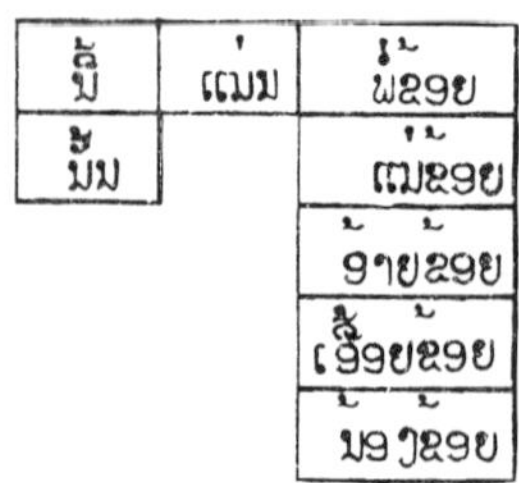

ນີ້	ແມ່ນ	ພໍ່ຂ້ອຍ
ນັ້ນ		ແມ່ຂ້ອຍ
		ອ້າຍຂ້ອຍ
		ເອື້ອຍຂ້ອຍ
		ນ້ອງຂ້ອຍ

(See also p.153/5.5)

ni^5	$maen^2$	poh^2 $kohy^6$
$na:n^5$		mae^2 $kohy^6$
		ay^5 $kohy^6$
		$euay^5$ $kohy^6$
		$nohng^5$ $kohy^6$

This	is	my father.
That		my mother.
		my older brother.
		my older sister.
		my younger sibling.

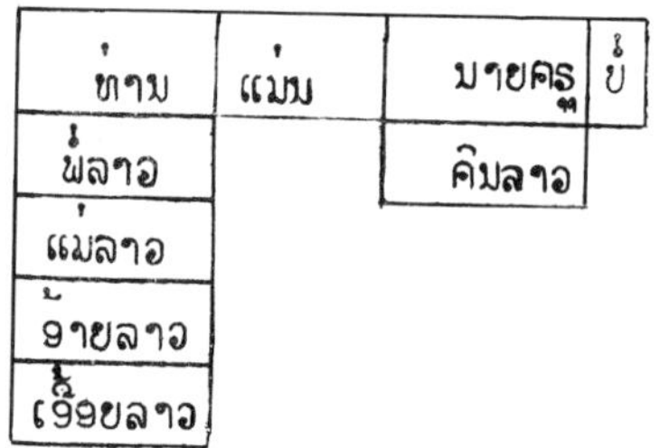

ທ່ານ	ແມ່ນ	ນາຍຄູ	ບໍ່
ພໍ່ລາວ		ຄົນລາວ	
ແມ່ລາວ			
ອ້າຍລາວ			
ເອື້ອຍລາວ			

tan^2	$maen^2$	nai^3 ku^3	boh^2
poh^2 lao^3		$ko:n^3$ lao^3	
mae^2 lao^3			
ay^5 lao^3			
$euay^5$ lao^3			

Sir	is	a teacher	?
His father		a Lao.	
His mother			
His older brother			
His older sister			

Vocabulary Exercise

2-1	ສອນ	sohn^4	To teach
	ເພິ່ນສອນ ໜັງສື ຢູ່ວິທຍາລັຍ	per:n^2 sohn^4 na:ng^4 seu^4 yu^2 wi:^{2} ta:^{2} nya^3 lai:^{3}	He (she) teaches at high school.
	ຂ້ອຍສອນພາສາລາວ ຢູ່ວິທຍາລັຍ	kohy^6 sohn^4 pa^3 sa^4 lao^3 yu^2 wi:^{2} ta:^{2} nya^3 lai:^{3}	I teach Lao at a high school.
	ລາວສອນໜັງສືຢູ່ບ້ານ	lao^3 sohn^4 na:ng^4 seu^4 yu^2 ban^5	He (she) teaches at home.
	ເອື້ອຍຂ້ອຍ ສອນໜັງສື	euay^5 kohy^6 sohn^4 na:ng^4 seu^4	My elder sister teaches.
2-2	ຮຽນ	hian^3	To study
	ນ້ອງຂ້ອຍຮຽນໜັງສືຢູ່ບ້ານ	nohng^5 kohy^6 hian^3 na:ng^4 seu^4 yu^2 ban^5	My younger brothers (sisters) study at home.
	ຂ້ອຍຮຽນຢູ່ ວິທຍາລັຍ	kohy^6 hian^3 yu^2 wi:^{2} ta:^{2} nya^{3}lai:^{3}	I study at high school.
	ເພິ່ນຮຽນ ພາສາລາວ ນຳນາຍຄູຄົນລາວ	per:n^2 hian^3 pa^3 sa^4 lao^3 na:m^3 nai^3 ku^3 ko:n^3 lao^3	He (she) studies the Lao language with a Lao teacher.
	ລາວຮຽນນຳໝູ່ລາວ	lao^3 hian^3 na:m^3 mu^2 lao^3	He (she) studies with his friend(s).
2-3	ປາກ	bpak^6	To speak
	ເຈົ້າ ປາກພາສາລາວບໍ່	chao:^{5} bpak^6 pa^3 sa^4 lao^3 boh^2	Do you speak Lao?
	ລາວ ປາກພາສາລາວ	lao^3 bpak^6 pa^3 sa^4 lao^3	He (she) speaks Lao.
	ຄົນລາວ ປາກພາສາລາວ	ko:n^3 lao^3 bpak^6 pa^3 sa^4 lao^3	Lao people speak Lao.
	ເພິ່ນປາກຫຼາຍພາສາ	per:n^2 bpak^6 lai^4 pa^3 sa^4	They speak many languages.

2-4	ເກັ່ງ	ge:ng^2	To be good at..., skillful, can (do something) well.
	ເຈົ້າ ປາກພາສາລາວເກັ່ງ	chao:^{5} bpak^6 pa^3 sa^4 lao^3 ge:ng^2	You speak Lao well.
	ນາຍຄູ ສອນໜັງສືເກັ່ງຫຼາຍ	nai^3 ku^3 sohn^4 na:ng^4 seu^4 ge:ng^2 lai^4	The teacher teaches very well.
	ລາວຮຽນເກັ່ງ	Lao^3 hian^3 ge:ng^2	He learns well.
2-5	ຮູ້ຈັກ	hu^5 cha:k^3	To know
	ເຈົ້າຮູ້ຈັກລາວບໍ່	chao:^{5} hu^5 cha:k^3 lao^3 boh^2	Do you know him?
	ລາວ ຮູ້ຈັກພາສາລາວ	lao^3 hu^5 cha:k^3 pa^3 sa^4 lao^3	He (she) knows Lao.
	ຂ້ອຍບໍ່ຮູ້ຈັກລາວ	kohy^6 boh^2 hu^5 cha:k^3 lao^3	I don't know him.
	ຂ້ອຍຮູ້ຈັກວິທຍາລັຍ ຢູ່ໃສ	kohy^6 hu^5 cha:k^3 wi:^{2} ta:^{2}nya^3 lai:^{3} yu^2 sai:^{4}	I know where the high school is.
	ລາວ ບໍ່ຮູ້ຈັກ ບ້ານນາຍຄູ ຢູ່ໃສ	lao^3 boh^2 hu^5 cha:k^3 ban^5 nai^3 ku^3 yu^2 sai:^{4}	He (she) does not know where the teacher's house is.
2-6	ໄປຮຽນ (See also p.153/5.3)	bpai:^{1} hian^3	To go to study
	ໄປວິທຍາລັຍ ຮຽນໜັງສື	bpai:^{1} wi:^{2} ta:^{2}nya^3 lai:^{3} hian^3 na:ng^4 seu^4	I go to high school to study.
	ມາບ້ານ ສອນພາສາລາວ	ma^3 ban^5 sohn^4 pa^3 sa^4 lao^3	He comes to my home and teach Lac.
	ໄປບ້ານນາຍຄູ ຮຽນພາສາລາວນຳເພິ່ນ	bpai:^{1} ban^5 nai^3 ku^3 hian^3 pa^3 sa^4 lao^3 na:m^3 per:n^2	I go to the teacher's house and study Lao with him.

2-7	<u>ຫຼາຍ</u> (See also p.143/2.1.1)	<u>lai^{4}</u>	<u>Very, Much, Many</u>
	ຂ້ອຍມີອ້າຍນ້ອງຫຼາຍຄົນ	kohy^{6} mi^{3} ay^{5} nohng^{5} lai^{4} ko:n^{3}	I have many brothers and sisters.
	ລາວ ມີໝູ່ຄົນລາວຫຼາຍ	lao^{3} mi^{3} mu^{2} ko:n^{3} lao^{3} lai^{4}	He (she) has many Lao friends.
	ມີຫຼາຍ	mi^{3} lai^{4}	There are many things.
	ພໍ່ຮູ້ຈັກຫຼາຍ	poh^{2} hu^{5} cha:k^{3} lai^{4}	Father knows a lot.
	ລາວຮຽນໜັງສືຫຼາຍ	lao^{3} hian^{3} na:ng^{4} seu^{4} lai^{4}	He learns a lot.
	ດີຫຼາຍ	di^{1} lai^{4}	Very good.
2-8	<u>ຍັງ</u>	<u>nya:ng^{3}</u>	<u>Still, Not yet</u>.
	ລາວຍັງມີຫຼາຍ	lao^{3} nya:ng^{3} mi^{3} lai^{4}	He still has much (many).
	ຂ້ອຍຍັງຮູ້ຈັກ	kohy^{6} nya:ng^{3} hu^{5} cha:k^{3}	I still know about it.
	ເພິ່ນ ຍັງຢູ່ບ້ານ	per:n^{2} nya:ng^{3} yu^{2} ban^{5}	He is still at home.
	ພໍ່ແລະແມ່ ຍັງຢູ່ນາ	poh^{2} lae:^{2} mae^{2} nya: ng^{3} yu^{2} na^{3}	Father and mother are still in the rice-field.
2-9	<u>ແຕ່</u>	<u>dtae^{2}</u>	<u>But</u>
	ພໍ່ ຢູ່ບ້ານ ແຕ່ແມ່ບໍ່ຢູ່	poh^{2} yu^{2} ban^{5} dtae^{2} mae^{2} boh^{2} yu^{2}	Father is at home, but mother is not.
	ລາວ ປາກພາສາລາວ ແຕ່ຂ້ອຍບໍ່ເປັນ	lao^{3} bpak^{6} pa^{3} sa^{4} lao^{3} dtae^{2} kohy^{6} boh^{2} bpe:n^{1}	He speaks Lao but, I can't.

	Lao	Transcription	English
	ເພິ່ນ ປາກເປັນ ແຕ່ ນ້ອງເພິ່ນ ປາກບໍ່ເປັນ	per:n^{2} bpak^{6} bpe:n^{1} dtae^{2} nohng^{5} per:n^{2} bpak^{6} boh^{2} bpe:n^{1}	He can speaks, but his younger brother (sister) can't.
	ດຽວນີ້ ບໍ່ໄປ ແຕ່ ຕອນແລງຊິໄປ	diaw^{1} ni^{5} boh^{2} bpai:^{1} dtae^{2} dtohn^{1} laeng^{3} si:^{2} bpai:^{1}	Now I won't go, but in the evening I will.
	ອ້າຍໄປແລ້ວ ແຕ່ ເອື້ອຍຍັງຢູ່ບ້ານ	ay^{5} bpai:^{1} laew^{5} dtae^{2} euay^{5} nya:ng^{3} yu^{4} ban^{5}	Elder brother went, but elder sister is still at home.
2-10	<u>ເຊີນ</u>	<u>sern</u>^{3}	<u>Please</u>
	ເຊີນ ນັ່ງຢູ່ນີ້	sern^{3} na:ng^{2} yu^{2} ni^{5}	Please sit here.
	ເຊີນ ໄປດີ	sern^{3} bpai:^{1} di^{1}	So long.
	ເຊີນ ມາບ້ານຂ້ອຍ	sern^{3} ma^{3} ban^{5} kohy^{6}	Please come to my house.
2-11	<u>ນຳ</u>	<u>na:m</u>^{3}	<u>With</u>
	ໄປນຳເຈົ້າ	bpai:^{1} na:m^{3} chao:^{5}	(I'll) go with you.
	ມານຳລາວບໍ່	ma^{3} na:m^{3} lao^{3} boh^{2}	Did (you) come with him?
	ເຈົ້າມານຳຂ້ອຍບໍ່	chao:^{5} ma^{3} na:m^{3} kohy^{6} boh^{2}	Will you come with me?

Text

ບົດ ຮຽນ ທີ່ ສອງ

1. ຄຳ ນີ້ແມ່ນພໍ່ຂ້ອຍ
2. ນິມລາ ສບາຍດີ ຍິນດີ ຮູ້ຈັກທ່ານ
3. ພໍ່ຂອງຄຳ ສບາຍດີ ທ່ານ
4. ຄຳ ທ່ານນິມລາ ແມ່ນນາຍຄຣູສອນໜັງສື ຢູ່ວິທຍາລັຍ
5. ພໍ່ຂອງຄຳ ທ່ານປາກພາສາລາວເກັ່ງ ຮຽນຢູ່ໃສ
6. ນິມລາ ຈ້າງນາຍຄຣູຄົນລາວ ຮຽນຢູ່ບ້ານ
7. ພໍ່ຂອງຄຳ ໂອ່ ດີຫຼາຍ
8. ຄຳ ແມ່ ນີ້ ແມ່ນທ່ານນິມລາ ເພິ່ນປາກລາວເປັນ
   ນີ້ ແມ່ນແມ່ຂ້ອຍ ນັ້ນ ແມ່ນອ້າຍແລະເອື້ອຍ ຂ້ອຍຍັງມີນ້ອງຄົນນຶ່ງ
   ແຕ່ລາວບໍ່ຢູ່ບ້ານ ດຽວນີ້ ຫຼິ້ນຢູ່ນອກນຳໝູ່ລາວ.
9. ພໍ່ຂອງຄຳ ເຊີນນັ່ງຕີ ທ່ານ
10. ແມ່ຂອງຄຳ ເຊີນ
11. ນິມລາ ຂອບໃຈ

BO:T^{3} HIAN^{3} TI^{2} SOHNG^{4}

1. Ka:m^{3}: Ni^{5} maen^{2} poh^{2} kohy^{6}.
2. Mi:n^{3} la^{3}: Sa:^{3} bai^{4} di^{1}. Nyi:n^{3} di^{1} hu^{5} cha:k^{3} tan^{2}.
3. Poh^{2} kohng^{4} Ka:m^{3}: Sa:^{3} bai^{4} di^{1} tan^{2}.
4. Ka:m^{3}: Tan^{2} Mi:n^{3} la^{3} maen^{2} nai^{3} ku^{3} sohn^{4} nang^{4} seu^{4} yu^{2} wi:^{2} ta:^{2} nya^{3} lai:^{3}.
5. Poh^{2} kohng^{4} Ka:m^{3}: Tan^{2} bpak^{6} pa^{3} sa^{4} lao^{3} ge:ng.^{2} Hian^{3} yu^{2} sai:^{4}?
6. Mi:n^{3} la^{3}: Chang^{5} nai^{3} ku^{3} ko:n^{3} lao,^{3} hian^{3} yu^{2} ban^{5}.
7. Poh^{2} kohng^{4} Ka:m^{3}: O^{2}, di^{1} lai^{4}.
8. Ka:m^{3}: Mae^{2}, ni^{5} maen^{2} Tan^{2} Mi:n^{3} la^{3}. Per:n^{2} bpak^{6} lao^{3} bpe:n^{1}. ni maen^{2} mae^{2} kohy.^{6} Na:n^{5} maen^{2} ay^{5} lae:^{2} euay^{5}. Kohy^{6} nyang^{3} mi^{3} nohng^{5} ko:n^{3} neu:ng^{2} dtae^{2} lao^{3} boh^{2} yu^{2} ban^{5} diaw^{1} ni,^{5} lin^{6} yu^{2} nohk^{5} na:m^{3} mu^{2} lao^{3}.
9. Poh^{2} kohng^{4} Ka:m^{3}: Sern^{3} nang^{2} dti^{1}, tan^{2}.
10. Mae^{2} Kohng^{4} Ka:m^{3}: Sern^{3}.
11. Mi:n^{3} la^{3}: Kohp^{6} chai:^{1}.

LESSON 2: INTRODUCTIONS

1. Kham: This is my father.
2. Mr. Miller: Hello. I'm happy to know you sir.
3. Kham's father: Hello, sir.
4. Kham: Mr. Miller is a teacher teaching at the high school.
5. Kham's father: Sir, you speak Lao well. Where did you study?
6. Mr. Miller: I hired a Lao teacher and studied at home.
7. Kham's father: Oh, very good.
8. Kham: Mother, this is Mr. Miller. He can speak Lao. This is my mother. That's my older brother and older sister. Also I have one younger brother, but he's not at home now. He's still playing outside with his friends.
9. Kham's father: Please sit down, sir.
10. Kham's mother: Please.
11. Mr. Miller: Thank you.

Substitution Exercise

ຂ້ອຍ	ຊື່ວ່າ	ທ້າວແສງ
ລາວ		ນາງບຸນທອງ
ເພິ່ນ		
ນ້ອງຂ້ອຍ		
ນ້ອງລາວ		

kohy⁶	seu² wa²	tao⁵ saeng⁴
lao³		nang³ bu:n¹ tohng³
per:n²		
nohng⁵ kohy⁶		
nohng⁵ lao⁶		

My	name is	Mr. Seng.
Her		Mrs. Bounthong.
Their		
My younger sibling's		
His younger sibling's		

ເຈົ້າ	ກັບ	ຂ້ອຍ	ຮູ້ຈັກກັນດີ
ພໍ່		ເອື້ອຍ	ຮັກກັນຫຼາຍ
ແມ່		ເມັຽເຈົ້າ	
ອ້າຍ		ທ້າວແສງ	
		ນາງບຸນທອງ	

chao:⁵	ga:p³	kohy⁶	hu⁵ cha:k³ ga:n¹ di¹
poh²		euay⁵	ha:k² ga:n¹ lai⁴
mae²		mia:³ chao:⁵	
ay⁵		tao⁵ saeng⁴	
		nang³ bu:n¹ tohng³	

You	and	I	know each other well.
Father		older sister	like each other a lot.
My mother		your wife	
Older brother		Mr. Seng	
		Mrs. Bounthong	

ລາວ	ເຮັດການຢູ່	ກະຊວງ
ເພິ່ນ		ໂຮງການ
ທ້າວຄຳ		ໃສ
ນາງຄຳ		ວິທຍາລັຍ

lao^{3}	he:t^{2} gan^{1} yu^{2}	ga:^{3} suang^{3}
per:n^{2}		hong^{3} gan^{1}
tao^{5}ka:m^{3}		sai:^{4}
nang^{3} ka:m^{3}		wi:^{2} ta:^{2} nya^{3} lai:^{3}

He	is working at	the ministry.
He		the office.
Mr. Kham		where?
Mrs. Kham		at the high school.

(See also p.149/3.1)

ບ້ານ ຂ້ອຍ	ຢູ່ໃກ້	ບ້ານເຈົ້າ
ເພິ່ນ		ບ້ານທ້າວແສງ
ຂະເຈົ້າ		ໂຮງການ
		ກະຊວງ
		ວິທຍາລັຍ

ban^{5} kohy^{6}	yu^{2} gai:^{5}	ban^{5} chao:^{5}
per:n^{2}		ban^{5} tao^{5} saeng^{4}
ka:^{3} chao:^{5}		hong^{3} gan^{1}
		ga:^{3} suang^{3}
		wi:^{2} ta:^{2} nya^{3} lai:^{3}

My house	is near	your house.
He		Mr. Seng's house.
They		the office.
		the ministry.
		the high school.

ຂ້ອຍ	ມີ	ເຮືອນ	ຫຼັງນຶ່ງ
ລາວ			ສອງຫຼັງ
ຂະເຈົ້າ			ສາມຫຼັງ
		ລູກ	ຄົນດຽວ
			ສອງຄົນ
		ໝູ່ຄົນລາວ	ຄົນນຶ່ງ
			ສອງຄົນ
			ຫຼາຍຄົນ

(See also p.150/4.2)

kohy^{6}	mi^{3}	heuan^{3}	la:ng^{4} neu:ng^{2}
lao^{3}			sohng^{4} la:ng^{4}
ka:^{3} chao:^{5}			sam^{4} la:ng^{4}
		luk^{5}	ko:n^{3} diaw^{1}
			sohng^{4} ko:n^{3}
		mu^{2} ko:n^{3} lao	ko:n^{3} neu:ng^{2}
			sohng^{4} ko:n^{3}
			lai^{4} ko:n^{3}

I	have	house	one building.
He			two buildings.
They			three buildings.
		children	one person.
			two persons.
		Lao friend	one person.
			two persons.
			many persons.

Vocabulary Exercise

3-1	ຊື່ວ່າ	seu^{2} wa^{2}	Name is,...
	ຂ້ອຍຊື່ວ່າ ທ້າວຄຳ	kohy^{6} seu^{2} wa^{2} tao^{5} ka:m^{3}	My name is Thao Kham.
	ເຈົ້າ ຊື່ວ່າ ນາງບຸນທອງບໍ່	chao:^{5} seu^{2} wa^{2} nang^{3} bu:n^{1} tohng^{3} boh^{2}	Is your name Nang Bounthong?
	ເພິ່ນ ຊື່ວ່າ ທ່ານມິນລາ	per:n^{2} seu^{2} wa^{2} tan^{2} mi:n^{3} la^{3}	His name is Mr. Miller.
	ທ່ານ ຊື່ວ່າ ມິນລາບໍ່	tan^{2} seu^{2} wa^{2} mi:n^{3} la^{3} boh^{2}	Is your name Miller?
3-2	ກັນ	ga:n^{1}	To each other, together
	ຮູ້ຈັກກັນ ແຕ່ ບໍ່ຮັກກັນຫຼາຍ	hu^{5} cha:k^{3} ga:n^{1} dtae^{2} boh^{2} ha:k^{2} ga:n^{1} lai^{4}	We know each other, but don't like much.
	ເຈົ້າ ກັບ ລາວ ສອນກັນ ກໍໄດ້	chao:^{5} ga:p^{3} lao^{3} sohn^{4} ga:n^{1} goh^{1} dai:^{5}	You and he can teach each other.
	ຂະເຈົ້າ ອ້າຍນ້ອງກັນ	ka^{3} chao:^{5} ay^{5} nohng^{5} ga:n^{1}	They are brothers.
	ນ້ອງຫຼິ້ນກັນຢູ່ນອກ (ນ້ອງຫຼິ້ນນຳກັນຢູ່ນອກ)	nohng^{5} lin^{6} ga:n^{1} yu^{2} nohk^{5} (nohng^{5} lin^{6} na:m^{3} ga:n^{1} yu^{2} nohk^{5})	My little sisters and brothers are playing together outside.
3-3	ເຮັດການ	he:t^{2} gan^{1}	To work
	ເພິ່ນເປັນນາຍຄູ ເຮັດການ ຢູ່ວິທະຍາລັຍ	per:n^{2} bpe:n^{1} nai^{3} ku^{3} he:t^{2} gan^{1} yu^{2} wi:^{2} ta:^{2} nya^{3} lai:^{3}	He is teacher. He works at the school.
	ເຈົ້າເຮັດການ ຢູ່ໃສ	chao:^{5} he:t^{2} gan^{1} yu^{2} sai:^{4}	Where do you work?
	ແມ່ ບໍ່ເຮັດການຢູ່ບ້ານ	mae^{2} boh^{2} he:t^{2} gan^{1} yu^{2} ban^{5}	Mother does not go to work. She is at home.
	ລາວ ເຮັດການ ຢູ່ກະຊວງ	lac^{3} he:t^{2} gan^{1} yu^{2} ga:^{3} suang^{3}	He is working in the ministry.

	Lao	Romanization	English
3-4	ແລະ	lae:2	And
	ຂ້ອຍມີອ້າຍຄົນນຶ່ງ ແລະເອື້ອຍຄົນນຶ່ງ	kohy6 mi3 ay5 ko:n3 neu:ng2 lae:2 euay5 ko:n3 neu:ng2	I have one elder brother and one elder sister.
	ນ້ອງຂ້ອຍ ຮູ້ຈັກທ່ານມິນລາ ແລະເມັຽເພິ່ນດີ	nohng5 kohy6 hu5 cha:k3 tan2 mi:n3 la3 lae:2 mia:3 per:n2 di1	My younger brother knows Mr. Miller and his wife well.
	ຂະເຈົ້າ ຮູ້ຈັກກັນໄດ້ສາມປີແລວແຕ່ງງານແລ້ວ	ka:3 chao:5 hu5 cha:k3 ga:n1 dai:5 sam3 bpi1 lae:2 dtaeng2 gan3 laew5	They knew each other for three years and got married.
3-5	ເປັນ (See also p.153/5.5)	bpe:n1	To be
	ເພິ່ນເປັນ ຂ້າຣາຊການ	per:n2 bpe:n1 ka6 lat5 sa:2 gan1	He is an official.
	ລາວເປັນລູກຂອງທ່ານບຸນທອງ	lao3 bpe:n1 luk5 kohng4 tan2 bu:n1 tohng3	She is a child of Mr. Bounthong.
	ຂ້ອຍເປັນຄົນລາວ	kohy6 bpe:n1 ko:n3 lao3	I am a Lao.
	ອ້າຍຂອງລາວເປັນນາຍຄູ	ay5 kohng4 lao3 bpe:n1 nai3 ku3	His elder brother is a teacher
	ເພິ່ນເປັນເມັຽ	per:n2 bpe:n1 mia:3	She is (his) wife.
3-6	ທັມມະດາ	ta:m3 ma:2 da1	Usually, on the whole, as a rule
	ທັມມະດາ ລາວ ເຮັດການ ຢູ່ໂຮງການ	ta:m3 ma:2 da1 lao3 he:t2 gan1 yu2 hong3 gan1	He usually works at the office.
	ທັມມະດາ ເພິ່ນຢູ່ບ້ານຕອນແລງ	ta:m3 ma:2 da1 per:n2 yu2 ban5 dtohn1 laeng3	On the whole, he stays at home in the evening.
	ທັມມະດາ ເອື້ອຍຂ້ອຍໄປຕລາດ ແມ່ບໍ່ໄປ	ta:m3 ma:2 da1 euay5 kohy6 bpai:1 dta:3 lat5 mae2 boh2 bpai:1	As a rule, my elder sister goes to market. Mother doesn't (go).
	ທັມມະດາ ທ້າວແສງ ມາຫາຂ້ອຍ ຢູ່ບ້ານ	ta:m3 ma:2 da1 tao5 saeng4 ma3 ha4 kohy6 yu2 ban5	Usually Thao Seng comes to see me at home.
	ທັມມະດາ ນ້ອງໄປເບິ່ງວຽກຢູ່ນາ	ta:m3 ma:2 da1 nohng5 bpai:1 beung2 wiak5 yu2 na3	Usually, my brother goes to inspect work in the rice-field.

No.	Lao	Transcription	English
3-7	ບາງເທື່ອ	bang^1 teua^2	Sometimes
	ບາງເທື່ອ ລາວ ມາຫາຂ້ອຍ	bang^1 teua^2 lao^3 ma^3 ha^4 kohy^6	Sometimes he comes to see me.
	ບາງເທື່ອ ລາວບໍ່ມາ	bang^1 teua^2 lao^3 boh^2 ma^3	Sometimes he does not come.
	ບາງເທື່ອມີ ບາງເທື່ອບໍ່ມີ	bang^1 teua^2 mi^3 bang^1 teua^2 boh^2 mi^3	Sometimes we have it, sometimes we don't.
	ບາງເທື່ອ ນາຍຄູ ໄປເບິ່ງວຽກຢູ່ນາ	bang^1 teua^2 nai^3 ku^3 bpai:^{1} ber:ng^2 wiak^5 yu^2 na^3	Sometimes the teacher goes to look at the work in the rice-field.
3-8	....ກໍມີ	..goh^1 mi^3	It happens that..., also
	ບາງເທື່ອ ຂ້ອຍໄປບ້ານນອກກໍມີ	bang^1 teua^2 kohy^6 bpai:^{1} ban^5 nohk^5 goh^1 mi^3	Sometimes it happens that I go to the country-side.
	ບາງເທື່ອ ລາວບໍ່ໄປນາກໍມີ	bang^1 teua^2 lao^3 boh^2 bpai:^{1} na^3 goh^1 mi^5	Sometimes it happens that he does not go to rice-field.
	ຂ້ອຍມີຄອບຄົວ ອ້າຍກໍມີ ແລະນ້ອງກໍມີ	kohy^6 mi^3 kohp^5 kua^3 ay^5 goh^1 mi^3 lae:^{2} nohng^5 goh^1 mi^3	I have a family. I have elder brothers and younger siblings as well.
	ຢູ່ວິທະຍາລັຍ ນາຍຄູສອນພາສາລາວກໍມີ	yu^2 wi:^{2} ta:^{2} nya^3 lai:^{3} nai^2 ku^2 sohn^4 pa^3 sa^4 lao^3 goh^1 mi^3	At school we also have a Lao teacher.
3-9	ໄດ້..........ແລ້ວ (See also p.152/5.2a)	dai:^{5}.. laew^5	Since....., ago, for...
	ຂ້ອຍເປັນຂ້າຣາຊການ ໄດ້ສາມປີແລ້ວ	kohy^6 bpe:n^1 ka^6 lat^5 sa:^{2} gan^1 dai:^{5} sam^4 bpi^1 laew^5	I have been an official for 3 years.
	ເພິ່ນ ຢູ່ລາວໄດ້ຫ້າປີແລ້ວ	per:n^2 yu^2 lao^3 dai:^{5} ha^6 bpi^1 laew^5	He has been in Laos for 5 years.
	ຂະເຈົ້າ ໄປຢູ່ຫັ້ນ ໄດ້ນຶ່ງປີແລ້ວ	ka^3 chao:^{5} bpai:^{1} yu^2 ha:n^6 dai:^{5} bpi^1 neu:ng^2 laew^5	They went to live there a year ago.
	ເອື້ອຍຂ້ອຍແຕ່ງງານ ໄດ້ສີ່ປີແລ້ວ	euay^5 kohy^6 dtaeng^2 ngan^3 dai:^{5} si^2 bpi^1 laew^5	My elder sister got married 4 years ago.
	ຂ້ອຍ ຮູ້ຈັກລາວໄດ້ຫຼາຍປີແລ້ວ	kohy^6 hu^5 cha:k^3 lao^3 dai:^{5} lai^4 bpi^1 laew^5	I have known him for many years.

Text

ບົດ ຮຽນ ທີ ສາມ

1. ຂ້ອຍ ມີໝູ່ຄົນລາວຄົນນຶ່ງຊື່ວ່າທ້າວແສງ.
2. ທ້າວແສງກັບຂ້ອຍຮູ້ຈັກກັນດີ ແລະຮັກກັນຫລາຍ.
3. ທ້າວແສງເຮັດການຢູ່ກະຊວງ
4. ລາວເປັນຂ້າຣາຊການ.
5. ທັມມະດາ ລາວເຮັດການຢູ່ ໂຮງການ ແຕ່ບາງເທື່ອໄປບ້ານນອກເບິ່ງວຽກກໍມີ.
6. ລາວ ມີເຮືອນຫລັງນຶ່ງຢູ່ໃກ້ບ້ານຂ້ອຍ ແລະຢູ່ນຳຄອບຄົວຂອງລາວ
7. ລາວແຕ່ງ ງານໄດ້ສາມປີແລ້ວ
8. ເມັຽລາວຊື່ວ່າ ນາງບຸນທອງ
9. ຂະເຈົ້າມີລູກຄົນດຽວ.

BO:T^{3} HIAN^{3} TI^{2} SAM^{4}

1. Kohy^{6} mi^{3} mu^{2} ko:n^{3} lao^{3} ko:n^{3} neu:ng^{2} seu^{2} wa^{2} Tao^{5} Saeng^{4}.

2. Tao^{5} saeng^{4} ga:p^{3} kohy^{6} hu^{5} cha:k^{3} ga:n^{1} di^{1} lae:^{2} ha:k^{2} ga:n^{1}, lai^{4}.

3. Tao^{5} saeng^{4} he:t^{2} gan^{1} yu^{2} ga:^{3} suang^{3}.

4. Lao^{3} bpe:n^{1} ka^{6}la:t^{5}sa^{2} gan^{1}.

5. Ta:m^{3} ma^{2} da^{1} lao^{3} he:t^{2} gan^{1} yu^{2} hong^{3} gan^{1} dtae^{2} bang^{1} teua^{2} bpai:^{1} ban^{5} nohk^{5} ber:ng^{2} wiak^{5} goh^{1} mi^{3}.

6. Lao^{3} mi^{3} heuan^{3} lang^{4} neu:ng^{2} yu^{2} gai:^{5} ban^{5} kohy^{6} lae:^{2} yu^{2} na:m^{3} kohp^{5} kua^{3} kohng^{4} lao^{3}.

7. Lao^{3} dtaeng^{2} ngan^{3} dai:^{5} sam^{4} bpi^{1} laew^{5}.

8. Mia^{3} lao^{3} seu^{2} wa^{2} Nang^{3} Bu:n^{1} Tohng^{3}. Ka:^{3} chao:^{5} mi^{3} luk^{5} ko:n^{3} diaw^{1}.

LESSON 3: THE NEIGHBORS, PART 1

1. I have one Lao friend named Thao Seng.

2. Thao Seng and I know each other well and like each other very much.

3. Thao Seng works at a ministry.

4. He is a government official.

5. Usually he works at the office, but sometimes he goes to rural areas to inspect work.

6. He has one house near my house and he lives with his family.

7. He married 3 years ago.

8. His wife is named Nang Bounthong.

9. They have one child.

Substitution Exercise

(See also exercises pp. 51 and 101.)

ຂະເຈົ້າ	ມີລູກ	ຈັກຄົນ	ມີ	ສອງຄົນ
ລາວ	ມີນ້ອງ			ສີ່ຫ້າຄົນ
ເຈົ້າ	ມີຄອບຄົວ			ຄົນດຽວ
ຢູ່ນີ້	ມີຄົນ			ສາມສິບຄົນ
ບ້ານເຈົ້າ				ຫ້າຄົນ
ລາວ				ສິບຄົນ

ka:^{3} chao:^{5}	mi^{3} luk^{5}	cha:k^{3} ko:n^{3}	mi:^{3}	sohng^{4} ko:n^{3}
lao^{3}	mi^{3} nohng^{5}			si^{2} ha^{6} ko:n^{3}
chao:^{5}	mi^{3} kohp^{5} kua^{3}			ko:n^{3} diaw^{1}
yu^{2} ni^{5}	mi^{3} ko:n^{3}			sam^{4} si:p^{3} ko:n^{3}
ban^{5} chao:^{5}				ha^{6} ko:n^{3}
lao^{3}				si:p^{3} ko:n^{3}

They have	children	how many?	Have	2 persons.
He has	younger siblings			4 or 5 persons.
You have	family			one person.
Here are	people			35 people.
Your house has				5 people.
He has				10 people.

(See also p.148/2.3)

ເຈົ້າອາຍຸ	ຈັກປີ	ສີ່ສິບປີ
ອາຍຸເຈົ້າ		ອາຍຸຂ້ອຍ ສາມສິບຫ້າປີ
ນ້ອງລາວ ອາຍຸ		ສິບສາມປີ
ທ່ານ		ອາຍຸຂ້ອຍ ຫ້າສິບສີ່ປີ

chao:^{5} a^{1} nyu:^{2}	cha:k^{3} bpi^{1}	si^{2} si:p^{3} bpi^{1}
a^{1} nyu:^{2} chao:^{5}		a^{1} nyu:^{2} kohy^{6} sam^{4} si:p^{3} ha^{6} bpi^{1}
nohng^{5} lao^{3} a^{1} nyu:^{2}		si:p^{3} sam^{4} bpi^{1}
tan^{2}		a^{1} nyu:^{2} kohy^{6} ha^{6} si:p^{3} si^{2} bpi^{1}

Your age	how many years?	40 years old.
Your age		My age 35 years old.
His younger sibling age		30 years old.
Sir's age		My age 54 years old.

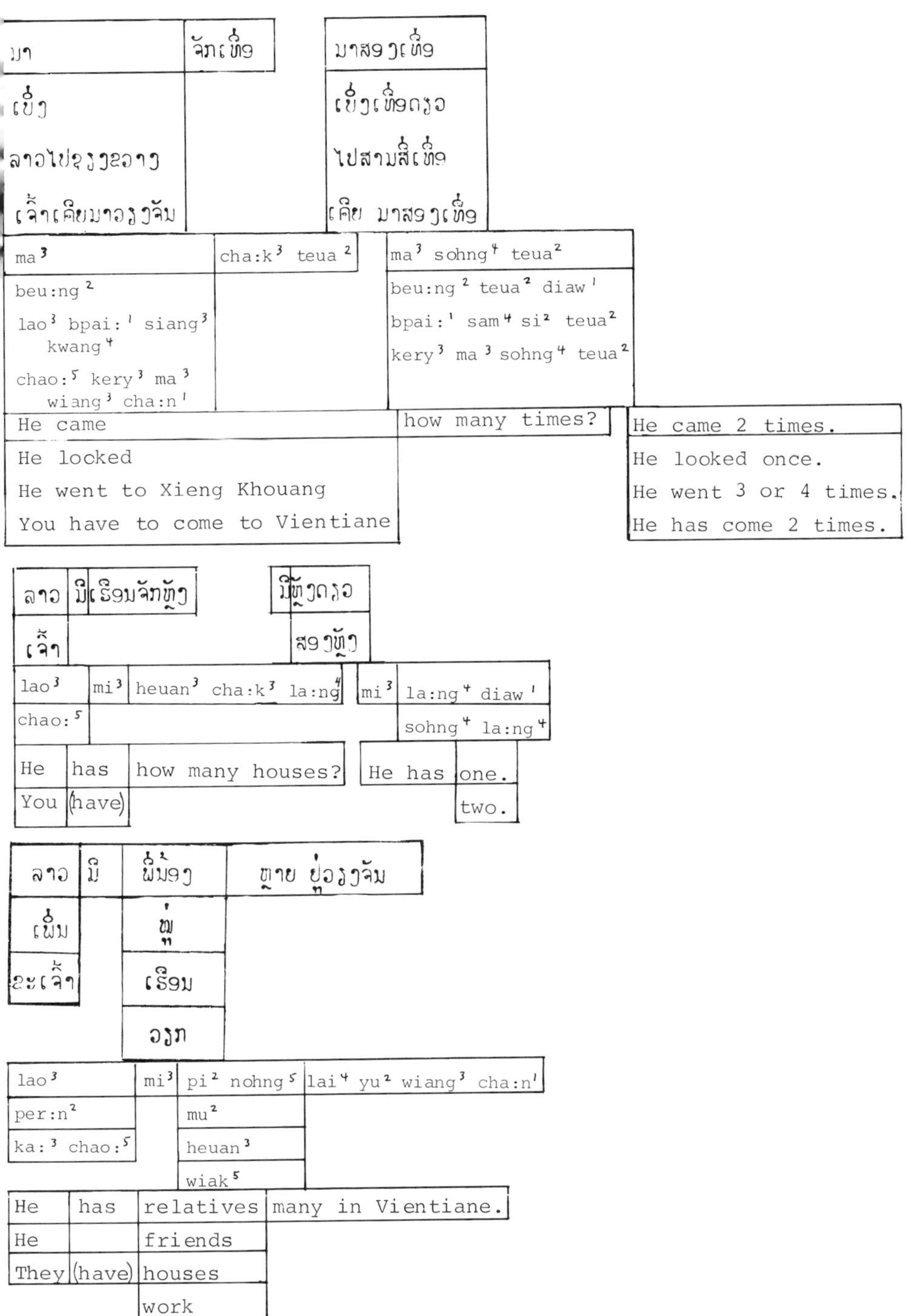

ມາ	ຈັກເທື່ອ
ເບິ່ງ	
ລາວໄປຊຽງຂວາງ	
ເຈົ້າເຄີຍມາວຽງຈັນ	

ມາສອງເທື່ອ
ເບິ່ງເທື່ອດຽວ
ໄປສາມສີ່ເທື່ອ
ເຄີຍ ມາສອງເທື່ອ

ma 3	cha:k 3 teua 2
beu:ng 2	
lao 3 bpai: 1 siang 3 kwang 4	
chao: 5 kery 3 ma 3 wiang 3 cha:n 1	

ma 3 sohng 4 teua 2
beu:ng 2 teua 2 diaw 1
bpai: 1 sam 4 si 2 teua 2
kery 3 ma 3 sohng 4 teua 2

He came	how many times?
He looked	
He went to Xieng Khouang	
You have to come to Vientiane	

He came 2 times.
He looked once.
He went 3 or 4 times.
He has come 2 times.

ລາວ	ມີ	ເຮືອນຈັກຫຼັງ
ເຈົ້າ		

ມີ	ຫຼັງດຽວ
	ສອງຫຼັງ

lao 3	mi 3	heuan 3 cha:k 3 la:ng 4
chao: 5		

mi 3	la:ng 4 diaw 1
	sohng 4 la:ng 4

He	has	how many houses?
You	(have)	

He has	one.
	two.

ລາວ	ມີ	ພີ່ນ້ອງ	ຫຼາຍ ຢູ່ວຽງຈັນ
ເພິ່ນ		ໝູ່	
ຂະເຈົ້າ		ເຮືອນ	
		ວຽກ	

lao 3	mi 3	pi 2 nohng 5	lai 4 yu 2 wiang 3 cha:n 1
per:n 2		mu 2	
ka: 3 chao: 5		heuan 3	
		wiak 5	

He	has	relatives	many in Vientiane.
He		friends	
They	(have)	houses	
		work	

ຂ້ອຍ ບໍ່ຮູ້ຈັກ	ລາວ	ມີອາຍຸຈັກປີ
	ຂະເຈົ້າ	ມີລູກຈັກຄົນ
		ເຮັດການຢູ່ໃສ
		ໄປໃສ
		ມາແຕ່ໃສ
		ໄປຈັກປີ
		ມາຈັກເທື່ອ

kohy^{6} boh^{2} hu^{5} cha:k^{3}	lao^{3}	mi^{3} a^{1} nyu:^{2} cha:k^{3} bpi^{1}
	ka:^{3} chao:^{5}	mi^{3} luk^{5} cha:k^{3} ko:n^{3}
		he:t^{2} gan^{1} yu^{2} sai:^{4}
		bpai:^{1} sai:^{4}
		ma^{3} dtae^{2} sai:^{4}
		bpai:^{1} cha:k^{3} bpi^{1}
		ma^{3} cha:k^{3} teua^{2}

I don't know	he	is how old?
	they	have how many children?
		work where?
		came from where?
		went for how many years?
		came how many times?

Vocabulary Exercise

	Lao	Transliteration	English
4-1	<u>ເກີດ</u>	<u>gert^6</u>	<u>To be born</u>
	ຂ້ອຍເກີດຢູ່ວຽງຈັນ	kohy^6 gert^6 yu^2 wiang^3 cha:n^1	I was born in Vientiane.
	ຂະເຈົ້າເກີດຢູ່ຕ່າງປະເທດ	ka:^{3} chao:^{5} gert^6 yu^2 dtang^2 bpa:^{3} tet^5	They were born abroad.
	ເຈົ້າເກີດຢູ່ໃສ ອາຍຸຈັກປີ	chao:^{5} gert^6 yu^2 sai:^{4} a^{1}nyu:^{2} cha:k^3 bpi^1	Where were you born? How old (are you)?
	ຂ້ອຍບໍ່ຮູ້ ລາວເກີດຢູ່ໃສ	kohy^6 boh^2 hu^5 lao^3 gert^6 yu^2 sai:^{4}	I don't know where he was born.
4-2	<u>ອາຍຸ</u>	<u>a^1 nyu:^{2}</u>	<u>Age</u>
	ອາຍຸເຈົ້າ ຈັກປີ	a^1 nyu:^{2} chao:^{5} cha:k^3 bpi^1	How old are you?
	ອາຍຸຂ້ອຍ ສິບປີ	a^1 nyu:^{2} kohy^6 si:p^3 bpi^1	I'm 10 years old.
	ເຈົ້າ ຮູ້ຈັກອາຍຸຂອງພໍ່ແມ່ເຈົ້າບໍ່	chao:^{5} hu^5 cha:k^3 a^1 nyu:^{2} kohng^4 poh^2 mae^2 chao:^{5} boh^2	Do you know your parent's age?
	ລາວບໍ່ຮູ້ ອາຍຸລາວຈັກປີ	lao^3 boh^2 hu^5 a^1 nyu:^{2} lao^3 cha:k^3 bpi^1	He doesn't know how old he is.
4-3	<u>ນຳກັນ</u>	<u>na:m^3 ga:n^1</u>	<u>Together</u>
	ລາວກັບຂ້ອຍເຄີຍຮຽນນຳກັນ	lao^3 ga:p^3 kohy^6 kery^3 hian^3 na:m^3 ga:n^1	He and I have studied together.
	ຂະເຈົ້າ ມານຳກັນ	ka:^{3} chao:^{5} ma^3 na:m^3 ga:n^1	They came together.
	ຂະເຈົ້າ ບໍ່ຢູ່ນຳກັນ	ka:^{3} chao:^{5} boh^2 yu^2 na:m^3 ga:n^1	They are not living together.
	ມີຄົນຫຼາຍຄົນ ຢູ່ນຳກັນ	mi^3 ko:n^3 lai^4 ko:n^3 yu^2 na:m^3 ga:n^1	There are many people. They live together.

4-4 <u>เลื้อยๆ</u> (See also p.154/6.3)	<u>leuay^{5} leuay^{5}</u>	<u>Always, all the time</u>
เพิ่นเว้าเรื่องนั้น เลื้อยๆ	per:n^{2} wao:^{5} leuang^{2} na:n^{5} leuay^{5} leuay^{5}	He always tells that story.
ลาว มาหาข้อย เลื้อยๆ	lao^{3} ma^{3} ha^{4} kohy^{6} leuay^{5} leuay^{5}	He always comes to see me.
ຂະເຈົ້າ มาซื้อของวຽງຈັນເລື້ອຍໆ	ka:^{3} chao:^{5} ma^{3} seu^{5} kohng^{4} wiang^{3} cha:n^{1} leuay^{5} leuay^{5}	They always come to shop in Vientiane.
ຂະເຈົ້າຮັກກັນຫຼາຍ ຢູ່ນຳກັນເລື້ອຍໆ	ka:^{3} chao:^{5} ha:k^{2} ga:n^{1} lai^{4} yu^{2} na:m^{3} ga:n^{1} leuay^{5} leuay^{5}	They like each other a lot, (they) are always together.
4-5 <u>ດົນໆ</u>	<u>do:n^{1} do:n^{1}</u>	<u>For a long time</u>
ທ້າວຄຳ ເຮັດການ ຢູ່ກະຊວງ ດົນໆ ໄດ້ ສາມສິບປີແລ້ວ	tao^{5} ka:m^{3} he:t^{2} gan^{1} yu^{2} ga:^{3}suang^{3} do:n^{1} do:n^{1} dai:^{5} sam^{4} si:p^{3} bpi^{1} laew^{5}	Thao Kham has been working in the ministry for a long time. It's been 30 years now.
ຂະເຈົ້າຢູ່ວຽງຈັນ ດົນໆ	ka:^{3} chao:^{5} yu^{2} wiang^{3} cha:n^{1} do:n^{1} do:n^{1}	They have lived in Vientiane for many years.
ເມັຽລາວໄປຕລາດ ດົນໆ ຊື້ຂອງຫຼາຍ	mia:^{3} lao^{3} bpai:^{1} dta:^{3} lat^{6} do:n^{1} do:n^{1} seu^{5} kohng^{4} lai^{4}	His wife went to market for a long time to do lots of shopping.
ຂ້ອຍຮູ້ຈັກລາວ ດົນໆ ຫຼາຍປີແລ້ວ	kohy^{6} hu^{5} cha:k^{3} lao^{3} do:n^{1} do:n^{1} lai^{4} bpi^{1} laew^{5}	I have known him for a long time; it's been many years.
4-6 <u>ເວົ້າ</u>	<u>wao:^{5}</u>	<u>To speak, tell</u>
ເຈົ້າເວົ້າພາສາລາວໄດ້ບໍ່	chao:^{5} wao:^{5} pa^{3} sa^{4} lao^{3} dai:^{5} boh^{2}	Can you speak Lao?
ລູກລາວເວົ້າເປັນແລ້ວບໍ່	luk^{5} lao^{3} wao:^{5} bpe:n^{1} laew^{5} boh^{2}	Can his son speak already?

	Lao	Transcription	English
	ຂະເຈົ້າເວົ້າເລື່ອງໝູ່	ka:^{3} chao:^{5} wao:^{5} leuang^2 mu^2	They talk about their friends.
	ລາວເວົ້າວ່າ ລາວຊິໄປຕ່າງປະເທດ	lao^3 wao:^{5} wa^2 lao^3 si:^{2} bpai:^{1} dtang^2 bpa:^{3} tet^5	He says that he is going abroad.
	ຂະເຈົ້າເວົ້າວ່າ ບໍ່ຮູ້ບ້ານເພິ່ນຢູ່ໃສ	ka:^{3} chao:^{5} wao:^{5} wa^2 boh^2 hu^5 ban^5 per:n^2 yu^2 sai:^{4}	They say that they don't know where his house is.
4-7	<u>ເຄີຍ</u> (See also p.153/5.2c)	<u>kery</u>^{3}	<u>Have ... ed</u>
	ເຈົ້າເຄີຍໄປຊຽງຂວາງບໍ່	chao:^{5} kery^3 bpai:^{1} siang^3 kwang^4 boh^2	Have you been to Xieng Khouang?
	ຂ້ອຍເຄີຍຢູ່ວຽງຈັນ	kohy^6 kery^3 yu^2 wiang^3 cha:n^1	I used to live in Vientiane.
	ລາວເຄີຍຮຽນພາສາລາວເທື່ອນຶ່ງ	lao^3 kery^3 hian^3 pa^3 sa^4 lao^3 teua^2 neu:ng^2	He once learned Lao before.
	ຂ້ອຍບໍ່ເຄີຍເດີນທາງໄປຕ່າງປະເທດ	kohy^6 boh^2 kery^3 dern^1 tang^3 bpai:^{1} dtang^2 bpa:^{3} tet^5	I have never travelled abroad.
4-8	<u>ມັກ</u>	<u>ma:k</u>^{2}	<u>To like</u>
	ເຈົ້າມັກລາວບໍ່	chao:^{5} ma:k^2 lao^3 boh^2	Do you like Lao?
	ລູກມັກພໍ່ແມ່ຫຼາຍ	luk^5 ma:k^2 poh^2 mae^2 lai^4	Children like (their) father and mother very much.
	ຂະເຈົ້າມັກເວົ້າດົນໆ	ka:^{3} chao:^{5} ma:k^2 wao:^{5} do:n^1 do:n^1	They like to talk for a long time.
	ຂ້ອຍມັກໄປຫຼິ້ນຢູ່ຫັ້ນ	kohy^5 ma:k^2 bpai:^{1} lin^6 yu^2 ha:n^6	I like to go there to play (for enjoyment.)
	ລາວມັກຊື້ຂອງ ຢູ່ຕລາດ	lao^3 ma:k^2 seu^5 kohng^4 yu^2 dta:^{3} lat^6	She likes to buy things at the market.

Text

ບົດ ຮຽນ ທີ່ ສີ່

1. ນາງບຸນທອງເປັນໄທວຽງຈັນ

2. ມີພີ່ນ້ອງຫຼາຍຢູ່ນີ້ ແຕ່ພໍ່ລາວ ທ້າວແສງມາແຕ່ຊຽງຂວາງ ເກີດຢູ່ຫັ້ນ.

3. ປີນີ້ ລາວ ອາຍຸ ສາມສິບປີ

4. ຂ້ອຍບໍ່ຮູ້ ອາຍຸເມັຽລາວ ຈັກປີ.

5. ເມັຽທ້າວແສງກັບເມັຽ ຂ້ອຍກໍຮັກກັນຫຼາຍ

6. ຂະເຈົ້າ ໄປຕລາດນຳກັນເລື້ອຍໆ

7. ນາງບຸນທອງຊື້ຂອງເກັ່ງ.

8. ມື້ວັນອາທິດ ພວກຂ້ອຍ ໄປຫາຂະເຈົ້າຢູ່ບ້ານ ແລະລົມກັນດົນໆ

9. ທ້າວແສງເຄີຍໄປຕ່າງ ປະເທດ ສາມສີ່ເທື່ອ

10. ລາວມັກເວົ້າເຣື່ອງການເດີນທາງຂອງລາວ.

BO:T^{3} HIAN^{3} TI^{2} SI^{2}

1. Nang^{3} Bu:n^{1} Tohng^{3} bpe:n^{1} tai^{3} wiang^{3} cha:n^{1}.
2. Mi^{3} pi^{2} nohng^{5} lai^{4} yu^{2} ni^{5} dtae^{2} pua^{4} lao^{3} Tao^{5} Saeng^{4} ma^{3} dtae^{2} siang^{3} kuang^{4}, gert^{6} yu^{2} ha:n^{6}.
3. Bpi^{1} ni^{5} lao^{3} a^{1} nyu^{2} sam^{4} si:p^{3} bpi^{1}.
4. Kohy^{6} boh^{2} hu^{5} a^{1} nyu^{2} mia^{3} lao^{3} cha:k^{3} bpi^{1}.
5. Mia^{3} Tao^{5} Saeng^{4} ga:p^{3} mia^{3} kohy^{6} goh^{1} ha:k^{2} ga:n^{1} lai^{4}.
6. Ka:^{3} chao:^{5} bpai:^{1} dta:^{3} lat^{6} na:m^{3} ga:n^{1} leuay^{5} leuay^{5}.
7. Nang^{3} Bu:n^{1} Tohng^{3} seu^{5} kohng^{4} geng^{2}.
8. Meu^{5} wan^{3} a^{1} ti:t^{2} puak^{5} kohy^{6} bpai:^{1} ha^{4} ka:^{3}chao:^{5} yu^{2} ban^{5} lae:^{2} lo:m^{3} ga:n^{1} do:n^{1} do:n^{1}.
9. Tao^{5} Saeng^{4} kery^{3} bpai:^{1} dtang^{2} pa:^{3} tet^{5} sam^{4} si^{2} teua^{2}.
10. Lao^{3} ma:k^{2} wao:^{5} leuang^{2} gan^{1} dern^{1} tang^{3} kohng^{4} lao^{3}.

LESSON 4: THE NEIGHBORS, PART 2

1. Nang Bounthong is a native of Vientiane.
2. She has many relatives here, but her husband Thao Seng comes from Xieng Khouang; he was born there.
3. This year, he is 30 years old.
4. I don't know how old his wife is.
5. Thao Seng's wife and my wife like each other very much.
6. They go to market together often.
7. Nang Bounthong is good at shopping.
8. On Sunday we go to see them at their home and talk a very long time.
9. Thao Seng has been abroad three or four times.
10. He likes to talk about his travels.

LESSON 5: GOING TO MARKET BY PEDICAB

Substitution Exercise

ໄປຫັ້ນເທົ່າໃດ	bpai:^{1} ha:n^{6} tao:^{2} dai:^{1}	How much to go there?
ທັງໝົດ ສອງຮ້ອຍສິບກີບ	ta:ng^{3} mo:t^{3} sohng^{4} hohy^{5} si:p^{3} gip^{6}	In all 210 kip.
ໄລ່ເງິນດຸ່	lai:^{2} nger:n^{3} du:^{2}	Count the money please.
ຕອນແລງມາຫາເພິ່ນແດ່ດຸ່	dton^{1} laeng^{3} ma^{3} ha^{4} per:n^{2} dae^{2} du^{2}	In the evening, please come look for them.
ນັ່ງນີ້ດຸ່	na:ng^{2} ni^{5} du:^{2}	Please sit here.
ໄປແດ່	bpai:^{1} dae^{2}	Please go.
ຊື້ໝາກກ້ວຍແດ່	seu^{5} mak^{6} guay^{5} dae^{2}	Please buy some bananas.
ຊິໄປໃສ	si:^{2} bpai:^{1} sai:^{4}	Where are you going?
ຂອບໃຈ	kohp^{6} chai:^{1}	Thanks.
ເຊີນ	sern^{3}	Please.
ເອົາເທົ່າໃດ	ao:^{1} tao:^{2} dai:^{1}	How much is it?
ໄປຕລາດເຊົ້າ	bpai^{1} dta:^{3} lat^{6} sao:^{5}	Go to the morning market.

ຊິໄປໃສ	ຊິໄປ	ຕລາດເຊົ້າ
		ວຽງຈັນ
		ຕ່າງປະເທດ

si:2 bpai:1 sai:4	si:2 bpai:1	dta:3 lat6 sao:5
		wiang3 cha:n1
		dtang2 bpa:3 tet5

Where are you going?	I will go to	the morning market.
		Vientiane.
		abroad.

(See also p.150/4.1)

ໄປຕລາດເຊົ້າ	ເທົ່າໃດ	ຫົກສິບກີບ
ໄປວິທຍາລັຍ		ຫ້າສິບ
ໝາກກ້ວຍຫວີນຶ່ງ		ຫວີນຶ່ງ ສອງຮ້ອຍກີບ
ໝາກຫຸ່ງໜ່ວຍນຶ່ງ		ໜ່ວຍນີ້ ຮ້ອຍຫ້າສິບ
ໝາກກ້ຽງ ກິໂລ		ກິໂລລະສອງຮ້ອຍ

bpai:1 dta:3 lat6 sao:5	tao:2 dai:1	ho:k3 si:p3 gip6
bpai:1 wi:2 ta:2 nya3 lai:3		ha6 si:p3
mak6 guay5 wi4 neu:ng2		wi4 neu:ng2 sohng4 hohy5 gip6
mak6 hu:ng2 nuay2 neu:ng2		nuay2 neu:ng2 hohy5 ha6 si:p3
mak6 giang5 gi1 lo3		gi1 lo3 la:2 sohng4 hohy5

To go to the morning market	how much?	60 kip.
To go to the high school		50.
Bananas one bunch		One bunch 200 kip.
Papaya one fruit		One fruit 150
Oranges one kilo		Per kilo 200.

(See also p.147/2.2.4b)

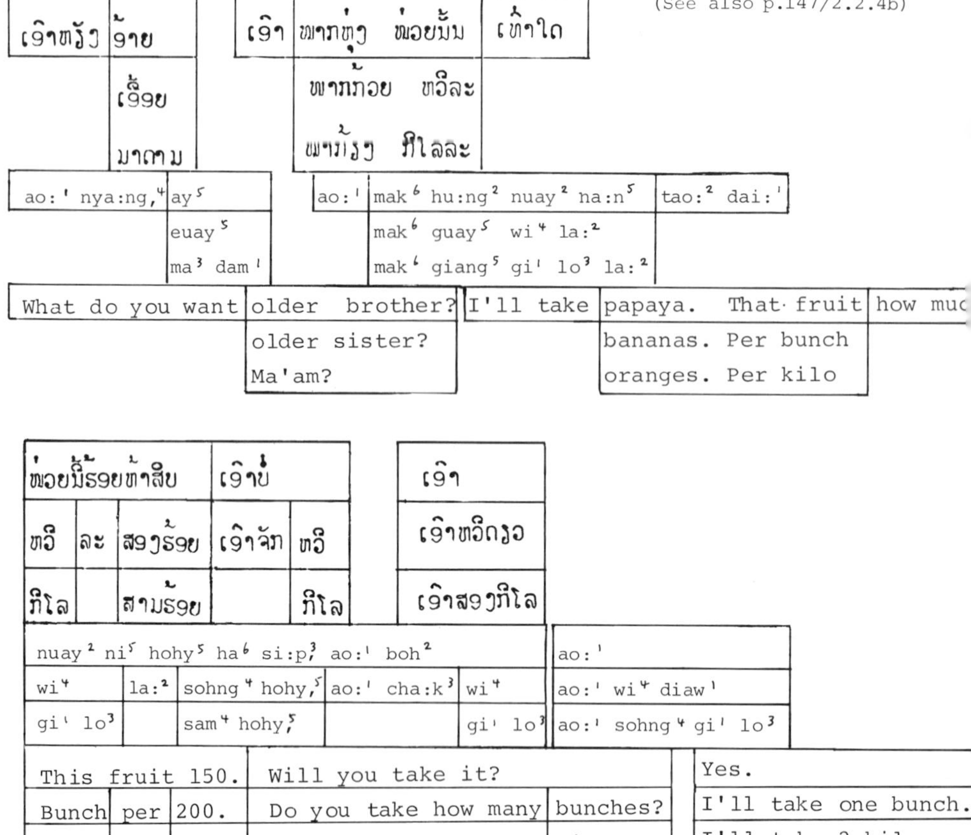

ເອົາຫຍັງ	ອ້າຍ
	ເອື້ອຍ
	ມາດາມ

ao:^{1} nya:ng,^{4}	ay^5
	euay^5
	ma^3 dam^1

What do you want	older brother?
	older sister?
	Ma'am?

ເອົາ	ໝາກຫຸ່ງ ໜ່ວຍນັ້ນ	ເທົ່າໃດ
	ໝາກກ້ວຍ ຫວີລະ	
	ໝາກກ້ຽງ ກິໂລລະ	

ao:^{1}	mak^6 hu:ng^2 nuay^2 na:n^5	tao:^{2} dai:^{1}
	mak^6 guay^5 wi^4 la:^{2}	
	mak^6 giang^5 gi^1 lo^3 la:^{2}	

I'll take	papaya. That fruit	how muc
	bananas. Per bunch	
	oranges. Per kilo	

ໜ່ວຍນີ້ຮ້ອຍຫ້າສິບ			ເອົາບໍ່	
ຫວີ	ລະ	ສອງຮ້ອຍ	ເອົາຈັກ	ຫວີ
ກິໂລ		ສາມຮ້ອຍ		ກິໂລ

ເອົາ
ເອົາຫວີດຽວ
ເອົາສອງກິໂລ

nuay^2 ni^5 hohy^5 ha^6 si:p,^{3}			ao:^{1} boh^2	
wi^4	la:^{2}	sohng^4 hohy,^{5}	ao:^{1} cha:k^3	wi^4
gi^1 lo^3		sam^4 hohy,^{5}		gi^1 lo^3

ao:^{1}
ao:^{1} wi^4 diaw^1
ao:^{1} sohng^4 gi^1 lo^3

This fruit 150.			Will you take it?	
Bunch	per	200.	Do you take how many	bunches?
Kilo		300.		kilos?

Yes.
I'll take one bunch.
I'll take 2 kilos.

ສອງ	ຄົນ
ສາມ	ຫຼັງ
ສີ່	ຄັນ
ຫ້າ	ໜ່ວຍ
ຫົກ	ຫວີ
ເຈັດ	ກິໂລ
ແປດ	ມື້
ເກົ້າ	ກີບ
ສິບ	
ຈັກ	

sohng^4	ko:n^3
sam^4	la:ng^4
si^2	ka:n^3
ha^6	nuay^2
ho:k^3	wi^4
che:t^3	gi^1 lo^3
bpaet^6	meu^5
gao:^{5}	gip^6
si:p^3	
cha:k^3	

2	people
3	buildings
4	machines.
5	fruits
6	bunches
7	kilos
8	days
9	kip
10	
How many	

ຄົນ	ນຶ່ງ
ຫຼັງ	ນີ້
ຄັນ	ນັ້ນ
ໜ່ວຍ	ໃໝ່
ຫວີ	

ko:n^3	neu:ng^2
la:ng^4	ni^5
ka:n^3	na:n^5
nuay^2	mai:^{2}
wi^4	

People	one
Building	this
Machines	that
Fruit	new
Bunches	

(See also p.150/4.2)

Vocabulary Exercise

	Lao	Transcription	English
5-1	ຖ້າ	ta6	To wait
	ສາມລໍ້ ຖ້າຢູ່ນີ້ແດ່	sam4 lo,5 ta6 yu2 ni5 dae2	Samloh, please wait here!
	ເຈົ້າຖ້າຂ້ອຍ ຢູ່ນີ້ແດ່	chao:5 ta6 kohy6 yu2 ni5 dae2	Please wait for me here.
	ຂ້ອຍຖ້າເຈົ້າ ດົນໆ ແຕ່ເຈົ້າບໍ່ມາ	kohy6 ta6 chao:5 do:n1 do:n1 dtae2 chao:5 boh2 ma3	I waited for you for a long time, but you did not come.
	ຂ້ອຍຖ້າເຈົ້າກໍໄດ້	kohy6 ta6 chao:5 goh1 dai:5	I can wait for you.
5-2	ແຕ່ (ນີ້) [ໄປ , ມາ]	dtae2 (ni5) [bpai:1, ma3]	From (here) to ...
	ແຕ່ນີ້ໄປມີຈັກກິໂລ	dtae2 ni5 bpai:1 mi3 cha:k6 gi1 lo3	How many kilometers from here?
	ແຕ່ວຽງຈັນໄປຫັ້ນມີຈັກກິໂລ	dtae2 wiang3 cha:n1 bpai:1 ha:n6 mi3 cha:k3 gi1 lo3	How many kilometers from Vientiane to there?
	ແຕ່ຕລາດມານີ້ ເຈັດສິບກີບ	dtae2 dta:3 lat6 ma3 ni5 che:t3 si:p3 gip6	From market to here, 70 kip.
	ແຕ່ຊຽງຂວາງມາວຽງຈັນ ຂ້ອຍມານຳຂະເຈົ້າ	dtae2 siang3 kwang4 ma3 wiang3 cha:n1 kohy6 ma3 na:m3 ka:3 chao:5	From Xieng Khouang to Vientiane I came with them.
5-3	ເປັນຫຍັງ	bpe:n1 nya:ng4	Why
	ເປັນຫຍັງ ຂະເຈົ້າບໍ່ມາ	bpe:n1 nya:ng4 ka:3 chao:5 boh2 ma3	Why don't they come?
	ເປັນຫຍັງ ເຈົ້າຢາກໄດ້	bpe:n1 nya:ng4 chao:5 yak6 dai:5	Why do you want it?
	ເປັນຫຍັງ ລາວເວົ້າວ່າລາວບໍ່ຮູ້	bpe:n1 nya:ng4 lao3 wao:5 wa2 lao5 boh2 hu5	Why does he say he doesn't know?

	Lao	Transcription	English
	ເປັນຫຍັງ ອ້າຍເຈົ້າບໍ່ໄປນຳ	bpe:n^1 nya:ng^4 ay^5 chao:^{5} boh^2 bpai:^{1} na:m^3	Why doesn't your brother go together (with you)?
	ເປັນຫຍັງ ລາວບໍ່ຮູ້	bpe:n^1 nya:ng^4 lao^3 boh^2 hu^5	Why doesn't he know?
5-4	<u>ແທ້</u>	<u>tae^5</u>	<u>Indeed, really</u>!
	ຫຼາຍແທ້	lai^4 tae^5	That's really a lot!
	ແພງແທ້	paeng^3 tae^5	It's expensive indeed!
	ມີຫຼາຍແທ້	mi^3 lai^4 tae^5	There are many indeed!
5-5	<u>ແຕ່</u>	<u>dtae^2</u>	<u>Only</u>
	ຂ້ອຍມີແຕ່ສາມຮ້ອຍກີບນຶ່ງ	kohy^5 mi^3 dtae^2 sam^4 hohy^5 gip^6 neu:ng^1	I have only 300 kip.
	ລາວມີລູກແຕ່ຄົນດຽວ	lao^3 mi^3 luk^5 dtae^2 ko:n^3 diaw^1	He has only one child.
	ມື້ນີ້ມີແຕ່ແນວນີ້	meu^5 ni^5 mi^3 dtae^2 naew^3 ni^5	Today there is only this variety (kind).
	ຂະເຈົ້າ ມາແຕ່ສາມຄົນ	ka:^{3} chao:^{5} ma^3 dtae^2 sam^4 ko:n^3	Just three persons came.
5-6	<u>ຈຶ່ງ</u> (See also p.155/7.2)	<u>cheu:ng^2</u>	<u>Then, so</u>
	ລາວຖ້າເຈົ້າ ດົນໆ ຈຶ່ງໄປ	lao^3 ta^6 chao:^{5} do:n^1 do:n^1 cheu:ng^2 bpai:^{1}	He waited for you quite a while and then went away.
	ຫ້າສິບ ລາວບໍ່ໄປ ເຈັດສິບຈຶ່ງໄປ	Ha^6 si:p^3 lao^3 boh^2 bpai:^{1} che:t^3 si:p^3 cheu:ng^2 bpai:^{1}	For 50 (kip) he won't go; for 70 (kip) he will.
	ລາວມາແລ້ວຈຶ່ງຈະໄປ	lao^3 ma^3 laew^5 cheu:ng^2 cha:^{3} bpai:^{1}	If he comes, then he'll go (with you)
	ສາມລໍ້ຄັນນັ້ນແພງຈຶ່ງບໍ່ເອົາ	sam^4 loh^5 ka:n^3 na:n^5 paeng^3 cheu:ng^2 boh^2 ao:^{5}	That samloh is expensive, so I won't take it.

	Lao	Romanization	English
5-7	<u>ໃໝ່</u> (See also p.154/6.2)	<u>mai:2</u>	<u>Another, New</u>
	ເຮືອນຫຼັງນີ້ແພງ ເອົາຫຼັງໃໝ່	heuan3 la:ng4 ni5 paeng3. ao:1 la:ng4 mai:2	This house is expensive. We'll take another house.
	ລາວໄປແລ້ວ ຂ້ອຍຊິເອົາຄົນໃໝ່	lao3 bpai:1 laew.5 kohy6 si:2 ao:1 ko:n3 mai:2	He is gone. I'll use another man.
	ໜ່ວຍນີ້ບໍ່ດີ ເອົາໜ່ວຍໃໝ່ຊະ	nuay2 ni5 boh2 di.1 ao:1 nuay2 mai:2 sa:2	This is not good. Why don't you have another.
	ບໍ່ມີແລ້ວຊິຊື້ແນວໃໝ່	boh2 mi3 laew.5 si:2 seu5 naew2 mai:2	It's used up. I'll buy a different kind.
5-8	<u>ເທົ່າໃດ</u>	<u>tao:2 dai:1</u>	<u>How much?</u>
	ໝາກກ້ວຍຫວີນີ້ເທົ່າໃດ	mak6 guay5 wi4 ni5 tao:2 dai:1	How much is this bunch of bananas?
	ໄປວຽງຈັນເທົ່າໃດ	bpai:1 wiang3 cha:n1 tao:2 dai:1	How much is the fare to Vientiane?
	ເຈົ້າຊື້ເທົ່າໃດ	chao:5 seu5 tao:2 dai:1	How much will you buy?
	ຂ້ອຍຊື້ສາມກິໂລ	kohy6 seu5 sam4 gi1 lo3	I'll buy 3 kilograms.
5-9	<u>ຂະນ້ອຍ</u> (See also p.145/2.2.4)	<u>ka:3 nohy5</u>	<u>Sir, Ma'am</u>
	ມີ ຂະນ້ອຍ	mi3 ka:3 nohy5	I have some (Here are some), sir (ma'am).
	ຢູ່ ຂະນ້ອຍ	yu2 ka:3 nohy5	(He) is here sir.
	ມາສອງຄົນ ຂະນ້ອຍ	ma3 sohng4 ko:n3 ka:3 nohy5	Two people came, sir.
	ມີຄົນມາຫາ ຂະນ້ອຍ	mi3 ko:n3 ma3 ha4 ka:3 nohy5	Someone has come to visit, sir.
5-10	<u>ຫຍັງ</u>	<u>nya:ng4</u>	<u>What?</u>
	ແມ່ນຫຍັງ	maen2 nya:ng4	What is it?
	ເຈົ້າ ຢາກຊື້ຫຍັງຢູ່ຕລາດເຊົ້າ	chao:5 yak6 seu5 nya:ng4 yu2 dta:3 lat6 sao:5	What do you want to buy at the morning market?

	Lao	Romanization	English
	ຂະເຈົ້າເວົ້າຫຍັງ	ka:3 chao:5 wao:5 nya:ng4	What did they say?
	ລາວເປັນຄົນຫຍັງ	lao3 bpe:n1 ko:n3 nya:ng4	Of what nationality is he?
5-11	<u>ລະ</u>	<u>la:2</u>	<u>Per, for</u>
	ຂ້ອຍຊື້ກິໂລລະສີ່ສິບກີບ	kohy6 seu5 gi1 lo3 la:2 si2 si:p3 gip6	I'll buy at 40 kip per kilo.
	ຂະເຈົ້າເອົາຄົນລະຮ້ອຍກີບ	ka:3 chao:5 ao:1 ko:n3 la:2 hohy5 gip6	They charge 100 kip per person.
	ລາວໄປຕລາດມື້ລະເທື່ອ	lao3 bpai:1 dta:3 lat6 meu5 la:2 teua2	She goes to market once a day.
	ໝາກກ້ຽງໜ່ວຍລະ ສິບຫ້າກີບ	mak6 giang5 nuay2 la:2 si:p3 ha6 gip6	Oranges are 15 kip each.
5-12	<u>ຢາກໄດ້</u>	<u>yak6 (dai:5)</u>	<u>To want</u>
	ເຈົ້າຢາກໄດ້ຫຍັງ	chao:5 yak6 dai:5 nya:ng4	What do you want?
	ຂ້ອຍຢາກໄດ້ເຮືອນຫຼັງນຶ່ງ	kohy6 yak6 dai:5 heuan3 la:ng4 neu:ng2	I want a house.
	ລາວບໍ່ຢາກໄດ້ໝາກກ້ຽງບໍ່	lao3 boh2 yak6 dai:5 mak6 giang5 boh2	Doesn't he want oranges?
	ຂ້ອຍຢາກໄດ້ແຕ່ໝາກຫຸ່ງ	kohy6 yak6 dai:5 dtae2 mak6 hu:ng2	I want only papaya.
5-13	<u>ແຊບ</u>	<u>saep5</u>	<u>Delicious</u>
	ໝາກກ້ຽງເຈົ້າຊື້ມື້ນີ້ແຊບຫຼາຍ	mak6 giang5 chao:5 seu5 meu5 ni5 saep5 lai4	The oranges you bought today are very delicious.
	ແນວນັ້ນແຊບບໍ່	naew3 na:n5 saep5 boh2	Is that one delicious?
	ດຽວນີ້ໝາກຫຸ່ງບໍ່ແຊບ	diaw1 ni5 mak6 hu:ng2 boh2 saep5	Now, papaya is not delicious.

5-14	<u>ມື້ນີ້</u>	<u>meu^{5} ni^{5}</u>	<u>Today</u>
	ມື້ນີ້ເຈົ້າບໍ່ໄປຕລາດບໍ່	meu^{5} ni^{5} chao:^{5} boh^{2} bpai:^{1} dta:^{3} lat^{6} boh^{2}	Don't you go to market today?
	ມື້ນີ້ຍັງມີຂອງຫຼາຍ ບໍ່ໄປຊື້ກໍໄດ້	meu^{5} ni^{2} nya:ng^{3} mi^{3} kohng^{4} lai^{4} boh^{2} bpai:^{1} seu^{5} goh^{1} dai:^{5}	We still have things today. We don't have to go shopping (yet).
	ເປັນຫຍັງມື້ນີ້ບໍ່ມີໝາກກ້ຽງ	bpe:n^{1} nya:ng^{4} meu^{5} ni^{5} boh^{2} mi^{3} mak^{6} giang^{5}	Why aren't there any oranges today?
	ມື້ນີ້ ລາວຊິມາຫາຂ້ອຍ	meu^{5} ni^{5} lao^{3} si:^{2} ma^{3} ha^{4} kohy^{6}	He will come to see me today.
5-15	<u>ເທົ່ານັ້ນ ເທົ່ານີ້</u>	<u>tao:^{2} na:n^{5}, tao:^{2} ni^{5}</u>	<u>Only that, only this.</u>
	ເຈົ້າມີເທົ່ານັ້ນບໍ່	chao:^{5} mi^{3} tao:^{2} na:n^{5} boh^{2}	Is that all you have?
	ມື້ນີ້ ຂ້ອຍມີເທົ່ານີ້ ຫຼະ	meu^{5} ni^{5} kohy^{6} mi^{3} tao:^{2} ni^{5} la:^{3}	Today I only have this.
	ສາມຮ້ອຍບໍ່ແພງແທ້ ສອງຮ້ອຍຫ້າສິບກີບ ເທົ່ານັ້ນ ຫຼະ	sam^{4} hohy^{5} boh^{2} paeng^{3} tae^{5} sohng^{4} hohy^{5} ha^{6} si:p^{3} gip^{6} tao:^{2} na:n^{5} la:^{3}	300 is not expensive at all. 250 kip is the last (price I can offer).
5-16	<u>ທັງໝົດ</u>	<u>ta:ng^{3} mo:t^{3}</u>	<u>In all</u>
	ຂະເຈົ້າມາທັງໝົດສິບຫ້າຄົນ	ka:^{3} chao:^{5} ma^{3} ta:ng^{3} mo:t^{3} si:p^{3} ha^{6} ko:n^{3}	In all 15 persons came.
	ລາວມີເຮືອນທັງໝົດ ສິບຫຼັງ	lao^{3} mi^{3} heuan^{3} ta:ng^{3} mo:t^{3} si:p^{3} la:ng^{4}	He has 10 houses in all.
	ທັງໝົດເທົ່າໃດ	ta:ng^{3} mo:t^{3} tao:^{2} dai:^{1}	How much are they in all?
	ໄລ່ເງິນທັງໝົດຈັກກີບ	lai:^{2} nger:n^{3} ta:ng^{3} mo:t^{3} cha:k^{3} gip^{6}	Count the money to see how much in all.

Text

ບົດ ຮຽນ ທີ່ ຫ້າ

1. ສາມລໍ້ ຖ້າແດ່

2. ສາມລໍ້ ຊິໄປໃສ

3. ໄປຕລາດເຊົ້າ ແຕ່ນີ້ໄປຫັ້ນເທົ່າໃດ

4. ສາມລໍ້ ຣ້ອຍນຶ່ງ

5. ເປັນຫຽັງ ເອົາແພງແທ້ ຂ້ອຍເຄີຍໄປແຕ່ຫົກສິບກີບນຶ່ງ

6. ສາມລໍ້ ແປດສິບຈຶ່ງຈະໄປ

7. ໄປຊະ ຂ້ອຍຊິເອົາຄັນໃໝ່...............

ສາມລໍ້ ໄປຕລາດເຊົ້າ ເອົາເທົ່າໃດ

8. ສາມລໍ້ ເຈັດສິບກີບຂ້ານ້ອຍ

9. ຫົກສິບກີບ ໄປບໍ່

10. ສາມລໍ້ ໄປ

11. ແມ່ຄ້າ ເອົາຫຽັງ ມາຖາມ ເອົາໝາກໄມ້ບໍ່.

12. ໝາກກ້ຽງກິໂລລະເທົ່າໃດ

13. ແມ່ຄ້າ ກິໂລລະສອງຣ້ອຍ ຢາກໄດ້ຈັກກິໂລ

14. ສອງກິໂລ ໝາກຫຸ່ງໜ່ອຍນັ້ນ ເທົ່າໃດ

15. ແມ່ຄ້າ ແນວນີ້ແຊບຫຼາຍ ເອົານຳ ມາຖາມ ຣ້ອຍຫ້າສິບ ຊະ

16. ຂ້ອຍ ຢາກໄດ້ໝາກກ້ວຍຫວີນຶ່ງ ຫວີຈັກກີບ

17. ແມ່ຄ້າ ຣ້ອຍແປດສິບ

18. ເປັນຫຽັງມື້ນີ້ ໝາກກ້ວຍແພງແທ້ ຣ້ອຍຫ້າສິບເທົ່ານັ້ນຫຼະ
ໄລ່ເງິນທັງໝົດເທົ່າໃດ

BO:T3 HIAN3 TI2 HA6

1. X: Sam4 loh5, ta6 dae2.

2. Sam4 loh5 #1: Si:2 bpai:1 sai:4?

3. X: Bpai:1 dta3 lat6 sao:5. Dtae2 ni5 bpai:1 ha:n6 tao:2 dai:1

4 Sam4 loh5 #1: Hohy5 neu:ng2.

5. X: Bpe:n1 nya:ng4 ao:1 paeng3 tae5. Kohy6 kery3 bpai:1 dtae2 ho:k3 si:p3 gi:p6 neu:ng2.

6. Sam4 loh5 #1: Bpaet6 si:p3 cheu:ng2 cha:3 bpai:1.

7. X: Bpai:1 sa2. Kohy6 si:2 ao:1 ka:n3 mai:2........
Sam4 loh5, bpai:1 dta:3 lat6 sao:5 ao:1 tao:2 dai:1?

8. Sam4 loh5 #2: Che:t3 si:p3 gip6 ka6 nohy5.

9. X: Ho:k3 si:p3 gip6 bpai:1 boh2?

10. Sam4 loh5 #2: Bpai:1.

11. Mae:2 ka5: Ao:1 nya:ng4 ma3 dam1? Ao:1 mak6 mai:5 boh2?

12. X: Mak6 giang5 gi1 lo3 la:2 tao:2 dai:1?

13. Mae2 ka5: Gi1 lo3 la:2 sohng4 hohy5. Yak6 dai:5 cha:k3 gi1 lo3?

14. X: Sohng4 gi1 lo3. Mak6 hu:ng2 nuay2 na:n5 tao:2 dai:1?

15. Mae2 ka5: Naew3 ni5 saep5 lai4. Ao:1 na:m3 ma3 dam1 hohy5 ha6 si:p3 sa2.

16. X: Kohy6 yak6 dai:5 mak6 guay5 wi4 neu:ng2. Wi4 cha:k3 gip6?

17. Mae2 ka5: Hohy5 bpaet6 si:p3.

18. X: Bpe:n1 nya:ng4 meu5 ni5 mak6 guay5 paeng3 tae5? Hohy5 ha6 si:p3 tao:2 nan5 lae:3 lai:2 nger:n3 ta:ng3 mo:t3 tao:2 dai:1?

LESSON 5: GOING TO MARKET BY PEDICAB
(Note: a Samloh is a 3-wheel pedicab)

1. X: Samloh please wait.

2. 1st Samloh: Where are you going?

3. X: I'm going to the Morning Market. From here to there, how much?

4. 1st Samloh: One hundred.

5. X: Why is your charge so expensive? I used to go for only 60.

6. 1st Samloh: 80 then I'll go.

7. X: Please go. I'll get a new samloh....Samloh to go to the Morning Market, how much?

8. 2nd Samloh: 70 sir.

9. X: 60, will you go?

10. 2nd Samloh: Yes.

11. Woman vendor: What do you want Ma'am? Do you want some fruit?

12. X: Oranges cost how much per kilo?

13. Woman vendor: Per kilo, 200. How many kilos do you want?

14. X: Two kilos. How much is that papaya?

15. Woman vendor: This kind is very delicious. Take it with you Ma'am at 150 please.

16. X: I want one bunch of bananas. A bunch is how many kip?

17. Woman vendor: 180.

18. X: Today,why are bananas so expensive? Only 150. Now add up the bill please, in all, how much?

LESSON 6: BARGAINING AT THE MARKET

Substitution Exercise

ຂອບໃຈຫຼາຍໆ	ບໍ່ເປັນຫຍັງດອກ
ຂ້ອຍມີແຕ່ໃບຫ້າຮ້ອຍ	ບໍ່ເປັນຫຍັງ ມີເງິນທອນໃຫ້
ຊິລົງໃສ	ລົງຢູ່ຕລາດ
kohp⁶ chai:¹ lai:⁴ lai:⁴	boh² bpe:n¹ nya:ng⁴ dohk⁶
kohy⁶ mi³ dtae² ha⁶ hohy⁵	boh² bpe:n¹ nya:ng⁴ mi³ nger:n³ tohn³ hai:⁶
si:² lo:ng³ sai:⁴	lo:ng³ yu² dta:³ lat⁶
Thank you very much	You're welcome.
I only have a 500 kip note.	Never mind, I have change.
Where are you going to get off?	I'll get out at the market.

ໝ່ວຍ	ນີ້	ຣາຄາເທົ່າໃດ	ຣາຄາ	ຫ້າສິບກີບ
ແກ້ວ				ສອງຮ້ອຍຫ້າສິບກີບ
ສະບູ່ແນວ				ເຈັດສິບກີບ
nuay²	ni⁵	la³ ka³ tao:² dai:¹	la³ ka³	si:p³ gip⁶
gaew⁵				sohng⁴ hohy⁵ ha⁶ si:p³ gip⁶
sa:³ bu¹ naew³				che:t³ si:p³ gip⁶
Fruit	this	the price is how much?	The price (is)	50 kip.
Bottle				250 kip.
Soap piece				70 kip.

ຢາກໄດ້	ຫຍັງອີກແດ່	ໝາກເລັ່ນໜ່ວຍງາມມີບໍ່
ຢາກໄດ້		ໝາກແຕງຣາຄາຄືເກົ່າບໍ່
ຢາກຊື້		ໝາກກ້ຽງມື້ນີ້ກິໂລເທົ່າໃດ
ເອົາ		ເອົາໝາກກ້ວຍຫວີນຶ່ງ ຊະ
yak⁶ dai:⁵	nya:ng⁴ ik⁶ dae²	mak⁶ le:n² nuay² ngam³ mi³ boh²
yak⁶ dai:⁵		mak⁶ dtaeng¹ la³ ka³ keu³ gao:² boh²
yak⁶ seu⁵		mak⁶ gian⁵ meu⁵ ni⁵ gi:¹ lo³ tao:² dai:¹
ao:¹		ao:¹ mak⁶ guay⁵ wi⁴ neu:ng² sa:²
Do you want	something else?	Do you have any good looking tomatoes?
Do you want		Is the price of cucumbers the same as before?
Will you buy		Per kilo for this bunch of oranges, how much?
Will you take		Give me one bunch of bananas please.

ກະລໍ່າປີ	ຫົວ	ເທົ່າໃດ
ຜັກສລັດ	ກິໂລ	
ໝາກແຕງ	ໜ່ວຍ	
ໝາກເລັ່ນ	ກິໂລ	
ຜັກບົ່ວ	ມັດ	
ດອກກະລໍ່າປີ	ຫົວ	
ກະຕ່າ	ໜ່ວຍ	
ສະບູ	ກ້ອນ	
ຢາຖູແຂ້ວ	ຫຼອດ	
ນໍ້າອົບ	ແກ້ວ	
ເຂົ້າແປ້ງເດັກນ້ອຍ	ກັບ	
ໝາກກ້ຽງ	ກິໂລ	
ໝາກຫຸ່ງ	ໜ່ວຍ	
ໝາກກ້ວຍ	ຫວີ	

(See also p.150/4.1)

ga:[3] la:m[3] bpi[1]	hua[4]	tao:[2] dai[1]
pa:k[3] sa:[3] la:t[2]	gi[1] lo[3]	
mak[6] dtaeng[1]	nuay[2]	
mak[6] le:n[2]	gi[1] lo[3]	
pa:k[3] bua[2]	ma:t[2]	
dohk[6] ga:[3] la:m[3] bpi[1]	hua[4]	
ga:[3] dta[2]	nuay[2]	
sa:[3] bu[1]	gohn[5]	
ya[1] tu[4] kaew[6]	loht[6]	
na:m[5] o:p[3]	gaew[5]	
kao:[6] bpaeng[6] de:k[3] nohy[5]	ga:p[3]	
mak[6] giang[5]	gi[1] lo[3]	
mak[6] hu:ng[2]	nuay[2]	
mak[6] guay[5]	wi[4]	

Cabbage	head	how much?
Lettuce	kilo	
Cucumber	piece	
Tomato	kilo	
Onion	bundle	
Cauliflower	head	
Basket	piece	
Soap	solid	
Toothpaste	tube	
Perfume	bottle	
Baby powder	box	
Oranges	kilo	
Papaya	fruit	
Bananas	bunch	

ຫົວ	ນຶ່ງ	____ ກີບ
ກິໂລ		
ໜ່ວຍ		
ກິໂລ		
ມັດ		
ຫົວ		
ໜ່ວຍ		
ກ້ອນ		
ຫຼອດ		

hua[4]	neu:ng[2]	____ gip[6]
gi[1] lo[3]		
nuay[2]		
gi[1] lo[3]		
ma:t[2]		
hua[4]		
nuay[2]		
gohn[5]		
loht[6]		

Head	one	____ kip.
Kilo		
Fruit		
Kilo		
Bundle		
Head		
Piece		
Solid		
Tube		

ເຈົ້າ	ຮັບເງິນ	ໂດລາບໍ່	ຮັບຢູ່
ຂະເຈົ້າ		ກີບບໍ່	
ຂະເຈົ້າ		ໂດລາບໍ່ ຢູ່ຕລາດ	ທັມມະດາ ຮັບຢູ່
ເງິນນີ້ຮັບບໍ່			ເງິນນັ້ນຮັບບໍ່ໄດ້ດອກ

chao:^{5}	la:p^{2} nger:n^{3}	do^{1} la^{3} boh^{2}	la:p^{2} yu^{2}
ka:^{3} chao:^{5}		gip^{6} boh^{2}	
ka:^{3} chao:^{5}		do^{1} la^{3} boh^{2} yu^{2} dta:^{3} lat^{6}	ta:m^{3} ma:^{2} da^{1} la:p^{2} yu^{2}
nger:n^{3} ni^{5} la:p^{2} boh^{2}			nger:n^{3} na:n^{5} la:p^{2} boh^{2} dai:^{5} dohk^{6}

You	receive money	can?	Yes.
You(pl.)		kip?	Yes.
You(pl.)		dollars at the market?	Normally they do.
Will you take this money?			We cannot accept that money.

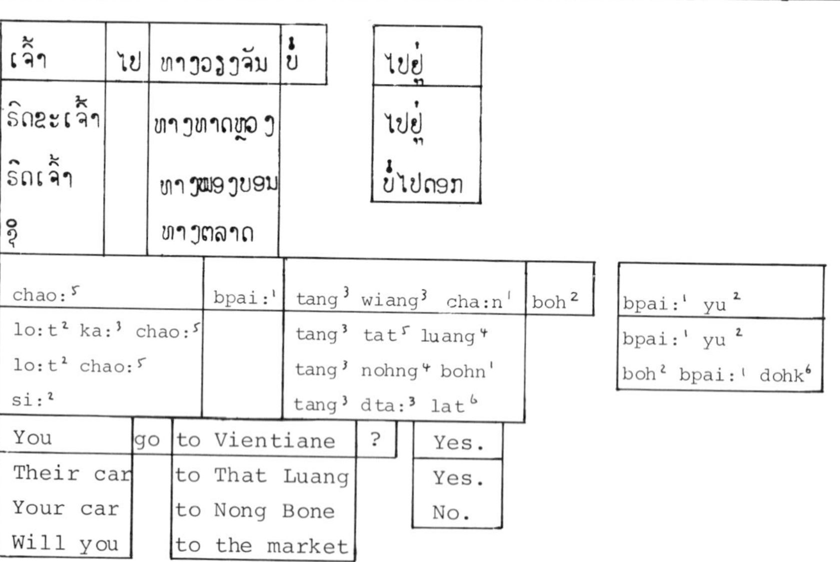

ເຈົ້າ	ໄປ	ທາງວຽງຈັນ	ບໍ່	ໄປຢູ່
ຣົດຂະເຈົ້າ		ທາງທາດຫຼວງ		ໄປຢູ່
ຣົດເຈົ້າ		ທາງໜອງບອນ		ບໍ່ໄປດອກ
ຊິ		ທາງຕລາດ		

chao:^{5}	bpai:^{1}	tang^{3} wiang^{3} cha:n^{1}	boh^{2}	bpai:^{1} yu^{2}
lo:t^{2} ka:^{3} chao:^{5}		tang^{3} tat^{5} luang^{4}		bpai:^{1} yu^{2}
lo:t^{2} chao:^{5}		tang^{3} nohng^{4} bohn^{1}		boh^{2} bpai:^{1} dohk^{6}
si:^{2}		tang^{3} dta:^{3} lat^{6}		

You	go	to Vientiane	?	Yes.
Their car		to That Luang		Yes.
Your car		to Nong Bone		No.
Will you		to the market		

ຄັນ	ເຈົ້າ	ບໍ່ຢູ່ ຂ້ອຍຊິບໍ່	ໄປ
	ລາວ		ໄປມື້ນີ້
	ຂະເຈົ້າ		ມາມື້ນີ້

ka:n^{3}	chao:^{5}	boh^{2} yu^{2} kohy si:^{2} boh^{2}	bpai:^{1}
	lao^{3}		bpai:^{1} meu^{5} ni^{5}
	ka:^{3} chao:^{5}		ma^{3} meu^{5} ni^{5}

If	you aren't	in, I won't	go.
	he isn't		go today.
	they aren't		come today.

ຂ້ອຍຊື້	ໝາກແຕງ	ນຳເຈົ້າ	ຫລາຍໜ່ວຍ
	ໝາກເລັ່ນ		ກິໂລ
	ຜັກບົ່ວ		ມັດ
	ນ້ຳອົບອີກ		ຫລາຍຢ່າງ
	ຢາ ອີກ		ຫລາຍຢ່າງ

kohy^{6} seu^{5}	mak^{6} dtaeng^{1}	na:m^{3} chao:^{5}	lai^{4} nuay^{2}
	mak^{6} le:n^{2}		gi^{1} lo^{3}
	pa:k^{3} bua^{2}		ma:t^{2}
	na:m^{5} o:p^{3} ik^{6}		lai^{4} yang^{2}
	ya^{1} ik^{6}		

I buy	cucumbers	from you	many pieces.
	tomatoes		kilo.
	onions		bundle.
	more perfume		many things.
	more medicine		

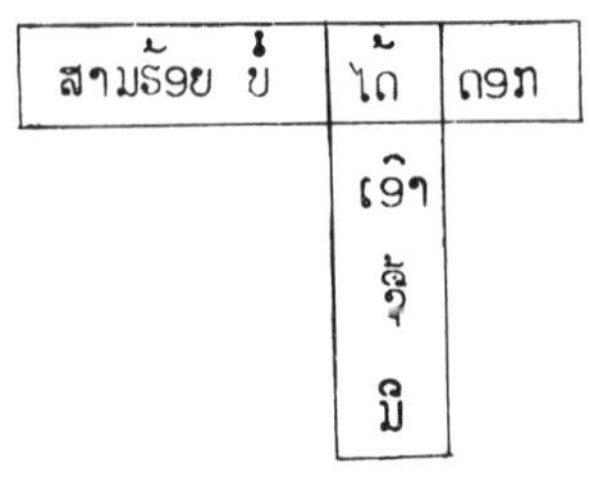

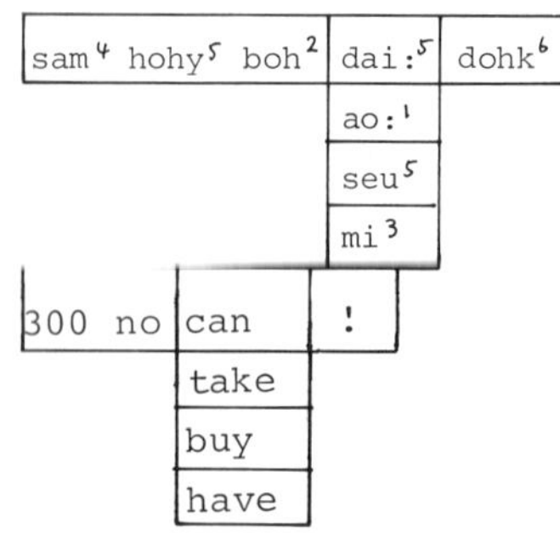

sam⁴ hohy⁵ boh²	dai:⁵	dohk⁶
	ao:¹	
	seu⁵	
	mi³	

300 no	can	!
	take	
	buy	
	have	

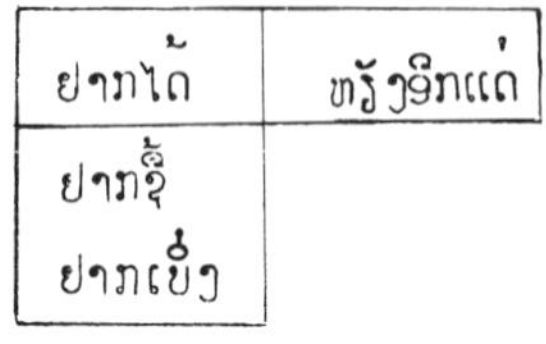

yak¹ dai:⁵	nya:ng⁴ ik⁶ dae²
yak¹ seu⁵	
yak¹ beu:ng²	

You want	What else?
You'll buy	
You want to see	

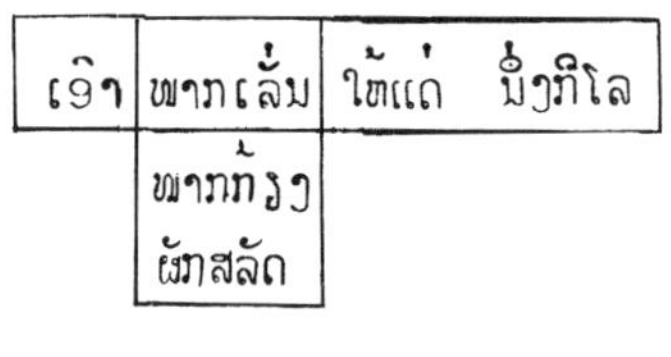

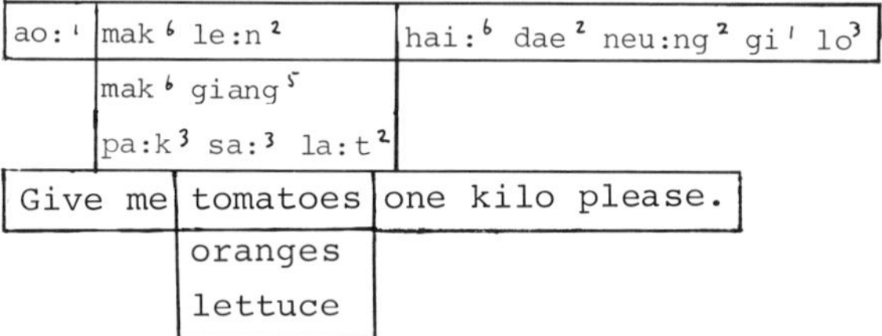

ao:¹	mak⁶ le:n²	hai:⁶ dae² neu:ng² gi¹ lo³
	mak⁶ giang⁵	
	pa:k³ sa:³ la:t²	

Give me	tomatoes	one kilo please.
	oranges	
	lettuce	

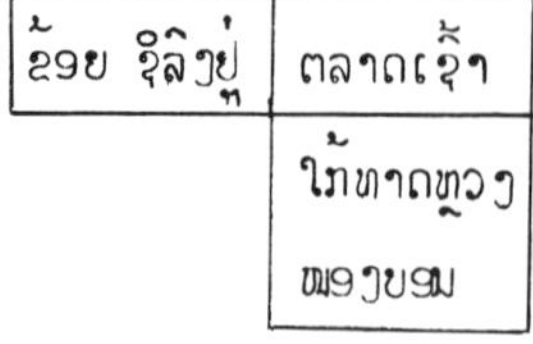

kohy⁶ si:² lo:ng³ yu²	dta:³ tat⁶ sao:⁵
	gai:⁵ tat⁵ luang⁴
	nohng⁴ bohn¹

I will get off at	the morning market.
	near That Luang.
	Nong Bone.

Vocabulary Exercise

6-1 **ຄັນ** — ka:n^3 — If, when

Lao	Transcription	English
ຄັນບໍ່ມີຣົດ ຂະເຈົ້າໄປບໍ່ໄດ້ດອກ	ka:n^3 boh^2 mi^3 lo:t^2, ka:^{3} chao:^{5} bpai:^{1} boh^2 dai:^{5} dohk^6	If they don't have a car, they can't go.
ຄັນບໍ່ມີໝາກກ້ຽງກໍຊື້ໝາກຫຸ່ງ ຊະ	ka:n^3 boh^2 mi^3 mak^6 giang,^{5} goh^1 seu^5 mak^6 hu:ng^2 sa:^{2}	If you don't have oranges, I'll buy papaya.
ຄັນເຈົ້າບໍ່ມີເງິນກີບ ກໍບໍ່ເປັນຫຍັງ ຂະເຈົ້າຮັບໂດລາ	ka:n^3 chao:^{5} boh^2 mi^3 nger:n^3 gip,^{6} goh^1 boh^2 bpe:n^1 nya:ng^4 ka:^{3} chao:^{5} ha:p^2 do^1 la^3	If you don't have kip, it's all right, they take dollars.
ຂ້ອຍຈະຫຼຸດຣາຄາ ຄັນເຈົ້າຊື້ນຳຂ້ອຍເລື້ອຍໆ	kohy^6 cha:^{3} lu:t^3 la^3 ka,^{3} ka:n^3 chao:^{5} seu^5 na:m^3 kohy^6 leuay^5 leuay^5	I'll lower the price, if you always buy from me.
ລາວຢາກໄປ ຄັນຂ້ອຍໄປ	lao^3 yak^6 bpai:^{1} ka:n^3 kohy^6 bpai:^{1}	He wants to go when I go.
ຂະເຈົ້າເອົາຣົດແທກຊີໄປ ຄັນສາມລໍ້ແພງຫຼາຍ	ka:^{3} chao:^{5} ao:^{1} lo:t^2 taek^5 si^3 bpai:^{1} ka:n^3 sam^4 loh^5 paeng^3 lai^4	They'll go by taxi if samloh is very expensive.
ເອົາແນວນີ້ກໍໄດ້ ຄັນເຈົ້າບໍ່ມີແນວນັ້ນ	ao:^{1} naew^3 ni^5 goh^1 dai:^{5} ka:n^3 chao:^{5} boh^2 mi^3	I can take these, if you don't have those.
ມື້ນີ້ບໍ່ໄປກໍໄດ້ ຄັນເຈົ້າບໍ່ຢາກໄດ້	meu^5 ni^5 boh^2 bpai:^{1} goh^1 dai:^{5} ka:n^3 chao:^{5} boh^2 yak^6 dai:^{5}	I don't mind not going today, if you don't want to.

6-2 **ຫຼຸດ** — lu:t^3 — To lower (prices), discount

Lao	Transcription	English
ຂະເຈົ້າຫຼຸດສາມຮ້ອຍກີບ	ka:^{3} chao:^{5} lu:t^3 sam^4 hohy^5 gip^6	They lower the price by 300 kip.
ລາວຫຼຸດຣາຄາ ໜ່ວຍລະ ສິບຫ້າກີບ	lao^3 lu:t^3 la^3 ka^3 nuay^2 la:^{2} si:p^3 ha^6 gip^6	He discounts 15 kip each.
ຫຼຸດໃຫ້ແດ່ ຫ້າສິບກີບ	lu:t^3 hai:^{6} dae^2 ha^6 si:p^3 gip^6	Give me a discount and make it 50 kip.
ຫຼຸດບໍ່ໄດ້ ຂ້ອຍຂາດທຶນ	lu:t^3 boh^2 dai:^{5} kohy^6 kat^6 teu:n^2	I can't lower the price; I'll lose money.
ລາວບໍ່ເຄີຍຫຼຸດໃຫ້	lao^3 boh^2 kery^3 lu:t^3 hai:^{6}	He never gives a discount to people.

6-3	<u>ລາຄາ</u>	<u>la^{3} ka^{3}</u>	<u>Price</u>
	ລາຄາແພງຫຼາຍ	la^{3} ka^{3} paeng^{3} lai^{4}	The price is very high.
	ຂ້ອຍບໍ່ຮູ້ຈັກລາຄາເທົ່າໃດ	kohy^{6} boh^{2} hu^{5} cha:k^{3} la^{3} ka^{3} tao:^{2} dai:^{1}	I don't know how much the price is.
	ລາຄາບໍ່ຄືເກົ່າ ດຽວນີ້	la^{3} ka^{3} boh^{2} keu^{3} gao:^{2} diaw^{1} ni^{5}	Now the price is the same as before.
	ນີ້ ລາຄາຄືເກົ່າ ສາມຮ້ອຍກີບ	ni^{5} la^{3} ka^{3} keu^{3} gao:^{2} sam^{4} hohy^{5} gip^{6}	This is the same price as before. 300 kip.
6-4	<u>ແບບ</u>	<u>baep^{6}</u>	<u>The way (of doing things), manner</u>
	ແບບນັ້ນບໍ່ແມ່ນແບບລາວ	baep^{6} na:n^{5} boh^{2} maen^{2} baep^{6} lao^{3}	That is not the way Lao people do it.
	ລາວເປັນແບບນັ້ນເລື້ອຍໆ	lao^{3} bpe:n^{1} baep^{6} na:n^{5} leuay^{5} leuay^{5}	He is always like that.
	ເວົ້າແບບນີ້ບໍ່ດີ	wao:^{5} baep^{6} ni^{5} boh^{2} di^{1}	(You) can't talk like that.
	ມີກະຕ່າແບບນີ້ບໍ່	mi^{3} ga:^{3} dta^{2} baep^{6} ni^{5} boh^{2}	Do you have this kind of basket?
6-5	<u>ງາມ</u>	<u>ngam^{3}</u>	<u>Beautiful, pretty</u>
	ແບບນີ້ງາມຫຼາຍ	baep^{6} ni^{5} ngam^{3} lai^{4}	This style is very beautiful
	ນ້ອງຂ້ອຍງາມ	nohng^{5} kohy^{6} ngam^{3}	My younger sister is pretty.
	ໝາກຫຸ່ງໜ່ວຍນີ້ງາມ	mak^{6} hu:ng^{2} nuay^{2} ni^{5} ngam^{3}	This papaya is beautiful.
	ເຮືອນຂອງລາວງາມຫຼາຍ	heuan^{3} kohng^{4} lao^{3} ngam^{3} lai^{4}	His house is very beautiful.
	ວັດທາດຫຼວງງາມ	wa:t^{2} tat^{5} luang^{4} ngam^{3}	Wat That Luang is beautiful.

	Lao	Romanization	English
6-6	ໝັ້ນ	ma:n^6	Strong (for things)
	ກະຕ່າແບບນີ້ໝັ້ນ ລາຄາບໍ່ແພງ	ga:^{3} dta^2 baep^6 ni^5 ma:n^6 la^3 ka^3 boh^2 paeng^3	These baskets are strong. The price is not expensive.
	ລົດຄັນນີ້ງາມ ແລະໝັ້ນດີ	lo:t^2 ka:n^3 ni^5 ngam^3 lae:^{2} ma:n^6 di^1	This car is beautiful and powerful.
	ຂ້ອຍມັກແບບນີ້ ໝັ້ນຫຼາຍ	kohy^6 ma:k^2 baep^6 ni^5 ma:n^6 lai^4	I like this style, it is very strong.
6-7	ດອກ	dohk^6	(Negative emphatic particle)
	ຂ້ອຍບໍ່ເຄີຍມາດອກ	kohy^6 boh^2 kery^3 ma^3 dohk^6	I have never been here before.
	ລາຄາບໍ່ແພງດອກ	la^3 ka^3 boh^2 paeng^3 dohk^6	The price is not high at all.
	ຂ້ອຍປາກພາສາລາວບໍ່ເປັນດອກ	kohy^6 bpak^6 pa^3 sa^4 lao^3 boh^2 bpe:n^1 dohk^6	I can't speak Lao!
	ແບບນັ້ນບໍ່ງາມດອກ	baep^6 na:n^5 boh^2 ngam^3 dohk^6	That is not beautiful at all.
6-8	ຂາດທຶນ	kat^6 teu:n^2	To lose money (in business)
	ລາວຂາດທຶນຫຼາຍ	lao^3 kat^6 teu:n^2 lai^4	He lost a lot of money.
	ແບບນີ້ບໍ່ຂາດທຶນ	baep^6 ni^5 boh^2 kat^6 teu:n^2	If you do it this way, you won't lose money.
	ແມ່ຄ້າບໍ່ຢາກຂາດທຶນ	mae^2 ka^5 boh^2 yak^6 kat^6 teu:n^2	Women vendors don't want to lose money.

	Lao	Romanization	English
6-9	<u>ອີກ</u>	<u>ik</u>^{6}	<u>Again, more</u>
	ມາຫາຂ້ອຍອີກ	ma^{3} ha^{4} kohy^{6} ik^{6}	Come to see me again.
	ມາຫຼິ້ນອີກ	ma^{3} lin^{6} ik^{6}	Come to visit again.
	ຂ້ອຍບໍ່ຢາກໄປອີກ	kohy^{6} boh^{2} yak^{6} bpai:^{1} ik^{6}	I don't want to go again.
	ລາວຍັງຊິໄປອີກເທື່ອນຶ່ງ	lao^{3} nyang^{3} si:^{2} bpai:^{1} ik^{6} teua^{2} neu:ng^{2}	He will go once again.
	ບໍ່ມີອີກແລ້ວ	boh^{2} mi^{3} ik^{6} laew^{5}	There is nothing left.
6-10	<u>ຢ່າງ</u>	<u>yang</u>^{2}	<u>Kind, sort</u>
	ຂ້ອຍຊື້ຫຼາຍຢ່າງຢູ່ຕລາດ	kohy^{6} seu^{5} lai^{4} yang^{2} yu^{2} dta:^{3} lat^{6}	I buy many kinds of things at the market.
	ມີຫຼາຍຢ່າງເຈົ້າຈະມັກ	mi^{3} lai^{4} yang^{2} chao:^{5} cha:^{3} ma:k^{2}	There are many things you would like to (have, buy, do etc.)
	ຂະເຈົ້າມີຫຼາຍຢ່າງ	ka:^{3} chao:^{5} mi^{3} lai^{4} yang^{2}	They have many things.
	ດຽວນີ້ມີແຕ່ສາມຢ່າງເທົ່ານັ້ນ	diaw^{1} ni^{5} mi^{3} dtae^{2} sam^{4} yang^{2} tao:^{5} na:n^{5}	Now we have only three kinds.
6-11	<u>ຢູ່</u>	<u>yu</u>^{2}	<u>(Reinforcing particle)</u>
	ມີຢູ່	mi^{3} yu^{2}	I really have. (There really is.)
	ຂ້ອຍຢາກເບິ່ງຢູ່	kohy^{6} yak^{6} beu:ng^{2} yu^{2}	I really want to see.
	ຢາກໄດ້ຫຼາຍຢູ່	yak^{6} dai:^{5} lai^{4} yu^{2}	I do want many.

	ງາມຢູ່ ແຕ່ແພງຫຼາຍ	ngam^3 yu^2 dtae^2 paeng^3 lai^4	Yes, it is beautiful, but very expensive.
	ດີຢູ່ ແຕ່ບໍ່ມີຫຼາຍ	di^1 yu^2 dtae^2 boh^2 mi^3 lai^4	Yes, it is good, but there are not many.
6-12	<u>ຄື</u>	<u>keu</u>^{3}	<u>(A) like, similar, to resemble</u>
	ລູກເຈົ້າຄືເຈົ້າຫຼາຍ	luk^5 chao:^{5} keu^3 chao:^{5} lai^4	Your child is just like you.
	ຂອງເຈົ້າບໍ່ຄືຂອງຂ້ອຍ	kohng^4 chao:^{5} boh^2 keu^3 kohng^4 kohy^6	Yours is not like mine.
	ຄືຫຼາຍແຕ່ບໍ່ແມ່ນແບບດຽວ	keu^3 lai^4 dtae^2 boh^2 maen^2 baep^6 diaw^1	It is very similar, but it is not the same kind.
	ລາວບໍ່ຄືອ້າຍລາວ ບໍ່ຢາກຮຽນໜັງສື	lao^3 boh^2 keu^3 ay^5 lao^3 boh^2 yak^6 hian^3 na:ng^4 seu^4	He is not like his elder brother. He doesn't like learning.
	ເພິ່ນປາກພາສາລາວຄືຄົນລາວຫຼາຍ	per:n^2 bpak^6 pa^3 sa^4 lao^3 keu^3 ko:n^3 lao^3 lai^4	He speaks Lao just like a Lao.
6-13	<u>ເອົາໃຫ້</u> (See also p.153/5.3)	<u>ao:^{1} hai:</u>^{6}	<u>To give (something) to</u>
	ເອົາໃຫ້ຂ້ອຍແດ່	ao:^{1} hai:^{6} kohy^6 dae^2	Give it to me, please.
	ຂ້ອຍເອົາໃຫ້ເຈົ້າ	kohy^6 ao:^{1} hai:^{6} chao:^{5}	I give it to you.
	ເອົາໝາກກ້ວຍໃຫ້ແດ່ ຫວີນຶ່ງ	ao:^{1} mak^6 guay^5 hai:^{6} dae^2 wi^4 neu:ng^2	Give (me) a bunch of bananas.
	ເອົາກະລໍ່າປີໃຫ້ແດ່ ກິໂລນຶ່ງ	ao:^{1} ga:^{3} la:m^3 bpi^1 hai^6 dae^2 gi^1 lo^3 neu:ng^2	Give (me) one kilo of cabbage.
	ຂ້ອຍບໍ່ເອົາໃຫ້ລາວ ແຕ່ເອົາໃຫ້ເຈົ້າ	kohy^6 boh^2 ao:^{1} hai:^{6} lao^3 dtae^2 ao:^{1} hai:^{6} chao:^{5}	I won't give it to him, but to you.

6-14	ຢາ	ya^{1}	Medicine
	ມີຢາຫຼາຍຢ່າງ	mi^{3} ya^{1} lai^{4} yang^{2}	There are many kinds of medicine.
	ນີ້ຢາຫຍັງ	ni^{5} ya^{1} nya:ng^{4}	What kind of medicine is this?
	ຢາແນວນີ້ດີ	ya^{1} naew^{3} ni^{5} di^{1}	This medicine is good.
	ຢານີ້ແຊບແລະດີຫຼາຍ	ya^{1} ni^{5} saep^{5} lae:^{2} di^{1} lai^{4}	This medicine is tasty and very effective.
6-15	ນ້ຳ	na:m^{5}	Water
	ມີນ້ຳຫຼາຍ	mi^{3} na:m^{5} lai^{4}	There is a lot of water.
	ໄປຊື້ນ້ຳແດ່	bpai:^{1} seu^{5} na:m^{5} dae^{2}	Go and buy water!
	ນ້ຳນີ້ແຊບຫຼາຍ	na:m^{5} ni^{5} saep^{5} lai^{4}	This water is tasty.
	ພວກຂ້ອຍຊື້ນ້ຳນຳລາວເລື້ອຍ ໆ	puak^{5} kohy^{6} seu^{5} na:m^{5} na:m^{5} lao^{3} leuay^{5} leuay^{5}	We buy water from him very often.
6-16	ຮັບ	ha:p^{2}	To meet, take
	ຂ້ອຍຊິໄປຮັບເຈົ້າ	kohy^{6} si:^{2} bpai:^{1} ha:p^{2} chao:^{5}	I'll go to meet you.
	ມີຫຼາຍຄົນມາຮັບເພິ່ນ	mi^{3} lai^{4} ko:n^{3} ma^{3} ha:p^{2} per:n^{2}	Many people came to meet him.
	ຂະເຈົ້າບໍ່ຮັບໂດລາ ແຕ່ເງິນກີບ	ka:^{3} chao:^{5} boh^{2} ha:p^{2} do^{1} la^{3} dtae^{2} nger:n^{3} gip^{6}	They don't take dollars but (they do take) kip.

	Lao	Transcription	English
6-17	ບໍ່ເປັນຫຍັງ	boh^2 bpe:n^1 nya:ng^4	That is all right, Don't worry, I don't mind, No sweat.
	ບໍ່ເປັນຫຍັງ ຂ້ອຍຊິຊື້ໃຫ້ເຈົ້າ	boh^2 bpe:n^1 nya:ng.^{4} kohy^6 si:^{2} seu^5 hai:^{6} chao:^{5}	That's all right, I'll buy you one.
	ບໍ່ເປັນຫຍັງຍັງມີຫຼາຍ	boh^2 bpe:n^1 nya:ng^4 mi^3 lai^4	Don't worry, there are still many.
	ເຈົ້າບໍ່ຢາກໄດ້ບໍ່ ບໍ່ເປັນຫຍັງ	chao:^{5} boh^2 yak^6 dai:^{5} boh.^{2} boh^2 bpe:n^1 nya:ng^4	You don't want it? That's all right with me.
	ບໍ່ເອົາບໍ່ ບໍ່ເປັນຫຍັງ	boh^2 ao:^{1} boh.^{2} boh^2 bpe:n^1 nya:ng^4	You don't want it? I don't mind.
	ບໍ່ມີເງິນ ບໍ່ເປັນຫຍັງ	boh^2 mi^3 nger:n.^{3} boh^2 bpe:n^1 nya:ng^4	You don't have any money. Don't worry.
6-18	ທອນ	tohn^3	To change money
	ເຈົ້າມີເງິນທອນບໍ່	chao:^{5} mi^2 nger:n^3 tohn^3 boh^2	Do you have change?
	ລາວທອນໃຫ້ຂ້ອຍ ຫ້າສິບ	lao^3 tohn^3 hai:^{6} kohy^6 ha^6 si:p^3	He gave me 5 kip change.
	ຂະເຈົ້າບໍ່ທອນໃຫ້ ເອົາໝົດແລ້ວ	ka:^{3} chao:^{5} boh^2 tohn^3 hai:^{5}, ao:^{1} mo:t^3 laew^5	They did not give (me) change. They took all (the money).
6-19	ໃຫຍ່	nyai:^{2}	Big, large
	ກະຕ່າພ່ວຍໃຫຍ່ພັນນຶ່ງກີບ	ga:^{3} dta^2 nuay^2 nyai:^{2} pa:n^3 neu:ng^2 gip^6	A big basket costs 1,000 kip.
	ລາວມີເຮືອນຫຼັງໃຫຍ່ຫຼັງນຶ່ງ	lao^3 mi^3 heuan^3 la:ng^4 nyai:^{2} la:ng^4 neu:ng^2	He has big house.
	ວັດນີ້ງາມແລະໃຫຍ່	wa:t^2 ni^5 ngam^3 lae:^{2} nyai:^{2}	This temple is beautiful and large.
	ນ້ຳອົບແກ້ວໃຫຍ່ເທົ່າໃດ	na:m^5 o:p^3 gaew^5 nyai:^{2} tao:^{2} dai:^{1}	How much is a big bottle of perfume?

Text

ບົດ ຮຽນ ທີ່ ຫົກ

1. X ກະລ່ຳປີນີ້ ຫົວເທົ່າໃດ

2. ແມ່ຄ້າ ກິໂລນຶ່ງສາມສິບຫ້າກີບ ຄັນເຈົ້າຊິເອົາຫຼາຍ ຂ້ອຍຈະຫຼຸດໃຫ້ ຫ້າກີບ .

3. X ເອົາສາມກິໂລ ແລະຜັກສລັດກິໂລນຶ່ງ ໝາກແຕງໜ່ອຍນຶ່ງ ໝາກເລັ່ນສອງກິໂລ ຜັກບົ່ວ ສອງມັດ ແລະດອກກະລ່ຳປີສອງຫົວ.

4. X ກະຕ່າໜ່ອຍນີ້ ຣາຄາເທົ່າໃດ

5. ແມ່ຄ້າ ແບບນີ້ງາມ ແລະກໍ່ພົ້ນຫຼາຍ ເອົານໍ ມາດາມແຕ່ສີ່ຮ້ອຍກີບ.

6. X ເປັນຫຍັງຈຶ່ງແພງແທ້ ສາມຮ້ອຍຊະ

7. ແມ່ຄ້າ ສາມຮ້ອຍບໍ່ໄດ້ດອກ ຂາດທຶນ ຄັນມາດາມຊິເອົາ ສາມຮ້ອຍເຈັດສິບ

8. X ສາມຮ້ອຍຫ້າສິບຊະ ຂ້ອຍຍັງຈະຊື້ນຳເຈົ້າອີກຫຼາຍຢ່າງຢູ່.

9. ແມ່ຄ້າ ມາດາມຢາກໄດ້ຫຍັງອີກແດ່

10. X ສະບູອາບນ້ຳ ຣາຄາຄືເກົ່າບໍ່ ເອົາໃຫ້ແດ່ຫົກກ້ອນ ຢາຖູແຂ້ວຫຼອດໃຫຍ່ຫຼອດນຶ່ງ ນ້ຳອົບແບບນີ້ແກ້ວນຶ່ງ ເຂົ້າແປ້ງເດັກນ້ອຍກັບນຶ່ງເທົ່ານັ້ນຫຼະ ທັງໝົດເທົ່າໃດ

11. ແມ່ຄ້າ ທັງໝົດ ພັນເກົ້າຮ້ອຍກີບ

12. X ເຈົ້າຮັບເງິນໂດລາບໍ່ ຢູ່ນີ້

13. ແມ່ຄ້າ ຮັບຢູ່

14. X ຂ້ອຍມີແຕ່ໃບຫ້າໂດລາ

15. ແມ່ຄ້າ ບໍ່ເປັນຫຍັງ ຂ້ອຍກໍ່ທອນໃຫ້ເຈົ້າຫົກຮ້ອຍ ຂອບໃຈຫຼາຍໆ

16. ຣົດໂດຍສານ (ແທັກຊີ) ມາດາມຊິລົງໃສ

17. X ເຈົ້າໄປທາງຫາດຫຼວງບໍ່ ຂ້ອຍຊິລົງຢູ່ວັດໜອງບອນ

18. ຣົດໂດຍສານ ໄປ

BO:T^{3} HIAN^{3} TI^{2} HO:K^{3}

1. X: Ga:^{3} la:m^{3} bpi^{1} ni^{5} hua^{4} tao:^{2} dai:^{1}?

2. Mae^{2} ka^{5}: Gi^{1} lo^{3} neu:ng^{2} sam^{4} si:p^{3} ha^{6} gip^{6}. Ka:n^{3} chao:^{5} si:^{2} ao:^{1} lai^{4}, kohy^{6} cha:^{3} lu:t^{3} hai:^{6} ha^{6} gip^{6}.

3. X: Ao:^{1} sam^{4} gi^{1} lo^{3}, lae:^{2} pa:k^{3} sa^{3} la:t^{2} gi^{1} lo^{3} neu:ng^{2}, mak^{6} dtaeng^{1} nuay^{2} neu:ng^{2}, mak^{6} le:n^{2} sohng^{4} gi^{1} lo^{3}, pa:k^{3} bua^{2} sohng^{4} ma:t^{2} lae:^{2} dohk^{6} ga:^{3} la:m^{3} bpi^{1} sohng^{4} hua^{4}.

4. X: Ga:^{3} dta^{2} nuay^{2} ni^{5} la^{3} ka^{3} tao:^{2} dai:^{1}.

5. Mae^{2} ka^{5}: Baep^{6} ni^{5} ngam^{3} lae:^{2} goh^{1} ma:n^{6} lai^{4}. Ao:^{1} na:m^{3} ma^{3} dam^{1} dtae^{2} si^{2} hohy^{5} gip^{6}.

6. X: Bpe:n^{1} nya:ng^{4} cheu:ng^{2} paeng^{3} tae^{5}. Sam^{4} hohy^{5} sa^{2}.

7. Mae^{2} ka^{5}: Sam^{4} hohy^{5} boh^{2} dai:^{5} dohk^{6}, Kat^{6} teu:n^{3}. Ka:n^{3} ma^{3} dam^{1} si:^{2} ao:^{1} sam^{4} hohy^{5} che:t^{3} si:p^{3}.

8. X: Sam^{4} hohy^{5} ha^{6} si:p^{3} sa^{2}. Kohy^{6} nya:ng^{3} cha:^{3} seu^{5} na:m^{3} chao:^{5} ik^{6} lai^{4} yang^{1} yu^{2}.

9. Mae^{2} ka^{5}: Ma^{3} dam^{1} yak^{6} dai:^{5} nya:ng^{4} ik^{6} dae^{2}.

10. X: Sa^{3} bu^{1} ap^{6} na:m^{5} la^{3} ka^{3} keu^{3} kao:^{2} boh^{2}? Ao:^{1} hai:^{6} dae^{2} hok^{3} gohn^{5}. Ya^{1} tu^{4} kaew^{6} loht^{6} nyai:^{2} loht^{6} neu:ng^{2}. Na:m^{5} o:p^{3} bpaep^{6} ni^{5} gaew^{5} neu:ng^{2}. Kao:^{6} bpaeng^{5} de:k^{3} nohy^{5} ga:p^{3} neu:ng^{2} tao:^{2} nan^{5} la:^{3}. Ta:ng^{3} mo:t^{3} tao:^{2} dai:^{1}?

11. Mae^{2} ka^{5}: Ta:ng^{3} mo:t^{3} pa:n^{3} kao:^{5} hohy^{5} gip^{6}.

12. X: Chao:^{5} la:p^{2} nger:n^{3} do^{1}la^{3} boh^{2} yu^{2} ni^{5}?

13. Mae^{2} ka^{5}: La:p^{2} yu^{2}.

14. X: Kohy^{6} mi^{3} dtae^{2} bai:^{1} ha^{6} do^{1} la^{3}.

15. Mae^{2} ka^{5}: Boh^{2} bpe:n^{1} nya:ng^{4}. Kohy^{6} goh^{1} tohn^{3} hai^{6} chao:^{5} ho:k^{3} hohy^{5} Kohp^{6} chai:^{1} lai^{4} la:^{4}.

16. Lo:t^{2} doy^{1} san^{4} (tae:k^{2} si^{3}) : Ma^{3} dam^{1} si:^{2} lo:ng^{3} sai:^{4}?

17. X: Chao:^{5} bpai:^{1} tang^{3} tat^{5} luang^{4} boh^{2}? kohy^{6} si:^{2} lo:ng^{3} yu^{2} wa:t^{2} nohng^{4} bohn^{1}.

18. Lo:t^{2} doy^{1} san^{3} : Bpai:^{1}.

LESSON 6: BARGAINING AT THE MARKET

1. X: How much is one head of cabbage?
2. Woman vendor: 35 kip for one kilo. If you buy a lot, I'll lower (the price) 5 kip.
3. X: I want 3 kilos of cabbages and 1 kilo of lettuce, a cucumber, 2 kilos of tomatoes, 2 bunches of onions and 2 heads of cauliflower.
4. X: How much is the price of this basket?
5. Woman vendor: These (baskets) are pretty and very solid too. Madam can take it for only 400.
6. X: How come so expensive? Make it 300.
7. Woman vendor: 300 is impossible. I lose money, if Ma'am will buy, (I sell) at 370.
8. X: Make it 350; I'll still buy many more things from you.
9. Woman vendor: What else does Ma'am want?
10. X: Bath soap prices are the same as before, aren't they? Give me six pieces (of bath soap), one big tube of tooth paste, one bottle of this (kind of) perfume, one box of baby powder and that is all. How much in all?
11. Woman vendor: In total 1,900 kip.
12. X: Do you accept dollars here?
13. Woman vendor: Yes, we do.
14. X: I only have a 5 dollar-note.
15. Woman vendor: Never mind, I'll give you 600 kip change. Thank you.
16. Taxi: Where will you be getting off, Ma'am?
17. X: Will you go to That Luang Street? I'll get off at Wat Nong Bone.
18. Taxi: (Okay) Let's go.

LESSON 7: RENTING A HOUSE

Substitution Exercise

ເຈົ້າ	ມາຢູ່ເມືອງລາວໄດ້ຈັກປີ		ປີປາຍ
ລາວ		ສອງ	
ຂະເຈົ້າ		ສາມ	

chao:⁵	ma³ yu² meuang³ lao³ dai:⁵ cha:k³ bpi¹		bpi¹ bpai¹
lao³		sohng⁴	
ka:³ chao:⁵		sam⁴	

You	came to live in Laos, how years ago?	1	years ago.
He		2	
They		3	

ເຈົ້າ	ເຊົ່າເຮືອນຢູ່ໃສ	ຂ້ອຍ	ເຊົ່າເຮືອນ	ຢູ່	ທາດຫຼວງ
ລາວ		ລາວ			ບ້ານໜອງບອນ
ຂະເຈົ້າ			ເຊົ່າເຮືອນຂອງທ້າວແສງ		ທາດຫຼວງ

chao:⁵	sao:² heuan³ yu² sai:⁴	kohy⁶	sao:² heuan³	yu²	tat⁵ luang⁴
lao³		lao³			ban⁵ nohng⁴ bohn¹
ka:³ chao:⁵			sao:² heuan³ kohng⁴ tao⁵ saeng⁴ yu²		tat⁵ luang⁶

You	rent a house, where?	I	rent a house	at	That Luang.
He		He			Ban Nong Bone.
They			rent a house from Mr. Seng at		That Luang.

ເຮືອນເຈົ້າມີຫ້ອງ	ຈັກຫ້ອງ	ມີຫ້ອງສີ່ຫ້ອງ
ຫຼັງນີ້ມີຫ້ອງນອນ		ມີສອງຫ້ອງ

heuan³ chao:⁵ mi³ hohng⁶	cha:k³ hohng⁶	mi³ hohng⁶ si² hohng⁶
la:ng⁴ ni⁵ mi³ hohng⁶ nohn³		mi³ sohng⁴ hohng⁶

Your house has rooms,	how many?	It has 4 rooms.
This building has bedrooms,		It has 2 rooms.

ເຮືອນຂ້ອຍມີ	ສອງຊັ້ນ
	ຊັ້ນດຽວ
	ສາມຊັ້ນ
	ສີ່ຊັ້ນ

heuan^{3} kohy^{6} mi^{3}	sohng^{4} sa:n^{5}
	sa:n^{5} diaw^{1}
	sam^{4} sa:n^{5}
	si^{2} sa:n^{5}

House I have	2 storeys.
	1 storey.
	3 storeys.
	4 storeys.

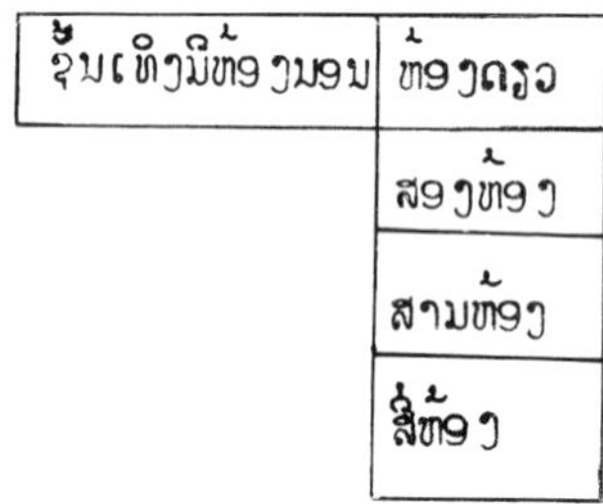

ຊັ້ນເທິງມີຫ້ອງນອນ	ຫ້ອງດຽວ
	ສອງຫ້ອງ
	ສາມຫ້ອງ
	ສີ່ຫ້ອງ

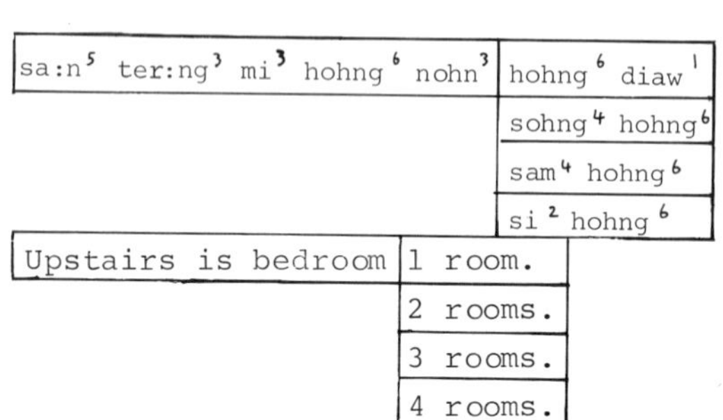

sa:n^{5} ter:ng^{3} mi^{3} hohng^{6} nohn^{3}	hohng^{6} diaw^{1}
	sohng^{4} hohng^{6}
	sam^{4} hohng^{6}
	si^{2} hohng^{6}

Upstairs is bedroom	1 room.
	2 rooms.
	3 rooms.
	4 rooms.

ຢູ່	ທາງໜ້າ	ບ້ານ	ມີ ບ່ອນຈອດລົດ
	ຂ້າງຫຼັງ	ເຮືອນ	
	ກ້ອງ		
	ອ້ອມ		

yu^{2}	tang^{3} na^{6}	ban^{5}	mi^{3} bohn^{2} choht^{6} lo:t^{2}
	kang^{6} la:ng^{4}	heuan^{3}	
	gohng^{5}		
	ohm^{5}		

In	front of	the home	is a parking place.
	behind	the house	
	under		
	around		

	Lao	Transcription	English
7-1	ເຊົ່າ	sao:^{2}	To rent
	ຂ້ອຍຢາກເຊົ່າເຮືອນແບບລາວ	kohy^{6} yak^{6} sao:^{2} heuan^{3} baep^{6} lao^{3}	I want to rent a Lao style house.
	ເຊົ່າຣົດຄັນນຶ່ງເທົ່າໃດ	sao:^{2} lo:t^{2} ka:n^{3} neu:ng^{2} tao:^{2} dai:^{1}	How much do you pay to rent a car?
	ລາວບໍ່ເຊົ່າເຮືອນ ເຊົ່າຫ້ອງ ຫ້ອງງື	lao^{3} boh^{2} sao:^{2} heuan^{3} sao:^{2} hohng^{6}	He does not rent a house. He rents a room.
	ຂະເຈົ້າຢາກເຊົ່າແຕ່ຊັ້ນເທິງ	ka:^{3} chao:^{5} yak^{6} sao:^{2} dtae^{2} sa:n^{5} ter:ng^{2}	They want to rent only the upstairs.
7-2	ໃນ	nai:^{3}	In
	ພໍ່ຢູ່ໃນບ້ານ	poh^{2} yu^{2} nai:^{3} ban^{5}	Father is in the house.
	ລາວເຮັດວຽກຢູ່ໃນຫ້ອງ	lao^{3} he:t^{2} wiak^{5} yu^{2} nai:^{3} hohng^{6}	He works in the room.
	ຢູ່ໃນວຽງຈັນມີຕລາດຈັກບ່ອນ	yu^{2} nai:^{3} wiang^{3} cha:n^{1} mi^{3} dta:^{3} lat^{6} cha:k^{3} bohn^{2}	How many markets are there in Vientiane?
7-3	ຄື	keu^{3}	Such as, like
	ມີຫລາຍແນວຄືໝາກກ້ວຍ, ໝາກກ້ຽງ, ໝາກຫຸ່ງ .	mi^{3} lai^{4} naew^{3} keu^{3} mak^{6} guay,^{5} mak^{6} giang,^{5} mak^{6} hu:ng^{2}	There are many kinds, such as banana, orange and papaya.
	ມີຫລາຍຄົນມາຄືທ້າວແສງກັບເມັຍລາວ ທ່ານບຸນທອງ ທ່ານມິນລາ .	mi^{3} lai^{4} ko:n^{3} ma^{3} keu^{3} tao^{5} saeng^{4} ga:p^{3} mia^{3} lao^{3} tan^{2} bu:n^{1} tohng,^{3} tan^{2} mi:n^{3} la^{3}	There are many people present such as Mr. Seng and his wife, Mrs. Bounthong and Mr. Miller.
	ເມືອງລາວມີເມືອງໃຫຍ່ຄື ວຽງຈັນ.	meuang^{3} lao^{3} mi^{3} meuang^{3} nyai:^{2} keu^{3} wiang^{3} cha:n^{1}.	Laos has big cities such as Vientiane.
	ຢູ່ຕລາດມີຫລາຍຢ່າງຄື ໝາກເລັ່ນ ກະລໍ່າປີ ຜັກບົ່ວ	yu^{2} dta:^{3} lat^{6} mi^{3} lai^{4} yang^{2} keu^{3} mak^{6} le:n,^{2} ga:^{3} la:m^{3} bpi,^{1} pa:k^{3} bua^{2}	In the market there are many things like tomatoes, cabbages, and onions.

7-4	<u>ຊັ້ນລຸ່ມ , ຊັ້ນເທິງ</u>	<u>sa:n^5 lu:m^2, sa:n^5 ter:ng^2</u>	<u>Downstairs, upstairs</u>
	ມີແຂກມາຫາເຈົ້າຢູ່ຊັ້ນລຸ່ມ	mi^3 kaek^6 ma^3 ha^4 chao:^{5} yu^2 sa:n^5 lu:m^2	A visitor came to see you downstairs.
	ແມ່ນອນຢູ່ຊັ້ນເທິງ	mae^2 nohn^3 yu^2 sa:n^5 ter:ng^2	Mother sleeps upstairs.
	ຢູ່ຊັ້ນເທິງມີຄົນເຊົ່າຢູ່	yu^2 sa:n^3 teu:ng^2 mi^3 ko:n^3 sao:^{2} yu^2	There is a tenant upstairs.
	ຂ້ອຍໄປເອົາເງິນຢູ່ຊັ້ນເທິງ	kohy^6 bpai:^{1} ao:^{1} nger:n^3 yu^2 sa:n^5 ter:ng^2	I'll go upstairs to get (my) money.
7-5	<u>ດ້ວຍ</u>	<u>duay^5</u>	<u>By (means of), with, of</u>
	ເຮືອນຂ້ອຍເຮັດດ້ວຍດິນຈີ່	heuan^3 kohy^6 he:t^2 duay^5 di:n^1 chi^2	My house is made of bricks.
	ຫຼັງຄາບ້ານຂ້ອຍມຸງດ້ວຍດິນຂໍ	la:ng^4 ka^3 ban^5 kohy^6 mu:ng^3 duay^5 di:n^1 koh^4	The roof of my house is covered with tiles.
	ນີ້ເຮັດດ້ວຍຫຍັງ	ni^5 he:t^2 duay^5 nya:ng^4	What is this made of?
7-6	<u>ກິນເຂົ້າ</u>	<u>gi:n^1 kao:^{6}</u>	<u>To have a meal, to eat</u>
	ເຈົ້າກິນເຂົ້າແລ້ວບໍ່	chao:^{5} gi:n^1 kao:^{6} laew^5 boh^2	Have you had a meal yet?
	ລາວກິນເຂົ້າແລງນຳກັນກັບຄອບຄົວຂອງລາວ	lao^3 gi:n^1 kao:^{6} laeng^3 na:m^3 ga:n^3 ga:p^3 kohp^5 kua^3 kohng^4 lao^3	He eats his dinner with his family.
	ກິນເຂົ້ານຳກັນຊະ	gi:n^1 kao:^{6} na:m^3 ga:n^1 sa:^{2}	Let's have a meal together.
	ຂະເຈົ້າໄປກິນເຂົ້າຢູ່ໃນເມືອງ	ka:^{3} chao:^{5} bpai:^{1} gi:n^1 kao:^{6} yu^2 nai:^{3} meuang^3	They went to eat in town.

7-7	<u>ນອນ</u>	<u>nohn^{3}</u>	<u>To sleep</u>
	ເດັກນ້ອຍໄປນອນແລ້ວບໍ່	de:k^{3} nohy^{5} bpai:^{1} nohn^{3} laew^{5} boh^{2}	Did the children go to bed yet?
	ຂ້ອຍຢາກນອນ	kohy^{6} yak^{6} nohn^{3}	I want to sleep. (I'm sleepy)
	ຂ້ອຍບໍ່ຢາກນອນ ເຮັດວຽກອີກກໍໄດ້	kohy^{6} boh^{2} yak^{6} nohn^{2}. he:t^{2} wiak^{5} ik^{6} goh^{1} dai:^{5}	I don't want to sleep. I can still work.
	ລາວນອນດົນໆ	lao^{3} nohn^{3} do:n^{1} do:n^{1}	He slept for a long time.
7-8	<u>ຂ້າງຫຼັງ</u>	<u>kang^{6} la:ng^{4}</u>	<u>Behind</u>
	ບ້ານຂ້ອຍຢູ່ຂ້າງຫຼັງວັດ	ban^{5} kohy^{6} yu^{2} kang^{6} la:ng^{4} wa:t^{2}	My house is behind a temple.
	ທັມມະດາເຮືອນຄົວຕັ້ງຢູ່ຂ້າງຫຼັງເຮືອນໃຫຍ່	ta:m^{3} ma:^{2} da^{1} heuan^{3} kua^{3} ta:ng^{5} yu^{2} kang^{6} la:ng^{4} heuan^{3} nyai^{2}	Usually the kitchen is behind the main house.
	ຂະເຈົ້າຢູ່ຂ້າງຫຼັງ	ka:^{3} chao:^{5} yu^{2} kang^{6} la:ng^{4}	They are in back of it.
	ຢູ່ຂ້າງຫຼັງບໍ່ມີບ່ອນ	yu^{2} kang^{6} la:ng^{4} boh^{2} mi^{3} bohn^{2}	There is no place behind it.
7-9	<u>ອື່ນ</u>	<u>eun^{2}</u>	<u>Other</u>
	ຂ້ອຍຢູ່ແຕ່ວຽງຈັນ ບໍ່ເຄີຍໄປເມືອງອື່ນ	kohy^{6} yu^{2} dtae^{2} wiang^{3} cha:n,^{1} boh^{2} kery^{3} bpai:^{1} meuang^{3} eun^{2}	I have lived only in Vientiane and never been to other cities.
	ທາງນີ້ບໍ່ດີ ໄປທາງອື່ນ ຊະ	tang^{3} ni^{5} boh^{2} di^{1}. bpai:^{1} tang^{3} eun^{2} sa:^{2}	This road is not good. Why don't you take another road?
	ຢູ່ໃນຫ້ອງນີ້ບໍ່ມີ ໄປເບິ່ງຫ້ອງອື່ນ	yu^{2} nai^{3} hohng^{6} ni^{5} boh^{2} mi^{3}. bpai:^{1} beu:ng^{2} hohng^{6} eun^{2}	It's not in this room. Go and look in the other rooms.

7-10	<u>ສ່ວນ</u>	<u>suan^{2}</u>	<u>A part, section, portion</u>
	ທາງນີ້ມີສ່ວນນຶ່ງບໍ່ດີ ໄປບໍ່ໄດ້	tang^{3} ni^{5} mi^{3} suan^{2} neu:ng^{2} boh^{2} di^{1} bpai:^{1} boh^{2} dai:^{5}	This road has one bad section. You can't go.
	ນີ້ມີແຕ່ສ່ວນນຶ່ງ ບໍ່ແມ່ນໝົດ	ni^{5} mi^{3} dtae^{2} suan^{2} neu:ng^{2} boh^{2} maen^{2} mo:t^{3}	This is just a part of it, not the whole.
	ສ່ວນຂອງຂ້ອຍ ຂ້ອຍເຮັດວຽກອື່ນ	suan^{2} kohng^{4} kohy,^{6} kohy^{6} he:t^{2} wiak^{5} eun^{2}	For my part, I'll do some other work.
	ຂ້ອຍບໍ່ຮູ້ຈັກເຣື່ອງສ່ວນຂອງລາວ	kohy^{6} boh^{2} hu^{5} cha:k^{3} leuang^{2} suan^{2} kohng^{4} lao^{3}	I don't know his side of the story.
	ພໍ່ເອົາມາໃຫ້ຂ້ອຍສ່ວນນຶ່ງ, ໃຫ້ລາວສ່ວນນຶ່ງ	poh^{2} ao:^{1} ma^{3} hai:^{6} kohy^{6} suan^{2} neu:ng^{2}, hai:^{6} lao^{3} suan^{2} neu:ng^{2}	Father gave me a portion and him a portion, too.
7-11	<u>ບ່ອນ</u>	<u>bohn^{2}</u>	<u>Place</u>
	ມີບ່ອນນັ່ງບໍ່	mi^{1} bohn^{2} na:ng^{2} boh^{2}	Is there any place to sit?
	ບ່ອນນີ້ງາມຂ້ອຍມັກຫຼາຍ	bohn^{3} ni^{5} ngam^{3} kohy^{6} ma:k^{2} lai^{4}	This is a beautiful place. I like it very much.
	ຢາກກິນເຂົ້າຢູ່ນີ້ແຕ່ບໍ່ມີບ່ອນ	yak^{6} gi:n^{1} kao:^{6} yu^{2} ni^{5} dtae^{2} boh^{2} mi^{3} bohn^{2}	We want to eat here, but there isn't any place (to sit).
	ເຈົ້າເຮັດການຢູ່ບ່ອນເກົ່າບໍ່	chao:^{5} he:t^{2} gan^{1} yu^{2} bohn^{2} gao:^{2} boh^{2}	Do you still work at the (same) old place?

7-12	ຈອດ	choht^{6}	To park, to stop
	ຈອດຣົດຢູ່ບ່ອນນີ້ໄດ້ບໍ່	choht^{6} lo:t^{2} yu^{2} bohn^{2} ni^{5} dai:^{5} boh^{2}	Can I park a car here?
	ຈອດຣົດທາງໜ້າບ້ານຂະເຈົ້າບໍ່ມັກ	choht^{6} lo:t^{2} tang^{3} na^{6} ban^{5} ka:^{3} chao:^{5} boh^{2} ma:k^{2}	They don't like parking cars in front of the house.
	ຢູ່ນີ້ຕອນເຊົ້າຈອດຣົດບໍ່ໄດ້	yu^{2} ni^{5} dtohn^{1} sao:^{5} choht^{6} lo:t^{2} boh^{2} dai:^{5}	You can't park here in the morning.
	ຈອດນີ້ແດ່ ສາມລໍ້	choht^{6} ni^{5} dae^{2} sam^{4} loh^{5}	Stop here, Samloh.
7-13	ທາງໜ້າ	tang^{3} na^{6}	In front of
	ທາງໜ້າບ້ານເຈົ້າມີຫຍັງ	tang^{3} na^{6} ban^{5} chao:^{5} mi^{3} nya:ng^{4}	What is in front of your house?
	ຢູ່ທາງໜ້າມີສວນ ແລະຂ້ອຍປູກເຄື່ອງ	yu^{2} tang^{3} na^{6} mi^{3} suan^{4} lae:^{2} kohy^{6} bpuk^{6} keuang^{2}	In front, we have a garden and I plant trees and flowers.
	ຢູ່ທາງໜ້າຕລາດມີບ່ອນຈອດຣົດ	yu^{1} tang^{3} na^{6} dta:^{3} lat^{6} mi^{3} bohn^{2} choht^{6} lo:t^{2}	There is a parking lot in front of the market.
	ຂະເຈົ້າຖ້າເຈົ້າຢູ່ໜ້າໂຮງການ	ka:^{3} chao:^{5} ta^{6} chao:^{5} yu^{2} na^{6} hong^{3} gan^{1}	They are waiting for you in front of your office.
7-14	ກ້ອງ	gohng^{5}	Under, below
	ບໍ່ຢູ່ເທິງແຕ່ຢູ່ກ້ອງ	boh^{2} yu^{2} ter:ng^{2} dtae^{2} yu^{2} gohng^{5}	It is not upstairs, but downstairs.
	ຢູ່ກ້ອງເຮືອນມີບ່ອນຈອດຣົດ	yu^{2} gohng^{5} heuan^{3} mi^{3} bohn^{2} choht^{6} lo:t^{2}	There is a parking space under the house.

Text

ບົດຮຽນທີເຈັດ

1. ຂ້ອຍມາຢູ່ເມືອງລາວໄດ້ປີປາຍແລ້ວ
2. ດຽວນີ້ເຊົ່າເຮືອນຫຼັງນີ້ຢູ່ໃນວຽງຈັນ
3. ເຮືອນຂ້ອຍມີ ສອງຊັ້ນຄື ຊັ້ນລຸ່ມແລະຊັ້ນເທິງ ແລະເປັນເຮືອນດິນຈີ່
4. ຫຼັງຄາມຸງດ້ວຍດິນຂໍສີແດງ.
5. ຢູ່ຊັ້ນລຸ່ມມີຫ້ອງສາມຫ້ອງຄື ຫ້ອງຮັບແຂກ ຫ້ອງກິນເຂົ້າ ແລະຫ້ອງເຮັດວຽກ ຂອງຂ້ອຍ
6. ເຮືອນຄົວຕັ້ງຢູ່ຂ້າງຫຼັງຄືກັນກັບບ້ານອື່ນໆຢູ່ໃນເມືອງລາວ.
7. ຢູ່ຊັ້ນເທິງມີຫ້ອງນອນ ແລະຫ້ອງອາບນໍ້າ
8. ສ່ວນນຶ່ງຂອງຊັ້ນເທິງແມ່ນເຊັ່ງຄືເຮືອນຮ້ານແບບລາວ ແລະມີບ່ອນຈອດ ລົດຢູ່ກ້ອງ
9. ຢູ່ທາງໜ້າແລະອ້ອມເຮືອນມີສວນທີ່ເຮົາປູກເຄື່ອງປູກຫຼາຍຢ່າງ.

BO:T^{3} HIAN^{3} TI^{2} CHE:T^{3}

1. Kohy^{6} ma^{3} yu^{2} meuang^{3} lao^{3} dai:^{5} bpi^{1} bpai^{1} laew^{5}.

2. Diaw^{1} ni^{5} sao:^{2} heuan^{3} la:ng^{4} neu:ng^{2} yu^{2} nai:^{3} wiang^{3} cha:n^{1}.

3. Heuan^{3} kohy^{6} mi^{3} sohng^{4} sa:n^{5} keu^{3} sa:n^{5} lu:m^{2} lae:^{2} sa:n^{5} ter:ng lae: bpe:n heuan^{3} di:n^{1} chi^{1}.

4. La:ng^{4} ka^{3} mu:ng^{3} duay^{5} di:n^{1} koh^{4} si^{4} daeng^{1}.

5. Yu^{2} sa:n^{5} lu:m^{2} mi^{3} hohng^{5} sam^{4} hohng^{6} keu^{3} hohng^{6} la:p^{2} kaek^{6} hohng^{6} gi:n^{1} kao:^{6} lae:^{2} hohng^{6} he:t^{2} wiak^{5} kohng^{4} kohy^{6}.

6. Heuan^{3} kua^{3} dta:ng^{5} yu^{2} kang^{6} la:ng^{4} keu^{3} ga:n^{1} ga:p^{3} ban^{5} eun^{2} eun^{2} nai:^{3} meuang^{3} lao^{3}.

7. Yu^{2} sa:n^{5} ter:ng^{3} mi^{3} hohng^{6} nohn^{3} lae:^{2} hohng^{6} ap^{6} na:m^{5}.

8. Suan^{2} neu:ng^{2} kohng^{4} sa:n^{5} ter:ng^{3} maen^{2} sia^{3} keu^{2} heuan^{3} han^{5} bpaep^{6} lao^{3}, lae:^{2} mi^{3} bohn^{2} choht^{6} lo:t^{2} yu^{2} kohng^{5}.

9. Yu^{2} tang^{3} na^{6} lae:^{2} ohm^{5} heuan^{3} mi^{3} suan^{4} ti^{2} hao:^{3} bpuk^{6} keuang^{2} bpuk^{6} lai^{4} yang^{2}.

LESSON 7: RENTING A HOUSE

1. I came to live in Laos more than a year ago.

2. At present I'm renting one house in Vientiane.

3. My house has two stories which are downstairs and upstairs and it is made of bricks.

4. The roof is covered with red tiles.

5. Downstairs (we have) 3 rooms which are a salon, a dining room and my study.

6. The kitchen stands behind like in other houses in Laos.

7. Upstairs (we have) bedrooms and a bathroom.

8. One part of the second floor is the veranda, like in Lao-style houses on stilts, and there is a place to park a car underneath it.

9. In front and all around the house, there is a garden where we grow many kinds of plants.

LESSON 8: PAYING A VISIT

Substitution Exercise

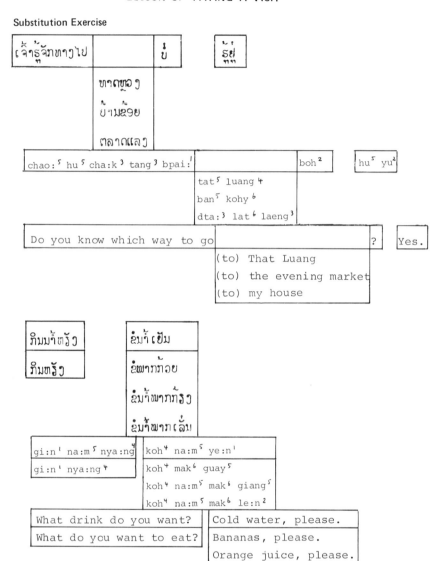

ເຈົ້າຮູ້ຈັກທາງໄປ		ບໍ່		ຮູ້ຢູ່
	ທາດຫຼວງ			
	ບ້ານຂ້ອຍ			
	ຕລາດແລງ			

chao:[5] hu[5] cha:k[3] tang[3] bpai:[1]		boh[2]		hu[5] yu[2]
	tat[5] luang[4]			
	ban[5] kohy[6]			
	dta:[3] lat[6] laeng[3]			

Do you know which way to go		?		Yes.
	(to) That Luang			
	(to) the evening market			
	(to) my house			

ກິນນ້ຳຫຍັງ	ຂໍນ້ຳເຢັນ
ກິນຫຍັງ	ຂໍໝາກກ້ວຍ
	ຂໍນ້ຳໝາກກ້ຽງ
	ຂໍນ້ຳໝາກເລັ່ນ

gi:n[1] na:m[5] nya:ng[4]	koh[4] na:m[5] ye:n[1]
gi:n[1] nya:ng[4]	koh[4] mak[6] guay[5]
	koh[4] na:m[5] mak[6] giang[5]
	koh[4] na:m[5] mak[6] le:n[2]

What drink do you want?	Cold water, please.
What do you want to eat?	Bananas, please.
	Orange juice, please.
	Tomato juice, please.

ໄປ	ນຳໃຜ
ມາ	
ຢູ່	
ຮຽນ	
ເວົ້າ	

ໄປນຳໝູ່ຂ້ອຍ
ມານຳໝູ່ຄົນຝຣັ່ງ
ຢູ່ນຳອ້າຍຂ້ອຍ
ຮຽນນຳນາຍຄູ
ເວົ້ານຳຜົວຂ້ອຍ

bpai:^{1}	na:m^3 pai:
ma^3	
yu^2	
hian^3	
wao:^{5}	

bpai:^{1} na:m^3 mu^2 kohy^6
ma^3 na:m^3 mu^2 ko:n^3 fa:^{3} la:ng^2
yu^2 na:m^3 ay^5 kohy^6
hian^3 na:m^3 nai^3 ku^3
wao:^{5} na:m^3 pua^4 kohy^6

(Do you)	Go	with who?
	Come	
	Stay	
	Study	
	Speak	

(I)	go with my friend.
	come with my foreign friend.
	stay with my older brother.
	study with my teacher.
	speak with my husband.

ເມື່ອໃດມີເວລາມາຫາຂ້ອຍແດ່
ສບາຍດີ ເປັນຢ່າງໃດ
ສບາຍເປັນຢ່າງໃດ
ເຊີນນັ່ງດີ
ແມ່ນບໍ່

ຂອບໃຈ ຊິໄປຫາເຈົ້າ
ສບາຍດີ ມື້ນີ້ຂ້ອຍມີວຽກຫຼາຍ
ສບາຍ ມື້ນີ້ບໍ່ມີວຽກຫຍັງ
ຂອບໃຈ. ຂໍນ້ຳເຢັນ
ແມ່ນ

meua^2 dai:^{1} mi^3 we^3 la^3 ma^3 ha^4 kohy^6 dae^2
sa:^{3} bai^4 di^1. bpe:n^1 yang^2 dai:^{1}
sa:^{3} bai^4. bpe:n^1 yang^2 dai:^{1}
seun^3 na:ng^2 dti:^{3}
maen^2 boh^2

kohp^6 chai:.^{1} si:^{2} bpai:^{1} ha^4 chao:^{5}
sa:^{3} bai^4 di^1. meu^5 ni^5 kohy^6 mi^3 wiak^5 lai^4
sa:^{3} bai.^{4} meu^5 ni^1 boh^2 mi^3 wiak^5 nya:ng^4
kohp^6 chai:^{1}. koh^4 na:m^5 ye:n^1
maen^2

When you have time come to see me please.
Hello! How are you?
Hello! How are you
Please sit down.
Isn't it so?

Thank you. I will go see you.
Hello. Today I have a lot of work.
Hello. Today I don't have any work.
Thank you. Could I have some cold water?
Yes.

ຈາກ	ນີ້	ໄປບໍ່ໄກ
	ວຽງຈັນ	
	ບ້ານຂ້ອຍ	
	ໂຮງການເຈົ້າ	
	ຕລາດ	

chak^6	ni^5	bpai:^{1} boh^2 gai:^{1}
	wiang^3 cha:n^1	
	ban^5 kohy^6	
	hohng^3 gan^1 chao:^{5}	
	dta:^{3} lat^6	

From	here	it isn't far to go.
	Vientiane	
	my house	
	your office	
	the market	

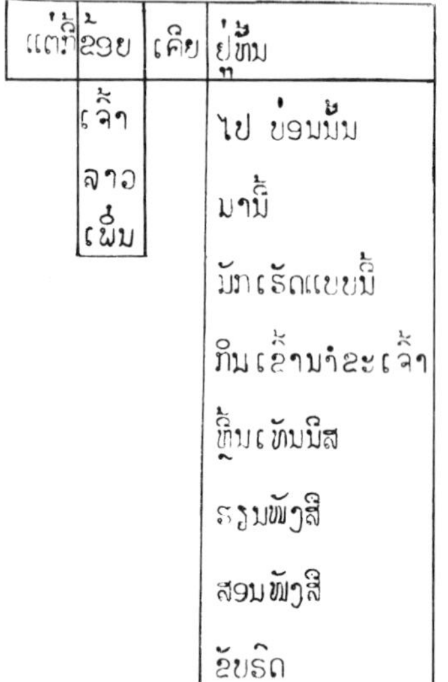

ແຕ່ກີ້	ຂ້ອຍ	ເຄີຍ	ຢູ່ຫັ້ນ
	ເຈົ້າ		ໄປ ບ່ອນນັ້ນ
	ລາວ		ມານີ້
	ເພິ່ນ		ມັກເຮັດແບບນີ້
			ກິນເຂົ້ານຳຂະເຈົ້າ
			ຫຼິ້ນເທັນນິສ
			ຮຽນໜັງສື
			ສອນໜັງສື
			ຂັບຣົດ

dtae^2 gi^5	kohy^6	kery^3	yu^2 ha:n^6
	chao:^{5}		bpai:^{1} bohn^2 na:n^5
	lao^3		ma^3 ni^5
	per:n^2		ma:k^2 he:t^2 baep^6 ni^5
			gi:n^1 kao:^{6} na:m^3 ka:^{3} chao:^{5}
			lin^6 te:n^3 nit^2
			hian^3 na:ng^4 seu^4
			sohn^4 na:ng^4 seu^4
			ka:p^3 lo:t^2

Before	I	used to	live there.
	you		go to that place.
	he		come here.
	they		like to work like this.
			eat with them.
			play tennis.
			study.
			teach.
			drive a car.

ເມື່ອໃດມີ	ເງິນຊື້
	ຄົນມາຫາ
	ຄົນຢາກໄປ
	ເວລາຫຼິ້ນເທັນນິສ
	ບ່ອນຈອດ
	ເຮືອນໃຫ້ເຊົ່າ
	ຣົດຂາຍ

meua^{2} dai:^{1} mi^{3}	nger:n^{3} seu^{5}
	ko:n^{3} ma^{3} ha^{4}
	ko:n^{3} yak^{6} bpai:^{1}
	we^{3} la^{3} lin^{6} te:n^{3} nit^{2}
	bohn^{2} chot^{6}
	heuan^{3} hai:^{6} sao:^{2}
	lo:t^{2} kai^{4}

When will you have	money to buy it?
	people to come to see it?
	people who want to go?
	time to play tennis?
	a space to stop?
	a house to let?
	a car for sale?

ມີ	ເຮືອນຂາຍ	ຢູ່ເບື້ອງ	ຂວາ	ບໍ່
	ຮ້ານຂາຍກາເຟ		ຊ້າຍ	
	ຮ້ານຂາຍຂອງ			
	ວັດນ້ອຍ			
	ໂຮງການ			
	ບ່ອນຈອດຣົດ			

mi^{3}	heuan^{3} kai^{4}	yu^{2} beuang^{5}	kwa^{4}	boh^{2}
	lan^{5} kai^{4} ga^{1} fe^{3}		sai^{5}	
	lan^{5} kai^{4} kohng^{4}			
	wat^{2} nohy^{5}			
	hohng^{3} gan^{1}			
	bohn^{2} choht^{6} lo:t^{2}			

Is there	a house for sale	on the side	right	?
	a coffee shop		left	
	a general store			
	a small temple			
	an office			
	a parking space			

ເຮືອນ	ທີ່ສອງແມ່ນ	ເຮືອນຂ້ອຍ
ຄົນ		ພໍ່
ຫ້ອງ		ຫ້ອງ
ຣົດ		ຣົດ
ຫຼັງ		ບ້ານ
ຄັນ		ຣົດ

heuan^{3}	ti^{2} sohng^{4} maen^{2}	heuan^{3}	kohy^{6}
ko:n^{3}		poh^{2}	
hohng^{6}		hohng^{6}	
lo:t^{2}		lo:t^{2}	
la:ng^{4}		ban^{5}	
ka:n^{3}		lo:t^{2}	

House	the second is	house	mine.
Person		father	
Room		room	
Car		car	
Building		house	
Machine		car	

Vocabulary Exercise

	Lao	Transcription	English
8-1	ຈາກນີ້ໄປ	chak6 ni5 bpai:1	From here to...
	ຈາກນີ້ໄປຕລາດເຊົ້າ ເທົ່າໃດ	chak6 ni5 bpai:1 dta:3 lat6 sao:5 tao:2 dai:1	How much is it from here to the morning market?
	ຈາກນີ້ໄປບ້ານເຈົ້າໄກບໍ່	chak6 ni5 bpai:1 ban5 chao:5 gai:1 boh2	It is far from here to your house?
	ຈາກນີ້ໄປຊຽງຂວາງຈັກກິໂລ	chak6 ni5 bpai:1 siang3 kwang4 cha:k6 gi1 lo3	How many kilometers are there from here to Xieng Khouang?
	ຈາກນີ້ໄປເມືອງນັ້ນ ມີສາມສິບກິໂລ	chak6 ni5 bpai:1 meuang3 na:n5 mi3 sam4 si:p3 gi1 lo3	It is 30 kilometers from here to that city.
8-2	ໄກ	gai:1	Far
	ບ້ານຂ້ອຍໄກຫຼາຍ	ban5 kohy6 gai:1 lai4	My house is very far.
	ຕລາດແລງໄກ ເອົາຣົດແທກຊີໄປດີ	dta:3 lat6 laeng3 gai:1 ao:1 lo:t2 taek5 si3 bpai:1 di1	The evening market is far. You'd better go by taxi.
	ໂຮງການຢູ່ໄກ ທັມມະດາກໍເອົາຣົດໄປ	hong3 gan1 yu2 gai:1 ta:m3 ma:2 da1 goh1 ao:1 lo:t2 bpai:1	The office is far. I usually go by car.
8-3	ແຕ່ກີ້	dtae2 gi5	Before, formerly
	ແຕ່ກີ້ເພິ່ນສອນຢູ່ວິທຍາລັຍ	dtae2 gi5 per:n2 sohn4 yu2 wi:2 ta:2 nya3 lai:3	Formerly he was teaching at the high school.
	ບ້ານຂ້ອຍແຕ່ກີ້ ຢູ່ໃກ້ວັດນັ້ນ	ban5 kohy6 dtae2 gi5 yu2 gai:5 wa:t2 na:n5	My old house was near that temple.
	ຣົດຄັນນີ້ ຂ້ອຍຊື້ແຕ່ກີ້ ດົນແລ້ວ ແຕ່ດຽວນີ້ເກົ່າຫຼາຍ	lo:t2 ka:n3 ni5 kohy6 seu5 dtae2 gi5 do:n1 laew5 dtae2 diaw1 ni5 gao:2 lai4	This car is the one I bought before, but it's very old now.
	ແຕ່ກີ້ ລາວມີເຮືອນຫຼັງໃຫຍ່ຢູ່ແຖວນີ້	dtae2 gi5 lao3 mi3 heuan3 la:ng4 nyai:2 yu2 taew4 ni5	Before he used to have a big house in this area.

8-4	<u>ບໍ່</u>	<u>boh^{1}</u>	<u>Is that so?</u>
	ບໍ່ ຂ້ອຍບໍ່ເຄີຍກິນ	boh^{1}, kohy^{6} boh^{2} kery^{3} gi:n^{1}	Is that so? I have never eaten it.
	ບໍ່ ບໍ່ຮູ້	boh^{1}, boh^{2} hu^{5}	Is that so? I don't know.
8-5	<u>ເມື່ອໃດ</u>	<u>meua^{2} dai:^{1}</u>	<u>When, whenever</u>
	ເມື່ອໃດມີເງິນຊື້ ຂ້ອຍຈະຊື້	meua^{2} dai:^{1} mi^{3} nger:n^{3} seu^{5} kohy^{6} cha:^{3} seu^{5}	When(ever) I have money, I'll buy it.
	ເມື່ອໃດມີເວລາຂ້ອຍຈະມາອີກ	meua^{2} dai:^{1} mi^{3} we^{3} la^{3} kohy^{6} cha:^{3} ma^{3} ik^{6}	When(ever) I have time, I'll come again.
	ເມື່ອໃດຂະເຈົ້າມາວຽງຈັນ ຂະເຈົ້າໄປຊື້ຂອງຢູ່ຕລາດ	meua^{2} dai:^{1} ka:^{3} chao:^{5} ma^{3} wiang^{3} cha:n^{1} ka:^{3} chao:^{5} bpai:^{1} seu^{5} kohng^{4} yu^{2} dta:^{3} lat^{6}	When they come to Vientiane, they go shopping at the market.
	ເມື່ອໃດລາວຢາກໄດ້ເງິນ ລາວຂໍນຳແມ່	meua^{2} dai:^{1} lao^{3} yak^{6} dai:^{1} nger:n^{3} lao^{3} koh^{4} na:m^{3} mae^{2}	When he wants money, he asks his mother for it.
8-6	<u>ເມື່ອໃດ</u>	<u>meua^{2} dai:^{1}</u>	<u>When?</u>
	ເມື່ອໃດຊິໄປ	meua^{2} dai:^{1} si:^{2} bpai:^{1}	When shall we go? When do you go?
	ຂ້ອຍບໍ່ຮູ້ວ່າ ຂະເຈົ້າ ຊິມາເມື່ອໃດ	kohy^{6} boh^{2} hu^{5} wa^{2} ka:^{3} chao:^{5} si:^{2} ma^{3} meua^{2} dai:^{1}	I don't know when they will come.
	ເມື່ອໃດເຈົ້າຢາກມາຢູ່ນີ້	meua^{2} dai:^{1} chao:^{5} yak^{6} ma^{3} yu^{2} ni^{5}	When do you want to come to live here?
	ເມື່ອໃດ ລາວຊິໄປຮຽນຢູ່ອະເມຣິກາ	meua^{3} dai:^{1} lao^{3} si:^{2} bpai:^{1} hian^{3} yu^{2} a:^{3} me^{3} li^{3} ga^{1}	When does he go to study in America?

	Lao	Transcription	English
8-7	ເວລາ	we3 la3	Time
	ເຈົ້າມີເວລາບໍ່ ດຽວນີ້	chao:5 mi3 we3 la3 boh2 diaw' ni5	Do you have time (to spare) now?
	ບໍ່ມີເວລາຫຼາຍ ມື້ໜ້າມາອີກໄດ້ບໍ່	boh2 mi3 we3 la3 lai.4 meu5 na6 ma3 ik6 dai:5 boh2	I don't have much time. Can you come again on another day?
	ເວລານີ້ ທັມມະດາຂ້ອຍຢູ່ບ້ານ	we3 la3 ni5 ta:m3 ma:2 da' kohy6 yu2 ban5	Now I usually stay home.
	ເວລານັ້ນ ຂ້ອຍບໍ່ຮູ້ວ່າ ລາວເປັນເຈົ້າຂອງ	we3 la3 na:n5 kohy6 boh2 hu5 wa2 lao3 bpe:n' chao:5 kohng4	At that time, I did not know that he was the owner.
8-8	ຮ້ານ	han5	Shop, store
	ແຖວນີ້ມີຮ້ານຫຼາຍ	taew4 ni5 mi3 han5 lai4	This street has many shops.
	ຂ້ອຍຊື້ຢູ່ຮ້ານນັ້ນ	kohy6 seu5 yu2 han5 na:n5	I buy at that store.
	ເປັນຮ້ານນ້ອຍ ໆ ແຕ່ຂາຍກາເຟແຊບ	bpe:n' han5 nohy5 nohy5 dtae2 kai4 ga' fe3 saep5	It is a small shop but (they) sell good coffee.
	ເຈົ້າຂອງຮ້ານນັ້ນ ມີຣົດໃຫຍ່ຄັນນຶ່ງ	chao:5 kohng4 han5 na:n5 mi3 lo:t2 nyai:2 ka:n3 neu:ng2	The owner of that store has a big car.
8-9	ກາເຟ	ga' fe3	Coffee
	ກາເຟລາວປູກຢູ່ໃສ	ga' fe3 lao3 bpuk6 yu2 sai:4	Where do they grow Lao coffee?
	ກາເຟແນວນີ້ແຊບ	ga' fe3 naew3 ni5 saep5	This kind of coffee is tasty.
	ເຈົ້າມັກກິນກາເຟບໍ່	chao:5 ma:k2 gi:n' ga' fe3 boh2	Do you like drinking coffee?
8-10	ຂ້າງ	kang6	At the side of, beside, next to
	ຢູ່ຂ້າງບ້ານລາວມີນາ (ກ້ວາງ)	yu' kang6 ban5 lao3 mi3 na3 (gwang5)	Next to his house is a (large) rice-field.
	ຮ້ານຂອງຂະເຈົ້າຢູ່ຂ້າງຕລາດເຊົ້າ	han5 kohng4 ka:3 chao:5 yu2 kang6 dta:3 lat6 sao:5	Their shop is at the side of the Morning market.
	ມີສວນງາມຢູ່ຂ້າງວິທຍາໄລ	mi3 suan4 gam3 yu2 kang6 wi:2 ta:nya3 lai:3	There is a nice garden beside the high school.

8-11	**ແມ່ນບໍ່**	maen boh	isn't it? (say, ...)
	ເຈົ້າຂັບຣົດເຈົ້າໄປແມ່ນບໍ່	chao:^{5} ka:p^3 lo:t^2 chao:^{5} bpai:^{1} maen^2 boh^2	You are going to drive your car, aren't you?
	ນີ້ແມ່ນຂອງເຈົ້າແມ່ນບໍ່	ni^5 maen^2 kohng^4 chao:^{5} mean^2 boh^2	This is yours, isn't it?
	ເຈົ້າເປັນເຈົ້າຂອງແມ່ນບໍ່	chao:^{5} bpe:n^1 chao:^{5} kohng^4 maen^2 boh^2	You are the owner, aren't you?
	ມື້ວັນເສົາ ຂະເຈົ້າບໍ່ເຮັດການ ແມ່ນບໍ່	meu^5 wa:n^3 sao:^{4} ka:^{3} chao:^{5} boh^2 he:t^2 gan^1 maen^2 boh^2	They don't work on Saturday, do they?
8-12	**ຕໍ່ໄປ**	dtoh^2 bpai:^{1}	Next to, after
	ວັນເສົາຕໍ່ໄປ ແມ່ນວັນທິດ	wa:n^3 sao:^{4} dtoh^2 bpai:^{1} maen^2 wa:n^3 ti:t^2	After Saturday, it is Sunday.
	ຕໍ່ບ້ານຂະເຈົ້າໄປແມ່ນບ້ານຂ້ອຍ	dto^2 ban^5 ka:^{3} chao:^{5} bpai:^{1} maen^2 ban^5 kohy^6	Next to their house is my house.
8-13	**ເຂົ້າໄປ (ມາ)**	kao:^{6} bpai:^{1} (ma^3)	To go in (to come in), enter
	ລາວເຂົ້າໄປຮ້ານກາເຟ	lao^3 kao:^{6} bpai:^{1} han^5 ga^1 fe^3	He went into a coffee shop.
	ມີທາງນ້ອຍເສັ້ນນຶ່ງ ເຂົ້າໄປນາ	mi^3 tang^3 nohy^5 se:n^6 neung^2 kao:^{6} bpai:^{1} na^3	There is a small lane going into the rice-field.
	ເຂົ້າມານັ່ງຕັ່ງນີ້ ຈະ	kao:^{6} ma^3 na:ng^2 dta:ng^2 ni^5 sa:^{2}	Come in and sit on this chair, won't you?
	ດຽວນີ້ເຂົ້າມາຫ້ອງບໍ່ໄດ້ດອກ	diaw^1 ni^5 kao:^{6} ma^3 hohng^6 boh^2 dai:^{5} dohk^6	Don't come into the room now.
8-14	**ຄືຊິ**	keu^3 si:^{2}	It seems to me, I think that
	ຂ້ອຍຄືຊິເຮັດໄດ້ຜູ້ດຽວ	kohy^6 keu^3 si:^{2} he:t^2 dai:^{5} pu^6 diaw^1	I think I can do it alone.
	ລາວຄືຊິບໍ່ຊື້ ລາວມີແລ້ວ	lao^3 keu^3 si:^{2} boh^2 seu.^{5} lao^3 mi^3 laew^5	I think he won't buy it. He already has one.
	ຂ້ອຍວ່າບໍ່ງາມ ເຈົ້າຄືຊິບໍ່ມັກດອກ	kohy^6 wa^2 boh^2 ngam^3, chao:^{5} keu^3 si:^{2} boh^2 ma:k^2 dohk^6	I say it's not nice. I think you won't like it at all.
	ຄືຊິມີຢູ່ໃນຫ້ອງນອນຂ້ອຍ	keu^3 si:^{2} yu^2 nai:^{3} hohng^6 nohn^3 kohy^6	I think it's in my bedroom.

	Lao	Transcription	English
8-15	ຫາ	ha^{4}	To look for
	ເຈົ້າຫາຫຍັງ	chao:^{5} ha^{4} nya:ng^{4}	What are you looking for?
	ຂ້ອຍຫາເຮືອນໃຫ້ເຊົ່າຫຼັງນຶ່ງ	kohy^{6} ha^{4} heuan^{3} hai:^{6} sao:^{2} la:ng^{4} neu:ng^{2}	I'm looking for a house to rent.
	ລາວຫານ້ອງລາວ ດົນ ດົນ ແຕ່ນ້ອງບໍ່ຢູ່	lao^{3} ha^{4} nohng^{5} lao^{3} do:n^{1} do:n^{1} dtae^{2} nohng^{5} boh^{2} yu^{2}	He looked for his younger sister for a long time, but he didn't find her.
	ລາວຫາເງິນໄດ້ແລ້ວບໍ່	lao^{3} ha^{4} nger:n^{3} dai:^{5} laew^{5} boh^{2}	Has he found the money yet?
8-16	ເປັນຢ່າງໃດ	bpe:n^{1} yang^{2} dai:^{1}	How is .../(everything)?
	ວຽກຂອງເຈົ້າເປັນຢ່າງໃດ	wiak^{5} kohng^{4} chao:^{5} bpe:n^{1} yang^{2} dai:^{1}	How is your work going on?
	ເມັຽເຈົ້າເປັນຢ່າງໃດ	mia^{3} chao:^{5} bpe:n^{1} yang^{2} dai:^{1}	How is your wife?
	ລູກລາວເປັນຢ່າງໃດ	luk^{5} lao^{3} bpe:n^{1} yang^{2} dai:^{1}	How is his child?
8-17	ບໍ່......ຫຍັງ (ໃສ , ຈັກ ...)	boh^{2}.. nya:ng^{4} (sai:^{4}, cha:k^{3})	Not any...
	ບໍ່ຊື້ຫຍັງ ເບິ່ງຊື່ໆ	boh^{2} seu^{5} nya:ng^{4}. beu:ng^{2} seu^{2} seu^{2}	I won't buy anything. I'm just looking.
	ຂ້ອຍບໍ່ຢາກໄດ້ຫຍັງ	kohy^{6} boh^{2} yak^{6} dai:^{5} nya:ng^{4}	I don't want anything.
	ລາວບໍ່ໄປໃສ ຢູ່ບ້ານຊື່ໆ	lao^{3} boh^{2} bpai:^{1} sai:^{4}. yu^{2} ban^{5} seu^{2} seu^{2}	He does not go anywhere; he's always at home.
	ເຈົ້າບໍ່ມາຫາຂ້ອຍຈັກເທື່ອ	chao:^{5} boh^{2} ma^{3} ha^{4} kohy^{6} cha:k^{3} teua^{2}	You never come to see me at all.

	Lao	Transliteration	English
8-18	<u>ກໍ</u> (See also p.155/7.3)	<u>goh1</u>	(Particle showing a change of subject or topic in the latter half of a sentence.)
	ຂ້ອຍຖ້າລາວດົນໆ ລາວກໍບໍ່ມາ	kohy6 ta6 lao3 do:n1 do:n1 lao3 goh1 boh2 ma3	I waited for her for a long time, but she didn't come.
	ລາວວ່າ ລາວມັກເຈົ້າຫຼາຍ ເຈົ້າກໍບໍ່ມັກລາວ	lao3 wa2 lao3 ma:k2 chao:5 lai,4 chao:5 goh1 boh2 ma:k2 lao3	He says he likes you a lot, but you don't like him.
	ໄປໃສກໍບໍ່ມີ	bpai:1 sai:4 goh1 boh2 mi3	I went everywhere, but I couldn't find any.
	ຫາຫຼາຍບ່ອນ ລາວກໍບໍ່ຢູ່	ha4 lai4 bohn,2 lao3 goh1 boh2 yu2	We looked many places, but could not find him.
8-19	<u>ຂໍ</u>	<u>koh4</u>	<u>To beg, to want</u>
	ຂໍເງິນແດ່ແມ່	koh4 nger:n3 dae2 mae2	Mother, I want some money.
	ຂ້ອຍຂໍນ້ຳ ນ້ຳເຢັນໆມີບໍ່	kohy6 koh4 na:m,5 na:m5 ye:n1 ye:n1 mi3 boh2	I want some water. Do you have very cold water?
	ລາວຂໍສິບພັນ ນາຍກໍເອົາໃຫ້ແຕ່ແປດພັນ	lao3 kch4 si:p3 pa:n3 nai3 goh1 ao:1 hai:6 dtae2 bpaet6 pa:n3	He wants 10,000,but the boss gave (him) only 8,000.
	ລາວຂໍເງິນນຳພໍ່ລາວ	lao3 koh4 nger:n3 na:m3 poh2 lao3	He asks his father for money.
8-20	<u>ຫິວນ້ຳ , ຫິວເຂົ້າ</u>	<u>hiw4 na:m,5 hiw4 kao:6</u>	<u>To be thirsty, to be hungry</u>
	ຫິວນ້ຳ ຂໍນ້ຳແດ່	hiw4 na:m5 koh4 na:m5 dae2	I'm thirsty. I want some water.
	ມື້ນີ້ຫິວນ້ຳຫຼາຍ	meu5 ni5 hiw4 na:m5 lai4	Today I'm very thirsty.
	ຫິວເຂົ້າແລ້ວບໍ່	hiw4 kao:6 laew5 boh2	Are you hungry yet?
	ກິນຫຼາຍກໍຍັງຫິວເຂົ້າ	gi:n1 lai4 goh1 nya:ng3 hiw4 kao:6	(He) eats a lot,but (he) is still hungry.

	Lao	Romanization	English
8-21	ຍາກ	nyak^{5}	Difficult, hard
	ພາສາລາວຮຽນຍາກ	pa^{3} sa^{4} lao^{3} hian^{3} nyak^{5}	Lao is hard to learn.
	ບໍ່ຍາກດອກ ຮຽນອີກຫຼາໆ	boh^{2} nyak^{5} dohk^{6} hian^{3} ik^{6} lai^{4} lai^{4}	It is not hard at all. Study it a lot.
	ບໍ່ຍາກ ບໍ່ງ່າຍ	boh^{2} nyak^{5} boh^{2} ngai^{2}	It is not hard and it's not easy either.
	ເຣື້ອງນີ້ເວົ້າຍາກ ຂ້ອຍບໍ່ຢາກເວົ້າ	leuang^{2} ni^{5} wao:^{5} nyak^{5} kohy^{6} boh^{2} yak^{6} wao:^{5}	In this case it's hard to say. I don't want to say (anything).
8-22	ງ່າຍ	ngai^{2}	Easy
	ພາສາລາວຮຽນງ່າຍບໍ່	pa^{3} sa^{4} lao^{3} hian^{3} ngai^{2} boh^{2}	Is Lao easy to learn?
	ຮຽນຂັບຣົດບໍ່ງ່າຍ	hian^{3} ka:p^{3} lo:t^{2} boh^{2} ngai^{2}	It is not easy to learn to drive a car.
	ເວົ້າງ່າຍ ແຕ່ເຮັດຍາກ	wao:^{5} ngai^{2} dtae^{2} he:t^{2} nyak^{5}	That's easy to say, but hard to do.
8-23	ຂັບ	ka:p^{3}	To drive (a vehicle)
	ເຈົ້າຂັບຣົດເປັນບໍ່	chao:^{5} ka:p^{3} lo:t^{2} bpe:n^{1} boh^{2}	Can you drive a car?
	ລາວຂັບບໍ່ເປັນ	lao^{3} ka:p^{3} boh^{2} bpe:n^{1}	He can't drive.
	ລາວເປັນຄົນຂັບຣົດ	lao^{3} bpe:n^{1} ko:n^{3} ka:p^{3} lo:t^{2}	He is a driver.
	ຂະເຈົ້າຂັບຣົດ ດົນໆ	ka:^{3} chao:^{5} ka:p^{3} lo:t^{2} do:n^{1} do:n^{1}	They've been driving for a long time.

8-24	ທີ່ສຸດ (See also p.149/3.5)	ti^2 $su:t^3$	The most, the --est (superlative)
	ໃຫຍ່ທີ່ສຸດ	$nyai:^2$ ti^2 $su:t^3$	The biggest.
	ດີທີ່ສຸດ	di^1 ti^2 $su:t^3$	The best.
	ຍາກທີ່ສຸດ	$nyak^5$ ti^2 $su:t^3$	The most difficult.
	ແພງທີ່ສຸດ	$paeng^3$ ti^2 $su:t^3$	The most expensive.
8-25	ຜູ້ດຽວ	pu^6 $diaw^1$	Alone
	ເຈົ້າມາຜູ້ດຽວບໍ່	$chao:^5$ ma^3 pu^6 $diaw^1$ boh^2	Did you come alone?
	ເຮັດຜູ້ດຽວຍາກຫຼາຍ	$he:t^2$ pu^6 $diaw^1$ $nyak^5$ lai^4	It is very difficult to do by yourself.
	ລາວມັກຢູ່ຜູ້ດຽວ	lao^3 $ma:k^2$ yu^2 pu^6 $diaw^1$	He likes being alone.
	ກິນເຂົ້າຜູ້ດຽວບໍ່ແຊບ	$gi:n^1$ $kao:^6$ pu^6 $diaw^1$ boh^2 $saep^5$	Meals are not tasty when you eat alone.
8-26	ພໍ	poh^3	Enough, sufficient
	ມີພໍບໍ່	mi^3 pch^3 boh^2	Did you have enough?
	ກິນເຂົ້າພໍແລ້ວ	$gi:n^1$ $kao:^6$ poh^3 $laew^5$	I have eaten enough.
	ພໍແລ້ວຢ່າກໄດ້ອີກ	poh^3 $laew^5$. boh^2 yak^6 $dai:^5$ ik^6	It is sufficient (they) don't want any more.

Text

ບົດ ຮຽນ ທີ່ ແປດ

1. ບ້ານເຈົ້າຢູ່ໃສ

2. ຢູ່ໃກ້ວັດສີຖານເໜືອ ເຈົ້າຮູ້ຈັກທາງໄປບໍ່ ຈາກນີ້ໄປບໍ່ໄກ

3. ຮູ້ຢູ່ ແຕ່ກີ້ຂ້ອຍເຄີຍເຊົ່າບ້ານຢູ່ແຖວນັ້ນ

4. ບໍ່ ເມື່ອໃດມີເວລາ ມາຫາຂ້ອຍແດ່

5. ຂອບໃຈ ຂ້ອຍຮູ້ວ່າ ມີຮ້ານຂາຍກາເຟຢູ່ຂ້າງວັດແມ່ນບໍ່

6. ແມ່ນ ຕໍ່ໄປມີທາງນ້ອຍເສັ້ນນຶ່ງເຂົ້າໄປເບື້ອງຂວາຮ້ານນັ້ນ , ເຮືອນທີ່ສອງເບື້ອງຊ້າຍ ສອງຊັ້ນ ແມ່ນເຮືອນຂ້ອຍ.

7. ຄືຊິຫາໄດ້ ວັນເສົາໜ້າຊິໄປຫາເຈົ້າຢູ່ບ້ານ

   (ວັນເສົາ)

8. ສບາຍດີ ເປັນຢ່າງໃດ

9. ສບາຍດີ ຂ້ອຍບໍ່ມີວຽກຫຍັງມື້ນີ້ ໄປ**ໂຮງການ**ກໍນາຍບໍ່ຢູ່ ເຊີນງັ່ຕັ່ງນີ້ , ກິນນ້ຳຫຍັງ

10. ນ້ຳເຢັນຊື່ໆ ຫຼິ້ນເທັນນິສຫິວນ້ຳຫຼາຍ

11. ຫຼິ້ນນຳໃຜ

12. ຫຼິ້ນນຳຄົນຝຣັ່ງ ຄົນອະເມຣິກາ ຂະເຈົ້າເກັ່ງຫຼາຍ

13. ຂັບຣົດເຈົ້າມາບ້ານຂ້ອຍຫາທາງຍາກບໍ່ ມາເທື່ອທຳອິດ

14. ບໍ່ຍາກຫາງ່າຍທີ່ສຸດ ເຮືອນນີ້ແມ່ນຂອງເຈົ້າບໍ່

15. ແມ່ນ ຂ້ອຍເປັນເຈົ້າຂອງ ແຕ່ຢູ່ຜູ້ດຽວ ກ້ວາງພໍ ຂ້ອຍຢາກໃຫ້ຄົນເຊົ່າ ຄົນມີຜູ້ໃດຜູ້ນຶ່ງຢາກເຊົ່າຢູ່

BO:T^{3} HIAN^{3} TI^{2} BPAET^{6}

1. A : Ban^{5} chao:^{5} yu^{2} sai:^{4}?

2. B : Yu^{2} gai:^{5} wa:t^{2} si^{4} tan^{4} neua^{4}. Chao:^{5} hu^{5} cha:k^{3} tang^{3} bpai:^{1} boh^{2}? Chak^{6} ni^{1} bpai:^{1} boh^{2} kai:^{1}.

3. A : Hu^{5} yu^{2}. Dtae^{2} gi^{5} kohy^{6} kery^{3} sao^{2} ban^{5} yu^{2} taew^{4} na:n^{5}.

4. B : Boh^{1}. Meua^{2} dai:^{1} mi^{3} we^{3} la^{3} ma^{3} ha^{4} kohy^{6} dae^{2}.

5. A : Kohp^{6} chai:^{1}. Kohy^{6} hu^{5} wa^{2} mi^{3} lan^{5} kai^{4} ga^{3} fe^{3} yu^{2} kang^{6} wa:t^{2} maen^{2} boh^{2}.

6. B : Maen^{2}. dtoh^{2} bpai:^{1} mi^{3} tang^{3} nohy^{5} se:n^{6} neu:ng^{2} kao:^{6} bpai:^{1} beuang^{5} kua^{4} han^{5} na:n^{5}. Heuan^{3} ti^{2} sohng^{4} beuang^{5} sai^{5} sohng^{4} sa:n^{5} maen^{2} heuan^{3} kohy^{5}.

7. A : Keu^{3} si:^{2} ha^{4} dai:^{5} wa:n^{3} sao:^{4} na^{6} si:^{2} bpai:^{1} ha^{4} chao:^{5} yu^{2} ban^{5}. wa:n sao: .

8. B : Sa:^{3} bai^{4} di^{1} bpe:n^{1} yang^{2} dai:^{1}?

9. A : Sa:^{3} bai^{4} di^{1}. Kohy^{6} boh^{2} mi^{3} wiak^{5} nya:ng^{4} meu^{5} ni^{2}. Bpai:^{1} hong^{3} gan^{1} goh^{1} nai^{3} boh^{2} yu^{2}. Seun^{3} na:ng^{2} dta:ng^{2} ni^{5}, gi:n^{1} na:m^{5} nya:ng^{4}?

10. B : Na:m^{5} ye:n^{1} seu^{2} seu^{2}. Lin^{6} te:n^{3} nit^{2} hiw^{4} na:m^{5} lai^{4}.

11. A : Lin^{6} na:m^{3} pai:^{4}?

12. B : Lin^{6} na:m^{3} ko:n^{3} fa:^{2} la:ng^{2}. Ka:^{3} chao:^{5} ge:ng^{2} lai^{4}.

13. A : Ka:p^{3} lo:t^{2} chao:^{5} ma^{3} ban^{5} kohy^{6} ha^{4} tang^{3} nyak^{5} boh^{2}? Ma^{3} teua^{2} ta:m^{3} i:t^{3}.

14. B : Boh^{2} nyak^{5} ha^{4} ngai^{2} ti^{2} su:t^{3}. Heuan^{3} ni^{5} maen^{2} kohng^{4} chao:^{5} boh^{2}.

15. A : Maen^{2}. Kohy^{6} bpe:n^{1} chao:^{5} kohng^{4} dtae^{2} yu^{2} pu^{6} diaw^{1}. Gwang^{5} poh^{3}. kohy^{6} yak^{6} hai:^{6} ko:n^{3} sao:^{2}. Ka:n^{3} mi^{3} pu^{6} dai:^{1} pu^{6} neu:ng^{2} yak^{6} sao:^{2} yu^{2}.

LESSON 8: PAYING A VISIT

1. A: Where is your house?

2. B: It's near Wat Si Thane Neua. Do you know the way? It's not far from here.

3. A: I know. Before I used to rent a house in that area.

4. B: Did you? Whenever you have times, do come to see me.

5. A: Thanks. I know there is a coffee shop beside the Wat, right

6. B: Right. Next to that shop, there is one small lane, (you) enter (that lane) to right, and the second house on the left (with) two stories is my house.

7. A: I think I can find it. I'll go to see you at your house next Saturday.

(Saturday)

8. A: Hello , how are things?

9. B: Hi, I don't have anything to do today. I went to office and my boss wasn't there. Please sit in this chair. What will you have (drink)?

10. A: Just give me cold water. (I) play(ed) tennis. I'm very thirsty.

11. B: Who did you play with?

12. A: I played with some foreigners. They are very good.

13. B: Did you drive your car here? Was it difficult to find my house (you) coming the first time?

14. A: No, it's not difficult; its very easy to find. Is this house yours?

15. B: Yes, I'm the owner, but I'm living alone. It is wide enough. I want to rent it if someone wants to come and live as a tenant.

LESSON 9: THE DAILY ROUTINE

ubstitution Exercise

...ຈົ້າ	ລຸກຈັກໂມງທຸກໆເຊົ້າ
...າວ	
...ພິ່ນ	
...ະເຈົ້າ	

ຂ້ອຍລຸກຫ້າໂມງ	ທຸກໆເຊົ້າ
ລາວລຸກຫ້າໂມງເຄິ່ງ	
ເພິ່ນລຸກກ່ອນຫົກໂມງ	
ຂະເຈົ້າລຸກແຕ່ເດິກ	

...ao:[5]	lu:k[2] cha:k[3] mong[3] tu:k[2] tu:k[2] sao:[5]
...o[3]	
...r:n[2]	
...:[3] chao:[5]	

kohy[6] lu:k[2] ha[6] mong[3]	tu:k[2] tu:k[2] sao:[5]
lao[3] lu:k[2] ha[6] mong[3] ker:ng[2]	
per:n[2] lu:k[2] gohn[2] ho:k[3] mong[3]	
ka:[3] chao:[5] lu:k[2] dtae[2] der:k[3]	

...u	get up, what time every morning?
	(gets)
...ey	

I get up at 5 o'clock	every morning.
He gets up at 5:30	
He gets up before 6 o'clock	
They get up only at dark	

...ງຈາກ	ລຸກແລ້ວ	ເຮັດຫຍັງ
	ລ້າງໜ້າ ຖູແຂ້ວ	
	ກິນເຂົ້າແລ້ວ	

ລຸກແລ້ວລ້າງໜ້າ ຖູແຂ້ວ
ຫຼັງຈາກນັ້ນກິນເຂົ້າເຊົ້າ
ຫຼັງຈາກນັ້ນໄປການ

...a:ng[4] chak[6]	lu:k[2] laew[5]	he:t[2] nya:ng[4]
	lang[5] na[6] tu[4] kaew[6]	
	gi:n[1] kao:[6] laew[5]	

lu:k[2] laew[5] lang[5] na[6] tu[4] kaew[6]
la:ng[4] chak[6] na:n[5] gi:n[1] kao:[6] sao:[5]
la:ng[4] chak[6] na:n[5] bpai:[1] gan[1]

After	getting up	what do you do?
	washing your face and brushing your teeth	
	eating	

After getting up I wash my face and brush my teeth.
After that I eat breakfast.
After that I go to the office.

ຈັກໂມງເຈົ້າ	ພາເດັກນ້ອຍໄປໂຮງຮຽນ	ເຈັດໂມງສິບຫ້າ
	ໄປການ	ເຈັດໂມງສາມສິບ
	ກັບມາກິນເຂົ້າຕອນທ່ຽງ	ສິບສອງໂມງເຄິ່ງ
	ຈະໄປການອີກ	ສອງໂມງເຄິ່ງ
	ເຂົ້ານອນ	ປະມານສິບໂມງຫຼືສິບໂມງເຄິ່ງ

cha:k^3 mong^3 chao:^{5}	pa^3 de:k^3 nohy^5 bpai:^{1} hong^3 hian^3	che:t^3 mong^3 si:p^3 ha^6
	bpai:^{1} gan^1	che:t^3 mong^3 sam^4 si:p^3
	ga:p^3 ma^3 gi:n^1 kao:^{6} dtohn^1 tiang^2	si:p^3 sohng^4 mong^3 ker:n
	cha:^{3} bpai:^{1} gan^1 ik^6	sohng^4 mong^3 ker:ng^2
	kao:^{6} nohn^3	bpa:^{3} man^3 si:p^3 mong^3 leu^4 si:p^3 mong^3 ker:ng

At what time	(do you)	take the children to go to school?	7:15
		go to the office?	7:30
		return to eat lunch?	12:30
	(will you)	go back to the office?	2:30
		fall asleep?	About 10:0[illegible] or 10:3[illegible]

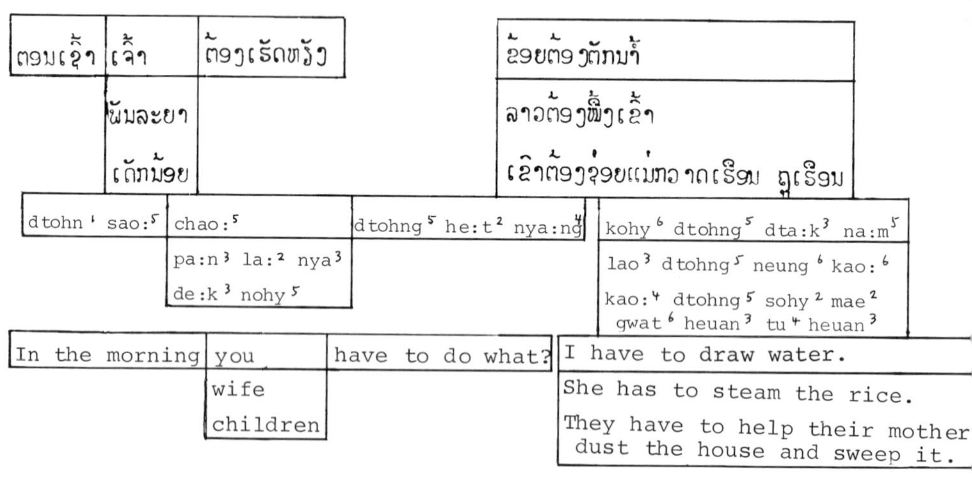

ຕອນເຊົ້າ	ເຈົ້າ	ຕ້ອງເຮັດຫຍັງ	ຂ້ອຍຕ້ອງຕັກນ້ຳ
	ພັນລະຍາ		ລາວຕ້ອງໜຶ້ງເຂົ້າ
	ເດັກນ້ອຍ		ເຂົາຕ້ອງຊ່ອຍແມ່ກວາດເຮືອນ ຖູເຮືອນ

dtohn^1 sao:^{5}	chao:^{5}	dtohng^5 he:t^2 nya:ng^4	kohy^6 dtohng^5 dta:k^3 na:m^5
	pa:n^3 la:^{2} nya^3		lao^3 dtohng^5 neung^6 kao:^{6}
	de:k^3 nohy^5		kao:^{4} dtohng^5 sohy^2 mae^2 gwat^6 heuan^3 tu^4 heuan^3

In the morning	you	have to do what?	I have to draw water.
	wife		She has to steam the rice.
	children		They have to help their mother dust the house and sweep it.

...ເລງ	ເຂົາຕ້ອງ	ເຮັດຫຍັງ	ເຂົາຕ້ອງຮຽນໜັງສື
	ມື້ນີ້ເຈົ້າຊິ		ຂ້ອຍຊິໄປຢາມພີ່ນ້ອງ
	ມື້ນີ້ລາວຊິ		ລາວຊິໄປເບິ່ງຊິເນ
	ມື້ນີ້ພວກເຈົ້າ		ພວກຂ້ອຍຊິພັກຜ່ອນຢູ່ບ້ານ

...tohn^{1} laeng^{3}	kao:^{4} dtohng^{5}	he:t^{2} nya:ng^{4}	kao:^{4} dtohng^{5} hian^{3} na:ng^{4} seu^{4}
	meu^{5} ni^{5} chao:^{5} si:^{2}		kohy^{6} bpai:^{1} yam^{1} pi^{2} nong^{5}
	meu^{5} ni^{5} lao^{3} si:^{2}		lao^{3} si:^{2} bpai:^{1} be:ng^{2} si^{3} ne^{3}
	meu^{5} ni^{5} puak^{5} chao:^{5}		puak^{5} kohy^{6} si:^{2} pa:k^{2} pohn^{2} yu^{2} ban^{5}

...the evening	they have	to do what?	They have to study.
	today you will		I will go meet my relatives.
	today he will		He will go see a movie.
	today you (pl.) will		We will hang around at home.

...ໂມງ	ນຶ່ງເຄິ່ງ	ຊິໄປ
ສອງ	ໂມງ	ຊິມາ
ສາມ		
ສີ່		
ຫ້າ		
ຫົກ		
ເຈັດ		
ແປດ		
ເກົ້າ		
ສິບ		
ສິບເອັດ		
ສິບສອງ		
ຈັກ		

mong^{3}	neu:ng^{2} ker:ng^{2}	si:^{2} bpai:^{1}
sohng^{4}	mong^{3}	si:^{2} ma^{3}
sam^{4}		
si^{2}		
ha^{6}		
ho:k^{3}		
che:t^{3}		
bpaet^{6}		
gao:^{5}		
si:p^{3}		
si:p^{3} e:t^{3}		
si:p^{3} sohng^{4}		
cha:k^{3}		

(At)	1:30	I'll go.
(At) 2	o'clock	I'll come.
3		
4		
5		
6		
7		
8		
9		
10		
11		
12		
What		

ເຈົ້າ	ລຸກ	ຈັກໂມງ
	ກິນເຂົ້າເຊົ້າ	
	ໄປການ	
	ມາການ	
	ກິນເຂົ້າແລງ	
	ເຂົ້ານອນ	

chao:^{5}	lu:k^2	cha:k^3 mong^3
	gi:n^1 kao:^{6} sao:^{5}	
	bpai:^{1} gan^1	
	ma^3 gan^1	
	gi:n^1 kao:^{6} laeng^3	
	kao:^{6} nohn^3	

You	get up	at what time?
	eat breakfast	
	go to the office	
	come to work	
	eat supper	
	fall asleep	

ຕອນ	ແລງ	ເຈົ້າຢູ່ບ້ານບໍ່
	ເຊົ້າ	
	ບ່າຍ	
	ທ່ຽງ	

dtohn^1	laeng^3	chao:^{5} yu^2 ban^5 boh^2
	sao:^{5}	
	bai^2	
	tiang^2	

In	the evening	will you be at home?
	the morning	
	the afternoon	
	noontime	

ຂ້ອຍ	ຕ້ອງລຸກຫົກໂມງ
ລາວ	ໄປການເຈັດໂມງເຄິ່ງ
ເຈົ້າ	ພາເດັກນ້ອຍໄປໂຮງຮຽນ
ຂະເຈົ້າ	ຮຽນໜັງສື
	ເຂົ້ານອນສິບໂມງ
	ຢາມພີ່ນ້ອງມື້ນີ້
	ໄປຕລາດ
	ເຮັດກິນ

kohy^6	dtohng^5 lu:k^2 ho:k^3 mong^3
lao^3	bpai:^{1} gan^1 che:t^3 mong^3 ker:ng^2
chao:^{5}	pa^3 de:k^3 nohy^5 bpai:^{1} hong^3 hian^3
ka:^{3} chao:^{5}	hian^3 na:ng^4 seu^4
	kao:^{6} nohn^3 si:p^3 mong^3
	yam^1 pi^2 nohng^5 meu^5 ni^5
	bpai:^{1} dta:^{3} lat^6
	he:t^2 gi:n^1

I	have to get up at 6:00.
He	go to the office at 7:30.
You	take the children to go to school
They	study.
	fall asleep at 10:00.
	meet relatives today.
	go to market.
	cook.

ເຈົ້າພາໝູ່ເຈົ້າ	ໄປໂຮງການ	ບໍ່
	ໄປເບິ່ງຊີເນ	
	ໄປກິນກາເຟ	
	ໄປຫານາຍຄູ	
	ມານີ້	
	ມາຫາຂ້ອຍ	
	ມາຫ້າໂມງ	
	ມາກິນເຂົ້ານຳກັນ	

chao:^{5} pa^3 mu^2 chao:^{5}	bpai:^{1} hong^3 gan^1	boh^2
	bpai:^{1} beu:ng^2 si^3 ne^3	
	bpai:^{1} gi:n^1 ga^1 fe^3	
	bpai:^{1} ha^4 nai^3 ku^3	
	ma^3 ni^5	
	ma^3 ha^4 kohy^6	
	ma^3 ha^6 mohng^3	
	ma^3 gi:n^1 kao:^{6} na:m^3 ga:n^1	

(Do) you bring your friend	to go to the office	?
	to go to see a movie	
	to go drink coffee	
	to find the teacher	
	to come here	
	to find me	
	to come at 5:00	
	to come eat together	

Vocabulary Exercise

	Lao	Transcription	English
9-1	ລຸກ	lu:k^2	To get up, to wake up
	ລາວລຸກໄປນາແຕ່ເດິກ	lao^3 lu:k^2 bpai:^{1} na^3 dtae^2 der:k^3	He gets up early to go to the rice-field.
	ລູກຂ້ອຍມັກລຸກສວຍ	luk^5 kohy^6 ma:k^2 lu:k^2 suay^4	My children like to get up late.
	ຕອນເຊົ້າຂ້ອຍລຸກແຕ່ຫ້າໂມງ	dtohn^1 sao:^{5} kohy^6 lu:k^2 dtae^2 ha^6 mong^3	I get up at five in the morning.
9-2	ພັນລະຍາ	pa:n^3 la:^{2} nya^3	Wife (formal)
	ທ່ານມິນລາແລະພັນລະຍາ	tan^2 mi:n^3 la^3 lae:^{2} pa:n^3 la:^{2} nya^3	Mr. Miller and his wife.
	ຂ້ອຍຮູ້ຈັກທ່ານບຸນທອງ ແຕ່ບໍ່ຮູ້ຈັກພັນລະຍາ	kohy^6 hu^5 cha:k^3 tan^2 bu:n^1 tohng^3 dtae^2 boh^2 hu^5 cha:k^3 pa:n^3 la:^{2} nya^3	I know Mr. Bounthong, but I don't know his wife.
	ນີ້ແມ່ນພັນລະຍາຂອງຂ້ອຍ	ni^5 maen^2 pa:n^3 la: nya^3 kohng^4 kohy^6	This is my wife.
	ພັນລະຍາລາວປາກລາວດີ	pa:n^3 la:^{2} nya^3 lao^3 bpak^6 lao^3 di^1	His wife speaks good Lao.
9-3	ກ່ອນ	gohn^2	Before
	ຂ້ອຍຊິມາຫາເຈົ້າກ່ອນເຈັດໂມງ	kohy^6 si:^{2} ma^3 ha^4 chao:^{5} gohn^2 che:t^3 mong^3	I'll come to see you before 7 o'clock.
	ລາວມາຖ້າຂ້ອຍກ່ອນແລ້ວ	lao^3 ma^3 ta^6 kohy^6 gohn^2 láew^5	He came before and waited for me.
	ກ່ອນຊິໄປ ຂ້ອຍຢາກເວົ້າກັບລາວ	gohn^2 si:^{2} bpai:^{1} kohy^6 yak^6 wao:^{5} ga:p^3 lao^3	Before going I want to speak with him.
	ຂ້ອຍຖູແຂ້ວທຸກໆແລງ ກ່ອນຊິໄປນອນ	kohy^6 tu^4 kaew^6 tu:k^2 tu:k^2 laeng^3 gohn^2 si:^{2} bpai:^{1} nohn^3	I brush my teeth every night before going to sleep.
9-4	ທຸກໆ	tu:k^2 tu:k^2	Every
	ທຸກໆຄົນກໍ່ຮູ້ຈັກ	tu:k^2 tu:k^2 ko:n^3 goh^1 hu^5 cha:k^3	Everybody knows about it.
	ໄປຕລາດທຸກໆເຊົ້າ	bpai:^{1} dta:^{3} lat^6 tu:k^2 tu:k^2 sao:^{5}	(I) go to market every morning.

	ລາວອາບນ້ຳທຸກໆແລງ	lao3 ap6 na:m5 tu:k2 tu:k2 laeng3	He takes a bath every evening.
	ທຸກໆບ່ອນມີວັດ	tu:k2 tu:k2 bohn2 mi3 wa:t2	Everyplace has a temple.
9-5	ຫຼັງ (ຈາກ)	la:ng4 chak6	After (... ing)
	ຫຼັງຈາກກິນເຂົ້າແລ້ວພັກຜ່ອນ	la:ng4 chak6 gi:n1 kao:6 laeng3 pa:k2 pohn2	After eating dinner, we have a rest.
	ຫຼັງຈາກເຮັດເທື່ອນຶ່ງແລ້ວ ເຮັດງ່າຍ	la:ng4 chak6 he:t2 teua2 neu:ng2 laew5 he:t2 ngai2	After doing it once, it is easy to do.
	ລາວສີຖູແຂ້ວຫຼັງຈາກກິນເຂົ້າ	lao3 si:2 tu4 kaew6 la:ng4 chak6 gi:n1 kao:6	He brushes his teeth after meals.
	ຂ້ອຍໄປການຫຼັງຈາກພາເດັກນ້ອຍໄປໂຮງຮຽນ	kohy6 bpai:1 gan1 la:ng4 chak6 de:k3 nohy5 bpai:1 hong3 hian3	I go to work after taking the children to school.
9-6	ລ້າງ	lang5	To wash
	ດຽວນີ້ ລາວລ້າງໜ້າຢູ່ໃນຫ້ອງອາບນ້ຳ	diaw1 ni5 lao3 lang5 na6 yu2 nai:3 hohng6 ap6 na:m5	Now he is washing his face in the bathroom.
	ຫຼັງຈາກກັບມາແຕ່ນອກ ຕ້ອງລ້າງໜ້າ	la:ng4 chak6 ga:p3 ma3 dtae2 nohk5 dtohng5 lang5 na6	After coming home from outside, you must wash you face.
	ມາຊ່ອຍລ້າງຣົດແດ່	ma3 sohy2 lang5 lo:t2 dae2	Come and help wash the car.
	ທຸກໆວັນອາທິດ ຂ້ອຍລ້າງຣົດຢູ່ທາງໜ້າບ້ານ	tu:k2 tu:k2 wa:n3 a1ti:t2 kohy6 lang5 lo:t2 yu2 tang3 na6 ban5	Every Sunday I wash my car in front of my house.
9-7	ໜ້າ	na6	Face
	ໜ້າລາວຄືໜ້າພໍ່ລາວຫຼາຍ	na6 lao3 keu3 na6 poh2 lao3 lai4	His face is very much like his father's face.
	ລາວໜ້າງາມ ທຸກໆຄົນຢາກເວົ້າກັບລາວ	lao3 na6 ngam3. tu:k2 tu:k2 ko:n3 yak6 wao:5 ga:p3 lao3	She is good looking. Everyone wants to talk with her.

	ໜ້າລາວບໍ່ຄືຄົນລາວແທ້	na^6 lao^3 boh^2 keu^3 ko:n^3 lao^3 tae^5	His face doesn't look like a real Lao.
	ເຈົ້າເບິ່ງໜ້າຂະເຈົ້າຈຶ່ງຮູ້ຈັກວ່າແມ່ນໃຜ	chao:^{5} ber:ng^2 na^6 ka:^{3} chao:^{5} cheu:ng^2 hu^5 cha:k^3 wa^2 maen^2 pai:^{4}	You look at their faces, then you'll know who they are.
9-8	<u>ຊ່ອຍ</u>	<u>sohy^2</u>	<u>Help</u>
	ເຈົ້າຊ່ອຍພວກຂ້ອຍດີໆ ຂອບໃຈຫຼາຍ	chao:^{5} sohy^2 puak^5 kohy^6 di' di' kohp^6 chai:' lai^4	You helped us a lot. Thank you very much.
	ນ້ອງຊ່ອຍອ້າຍຕັກນ້ຳ	nohng^5 sohy^2 ay^5 dta:k^3 na:m^5	Younger brother helps his elder brother to draw water.
	ຂະເຈົ້າໄປຊ່ອຍພີ່ນ້ອງເຮັດນາ	ka:^{3} chao:^{5} bpai:' sohy^2 pi^2 nohng^5 he:t^2 na^3	They go to help their relatives to farm in the rice-field.
	ຊ່ອຍຂ້ອຍຊັກເຄື່ອງນຸ່ງແດ່	sohy^2 kohy^6 sa:k^2 keuang^2 nu:ng^2 dae^2	Will you wash my clothes for me?
9-9	<u>ສ່ວນ</u>	<u>suan^2</u>	<u>For, as for</u>
	ສ່ວນພໍ່ຂ້ອຍເພີ່ນໄປເຮັດນາ	suan^2 poh^2 kohy^6 per:n^2 bpai:' he:t^2 na^3	As for my father, he went to work in the rice-field.
	ສ່ວນອ້າຍຂ້ອຍອີກຜູ້ນຶ່ງນັ້ນ ລາວເຮັດວຽກຢູ່ຕ່າງປະເທດ	suan^2 ay^5 kohy^6 ik^6 pu^6 neu:ng^2 na:n^5 lao^3 he:t^2 wiak^5 yu^2 dtang^2 bpa:^{3}tet^5	As for another elder brother, he is working abroad.
	ສ່ວນເມືອງລາວນີ້ຄົນບໍ່ຫຼາຍ	suan^2 meuang^3 lao^3 ni^5 ko:n^3 boh^2 lai^4	As for the country of Laos, it doesn't have many people.
	ສ່ວນຂ້ອຍ ໄປຕລາດເຮັດກິນ	suan^2 kohy^6 bpai:' dta:^{3} lat^6 he:t^2 gi:n'	As for me, I'll go to market and (then) cook food.
9-10	<u>ປັ້ນເຂົ້າເຊົ້າ</u>	<u>bpa:n^5 kao:^{6} sao:^{5}</u>	<u>To have a breakfast (Lit. to grip a glutinous rice ball in the morning.)</u>
	ເຈົ້າປັ້ນເຂົ້າເຊົ້າແລ້ວບໍ່	chao:^{5} bpa:n^5 kao:^{6} sao:^{5} laew^5 boh^2	Have you had breakfast?
	ຈັກໂມງປັ້ນເຂົ້າເຊົ້າທຸກໆມື້	cha:k^3 mong^3 bpa:n^5 kao:^{6} sao:^{5} tu:k^2 tu:k^2 meu^5	At what time do you have breakfast every morning?

	ຕອນເຊົ້ານີ້ລາວບໍ່ມີເວລາປັ້ນເຂົ້າເຊົ້າ	dtohn' sao:5 meu5 ni5 lao3 boh2 mi3 we3 la3 bpa:n5 kao:6 sao:5	This morning he did not have time to eat breakfast.
9-11	ເພາະ (ວ່າ)	poh:2 (wa2)	Because
	ຂ້ອຍບໍ່ໄປຫຼິ້ນເທນນິສ ເພາະວ່າໄປຫາໝູ່ຢູ່ບ້ານລາວ	kohy6 boh2 bpai:1 lin6 te:n3 nit2 poh:2 wa2 bpai:1 ha4 mu2 yu2 ban5 lao3	I don't go to play tennis because I'll go to see my friend at his house.
	ຂ້ອຍປັ້ນເຂົ້າເຊົ້າຫົກໂມງເຄິ່ງ ເພາະຕ້ອງພາເດັກນ້ອຍໄປໂຮງຮຽນເຈັດໂມງ	kchy6 bpa:n5 kao:6 sao:5 ho:k3 mong3 ker:ng2 poh:2 dtohng5 pa3 de:k3 nohy5 bpai:1 hong3 hian3 che:t3 mong3	I have my breakfast at six thirty because I have to take children to school at seven.
	ມື້ນີ້ບໍ່ຕ້ອງຊື້ຂອງ ເພາະຍັງມີຂອງຢູ່.	meu5 ni5 boh2 dtohng5 seu5 kohng4 poh:2 nya:ng3 mi3 kohng4 yu2	Today we don't have to go shopping because we still have some.
	ລາວຢາກຮຽນພາສາລາວ ເພາະລາວຈະເຮັດວຽກຢູ່ນີ້ສອງສາມປີ	lao3 yak6 hian3 pa3 sa4 lao3 poh:2 lao3 cha:3 he:t2 wiak5 yu2 ni5 sohng4 sam4 bpi1	He wants to learn Lao because he'll work here for 2 or 3 years.
9-12	ຕ້ອງ	dtohng5	Must, have to, should (imperative)
	ມື້ນີ້ຂ້ອຍຕ້ອງໄປຕລາດ	meu5 ni5 kohy6 dtohng5 bpai:1 dta:3 lat6	Today I have to go to market.
	ຂະເຈົ້າຕ້ອງຮູ້ຈັກເຣື່ອງນີ້	ka:3 chao:5 dtohng5 hu5 cha:k3 leuang2 ni5	They must know this story.
	ຂ້ອຍຕ້ອງກິນຢາມື້ນຶ່ງສາມເທື່ອ	kohy6 tohng5 gi:n1 ya1 meu5 neu:ng2 sam4 teua2	I must take medicine 3 times a day.
	ເດັກນ້ອຍຕ້ອງຮຽນໜັງສື	de:k3 nohy5 dtohng5 hian3 nang4 seu4	Children should study.

	Lao	Romanization	English
9-13	**ເຄິ່ງ**	ker:ng^2	Half
	ດຽວນີ້ເວລາແປດໂມງເຄິ່ງ	diaw^1 ni^5 we^3 la^3 bpaet^6 mong^3 ker:ng^2	Now the time is half past eight.
	ສິບສອງໂມງເຄິ່ງກັບບ້ານ	si:p^3 sohng^4 mong^3 ker:ng^2 ga:p^3 ban^5	We go home at twelve thirty.
	ຂ້ອຍບໍ່ຢາກເຮັດຫຼາຍ ເຮັດເຄິ່ງນຶ່ງ	kohy^6 boh^2 yak^6 he:t^2 lai^4 he:t^2 ker:ng^2 neu:ng^2	I don't want to do much. I'll do half of it.
	ເອົາເຄິ່ງນຶ່ງໃຫ້ລາວ ຊະ	ao:^{1} ker:ng^2 neu:ng^1 hai:^{6} lao^3 sa:^{2}	Give half **to** him.
9-14	**ຕັ້ງແຕ່......ຫາ....**	dta:ng^5 dtae^2.. ha^4..	From..... to....
	ຕັ້ງແຕ່ມື້ນີ້ຫາວັນເສົາ	dta:ng^5 dtae^2 meu^5 ni^5 ha^4 wa:n^3 sao:^{4}	From today until Saturday.
	ຂະເຈົ້າຂາຍຕັ້ງແຕ່ປະມານຫົກໂມງຫາສິບສອງໂມງ ຕອນເຊົ້າ	ka:^{3} chao:^{5} kai^4 dta:ng^5 dtae^2 bpa:^{3} man^3 ho:k^3 mong^3 ha^4 si:p^3 sohng^4 mong^3 dtohn^1 sao:^{5}	They're selling from about six o'clock to twelve o'clock in the morning.
	ຂ້ອຍຢູ່ອະເມຣິກາ ຕັ້ງແຕ່ພັນເກົ້າຮ້ອຍຫົກສິບເອັດ ຫາຫົກສິບຫ້າ	kohy^6 yu^2 a^3 me^3 li^3 ga^1 dta:ng^5 dtae^2 pa:n^3 gao:^{5} hohy^5 ho:k^3 si:p^3 e:t^3 ha^4 ho:k^3 si:p^3 ha^6	I was in the U.S. from 1961 until '65.
	ຂະເຈົ້າເຮັດການຕັ້ງແຕ່ແປດໂມງເຄິ່ງຫາສິບສອງ ໂມງ	ka:^{3} chao:^{5} he:t^2 gan^1 dta:ng^5 dtae^2 bpaet^6 mong^3 ha^4 si:p^3 sohng^4 mong^3	They work from eight thirty to twelve.
9-15	**ເຮັດກິນ**	he:t^2 gi:n^1	To cook
	ແມ່ເຮືອນເຮັດກິນ ຊັກເຄື່ອງນຸ່ງເບິ່ງເດັກນ້ອຍ	mae^2 heuan^3 he:t^2 gi:n^1 sa:k^2 keuang^2 nu:ng^2 beu:ng^2 de:k^3 nohy^5	Housewives cook, wash clothes and take care of children.
	ພັນລະຍາຂ້ອຍເຮັດກິນແຊບ	pa:n^3 la:^{2} nya^3 kohy^6 he:t^2 gi:n^1 saep^5	My wife cooks a delicious meal.
	ລາວມີຄົນໃຊ້ເຮັດກິນເກັ່ງ	lao^3 mi^3 ko:n^3 sai:^{5} he:t^2 gi:n^1 ge:ng^2	He has a servant who is good at cooking.
	ລາງເທື່ອຜົວຊ່ອຍເມັຍເຮັດກິນກໍ່ມີ	lang^3 teua^2 pua^4 sohy^2 mia^3 he:t^2 gi:n^1 goh^1 mi^3	Sometimes there are husbands

9-16	<u>ຊັກ</u>	<u>sa:k^2</u>	<u>To wash (clothes)</u>
	ແມ່ຊັກເຄື່ອງນຸ່ງຂອງເດັກນ້ອຍ	mae^2 sa:k^2 keuang^2 nu:ng^2 kohng^4 de:k^3 nohy^5	Mother washes the children's clothes.
	ເອົາສະບູໄປຊັກເຄື່ອງນຸ່ງ	ao:^{1} sa:^{3} bu^1 bpai:^{1} sa:k^2 keuang^2 nu:ng^2	Take the soap and wash the clothes.
	ຢູ່ບ້ານຂະເຈົ້າ ຊັກເຄື່ອງນຸ່ງທຸກໆວັນເສົາ	yu^1 ban^5 ka:^{3} chao:^{5} sa:k^2 keuang^2 nu:ng^2 tu:k^2 tu:k^2 wa:n^3 sao:^{4}	In their home they wash clothes every Saturday.
	ເຄື່ອງແບບນີ້ ຊັກຍາກ	keuang^2 baep^6 ni^5 sa:k^2 nyak^5	This kind of cloth is difficult to wash.
9-17	<u>ພວກ</u>	<u>puak^5</u>	<u>(Plural word stem)</u>
	ພວກເດັກນ້ອຍ ເຂົ້ານອນແລ້ວບໍ່	puak^5 de:k^3 nohy^5 kao:^{6} nohn^3 laew^5 boh^2	Have the children gone to sleep?
	ພວກເຈົ້າຕ້ອງເຮັດວຽກຕາມນາຍເວົ້າ (ບອກ)	puak^5 chao:^{5} dtohng^5 he:t^2 wiak^5 dtam^1 nai^3 wao:^{5} (bohk^6)	You must do what your boss told you to do.
	ຢູ່ຫ້ອງນັ້ນພວກນາຍຄູເຮັດການ	yu^2 hong^6 na:n^5 puak^5 nai^3 ku^3 he:t^2 gan^1	The teachers work in that room.
	ພວກຄົນຕ່າງປະເທດມາຊ່ວຍເມືອງລາວ	puak^5 ko:n^3 dtang^2 bpa:^{3} tet^5 ma^3 sohy^2 meuang^3 lao^3	Foreigners came to assist Laos.
9-18	<u>ປະມານ</u>	<u>bpa:^{3} man^3</u>	<u>About, approximately</u>
	ແຕ່ນີ້ໄປພຸ້ນມີປະມານຮ້ອຍກິໂລ	dtae^2 ni^5 bpai:^{1} ha:n^6 mi^3 bpa:^{3} man^3 hohy^5 gi^1 lo^3	It is about 100 kilometers from here to there.
	ຢູ່ວຽງຈັນມີຄົນປະມານຮ້ອຍຫ້າສິບພັນຄົນ	yu^2 wiang^3 cha:n^1 mi^3 ko:n^3 bpa:^{3} man^3 hohy^5 ha^6 si:p^3 pa:n^3 ko:n^3	There are about 150,000 people in Vientiane.
	ລາວອາຍຸປະມານສີ່ສິບປີ	lao^3 a^1 nyu:^{2} bpa:^{3} man^3 si^2 si:p^3 bpi^1	He is about forty years old.
	ລົດຄັນນີ້ ຂັບໄດ້ປະມານຫ້າປີ	lo:t^2 ka:n^3 ni^5 ka:p^3 dai:^{5} bpa:^{3} man^3 ha^6 bpi^1	You can drive this car about five years.

	Lao	Romanization	English
9-19	ເດິກ	der:k^3	Dark hours (late in the evening or very early in the morning)
	ເດິກແລ້ວ ເຮົາຕ້ອງກັບໄປນອນ	der:k^3 laew^5. hao:^{3} dtohng^5 ga:p^3 bpai:' nohn^3	It's getting late. We have to go back to sleep.
	ເມື່ອໃດໄປເບິ່ງຊີເນ ມາເດິກຫຼາຍ	meua^2 dai:' bpai:' beu:ng^2 si^3 ne^3 ma^3 der:k^3 lai^4	When they go to see the movies, they come back late.
	ພໍ່ຂ້ອຍຕື່ນແຕ່ເດິກ ໄປເຮັດວຽກຢູ່ນາ	poh^2 kohy^6 dteun^2 dtae^2 der:k^3 bpai:' he:t^2 wiak^5 yu^2 na^3	My father gets up very early and goes to work in the fields.
	ມື້ນີ້ເວລາຂ້ອຍຕື່ນຍັງເດິກຫຼາຍ	meu^5 ni^5 we^3 la^3 kohy^6 dteun^2 nya:ng^3 der:k^3 lai^4	Today when I got up it was still very dark.

	Lao	Romanization	English
9-20	ຫຼື	leu^4	Or
	ລາວວ່າລາວຊິມາວັນເສົາ ຫຼືວັນອາທິດ	lao^3 wa^2 lao^3 si:^{2} ma^3 wa:n^3 sao:^{4} leu^4 wa:n^3 a' ti:t^2	He says he'll come on Saturday or Sunday.
	ເຈົ້າມາຕອນເຊົ້າຫຼືຕອນບ່າຍ	chao:^{5} ma^3 dtohn' sao:^{5} leu^4 dtohn' bai^2	Will you come in the morning or in the afternoon?
	ເຈົ້າຢາກໄປທາງເສັ້ນນັ້ນ ຫຼືເສັ້ນນີ້	chao:^{5} yak^6 bpai:' tang^3 se:n^6 na:n^5 leu^4 se:n^6 ni^5	Do you want to go that way or this way?
	ລາຄາຣົດແບບນີ້ ປະມານພັນຫ້າຫຼືພັນຫົກໂດລາ	la^3 ka^3 lo:t^2 baep^6 ni^5 bpa:^{3} man^3 pa:n^3 ha^6 leu^4 pa:n^3 ho:k^3 do' la^3	The price of these cars is about one thousand five or six hundred dollars.

Text

ບົດ ຮຽນ ທີ ເກົ້າ

1. ຕາມທັມມະດາ ຂ້ອຍລຸກຫົກໂມງທຸກໆເຊົ້າ
2. ພັນລະຍາຂອງຂ້ອຍລຸກກ່ອນຫົກໂມງ
3. ເດັກນ້ອຍເຂົາລຸກສວຍ
4. ຫຼັງຈາກລຸກແລ້ວ ທຸກໆຄົນກໍລ້າງໜ້າຖູແຂ້ວ
5. ພັນລະຍາຂອງຂ້ອຍ ໜຶ້ງເຂົ້າ
6. ເດັກນ້ອຍຊ່ອຍແມ່ເຂົາກວາດເຮືອນ ຖູເຮືອນ
7. ສ່ວນຂ້ອຍໄປຕັກນ້ຳ
8. ເຈັດໂມງ ພວກຂ້ອຍປັ້ນເຂົ້າເຊົ້າເພາະຂ້ອຍຕ້ອງພາເດັກນ້ອຍໄປໂຮງຮຽນກ່ອນ
   ເຈັດໂມງເຄິ່ງ ແລ້ວຂ້ອຍກໍໄປການ
9. ຂ້ອຍເຮັດວຽກປະຈຳຢູ່ວຽງຈັນ ແຕ່ລາງເທື່ອຂ້ອຍຕ້ອງໄປເບິ່ງວຽກຢູ່ຕ່າງແຂວງ
10. ຕອນທ່ຽງຂ້ອຍກັບມາກິນເຂົ້າ
11. ຕອນບ່າຍ ຂ້ອຍເຮັດການຕັ້ງແຕ່ສອງໂມງເຄິ່ງຫາຫ້າໂມງ
12. ພັນລະຍາຂ້ອຍເປັນແມ່ເຮືອນ ບໍ່ໄດ້ເຮັດການຢູ່ໃສ.
13. ລາວໄປຕລາດເຮັດກິນ ແຕ່ມີຄົນໃຊ້ຊັກເຄື່ອງນຸ່ງໃຫ້
14. ຕອນແລງກິນເຂົ້າແລ້ວ ພວກເດັກນ້ອຍເຂົາຕ້ອງຮຽນໜັງສື ເມື່ອໃດບໍ່ໄດ້ໄປຢາມພີ່ນ້ອງ
15. ຂ້ອຍແລະພັນລະຍາໄປເບິ່ງພາບພະຍົນ ແຕ່ຕາມທັມມະດາ ພວກຂ້ອຍພັກຜ່ອນຢູ່ເຮືອນແລະ
    ເຂົ້ານອນປະມານສິບໂມງຫຼືສິບໂມງເຄິ່ງເພາະຂ້ອຍຕ້ອງໄດ້ຕື່ນແຕ່ເດິກ.

BO:T^{3} HIAN^{3} TI^{2} GAO:^{5}

1. Dtam^{1} ta:m^{3} ma:^{2} da^{1} kohy^{6} lu:k^{2} ho:k^{3} mong^{3} tu:k^{2} tu:k^{2} sao:^{5}.

2. Pa:n^{3} la:^{2} nya^{3} kohng^{4} kohy^{6} lu:k^{2} gohn^{2} ho:k^{3} mong^{3}.

3. De:k^{3} nohy^{5} kao:^{4} lu:k^{2} suay^{4}.

4. La:ng^{4} chak^{6} lu:k^{2} laew^{5} tu:k^{2} tu:k^{2} ko:n^{3} goh^{1} lang^{5} na^{6} tu^{4} kaeo^{6}.

5. Pa:n^{3} la^{2} nya^{3} kohng^{4} kohy^{6} neung^{6} kao^{6}.

6. De:k^{3} nohy^{5} sohy^{2} mae^{2} kao:^{4} gwat^{6} heuan^{3} tu^{4} heuan^{3}.

7. Suan^{2} kohy^{6} bpai:^{1} dta:k^{3} na:m^{5}.

8. Che:t^{3} mong^{3} puak^{5} kohy^{6} bpa:n^{5} kao:^{6} sao^{5}. Poh:^{2} kohy^{6} dtohng^{5} pa^{3} de:k^{3} nohy bpai:^{1} hong^{3} hian^{3} gohn^{2} che:t^{3} mong^{3} kerng^{2} laew^{5} kohy^{6} goh^{1} bpai:^{1} gan^{1}.

9. Kohy^{6} he:t^{2} wiak^{5} bpa:^{3} cha:m^{1} yu^{2} wiang^{3} cha:n^{1} dtae^{2} lang^{3} teua^{2} kohy^{6} dtohng^{5} bpai:^{1} ber:ng^{2}wiak^{5} yu^{2} dtang^{2} kwaeng^{4}.

10. Dtohn^{1} tiang^{2} kohy^{6} ga:p^{3} ma^{3} gi:n^{1} kao:^{6}.

11. Dtohn^{1} bai^{2} kohy^{6} he:t^{2} gan^{1} dta:ng^{5} dtae^{2} sohng^{4} mong^{3} ker:ng^{2} ha^{4} ha^{6} mong^{3}

12. Pa:n^{3} la:^{2} nya^{3} kohy^{6} bpe:n^{1} mae^{2} heuan^{3}. Boh^{2} dai:^{5} he:t^{2} gan^{1} yu^{2} sai:^{4}.

13. Lao^{3} bpai:^{1} dta:^{3} lat^{6} he:t^{2} gi:n^{1} dtae^{2} mi^{3} ko:n^{3} sai:^{5} sa:k^{2} keuang^{2} nu:ng^{2} hai:^{6}.

14. Dtohn^{1} laeng^{3} gi:n^{1} kao:^{6} laew^{5} puak^{5} de:k^{3} nohy^{5} Kao:^{4} dtohng^{5} hian^{3} na:ng^{4} seu^{4} meua^{2} dai:^{1} boh^{2} dai:^{5} bpai:^{1} yam^{1} pi^{2} nohng^{5}.

15. Kohy^{6} lae:^{2} pa:n^{3} la:^{2} nya^{3} bpai:^{1} ber:ng^{2} pap^{5} pa^{2} nyo:n^{3} dtae^{2} dtam^{1} ta:m^{3} ma:^{2} da^{1} puak^{5} kohy^{6} pa:k^{2} pohn^{2} yu^{2} heuan^{3} lae:^{2} kao^{6} nohn^{3} bpa:^{3} man^{3} si:p^{3} mong^{3} leu^{4} si:p^{3} mong^{3} ker:ng.^{2} Poh:^{2} kohy^{6} dtohng^{5} dai:^{5} dteun^{2} dtae der:k^{3}.

LESSON 9: THE DAILY ROUTINE

1. Usually I get up at six every morning.

2. My wife gets up before six.

3. The children, they get up late.

4. After having got up, everyone washes his face and brushes his teeth.

5. My wife steams rice.

6. The children help their mother to clean the house.

7. As for me, I go to get water.

8. At seven we have our breakfast because I have to take children to school before 7:30 and I too, go to work.

9. I usually work in Vientiane, but sometimes have to go to inspect works in the provinces.

10. At noon I come back to eat.

11. In the afternoon I work from 2:30 to 5:00.

12. My wife is a housewife and does not work elsewhere.

13. She goes to market and cooks, but we have a maid who washes clothes (for us).

14. In the evening after the meal, the children must study, if we don't go to visit relatives and friends.

15. Then my wife and I go to see a movie, but usually we rest at home and go to sleep at 10 o'clock or 10:30 because we have to wake up early.

LESSON 10: TOURING VIENTIANE

Substitution Exercise

ບ່ອນນີ້ເອີ້ນວ່າ	ຫຍັງ
	ເດີ່ນບິນ
	ວັດອົງຕື້
	ທ່າເດື່ອ
	ທາດຫຼວງ
	ນ້ຳພຸ

bohn^2 ni^5 ern^5 wa^2	nya:ng^4
	dern^2 nyo:n^3
	wa:t^2 o:ng^1 dteu^5
	ta^2 deua^2
	tat^5 luang^4
	na:m^5 pu:^{2}

This place is called	what?
	an airport.
	Wat Ongtu.
	Tha Deua.
	That Luang.
	a fountain.

ສຖານທູດ	ໄທ
ຄົນ	ວຽດນາມ
	ຂະເມນ
	ຝຣັ່ງ
	ອະເມຣິກາ
	ຍີ່ປຸ່ນ
	ອັງກິດ
	ຈີນ

sa:^{3} tan^4 tut^5	tai:^{3}
ko:n^3	wiat^5 nam^3
	ka:^{3} men^3
	fa:^{3} la:ng^2
	a:^{3} me^3 li^3 ga^1
	nyi^2 bpu:n^2
	a:ng^1 gi:t^3
	chin^1

Embassy	Thai
Person	Vietnam
	Kampuchea
	foreigner
	American
	Japanese
	English
	Chinese

ກະຊວງ	ຄັງ
	ໂຍທາ
	ສຶກສາ
	ຕ່າງປະເທດ
	ຖແລງຂ່າວ

ga:^{3} suang^3	ka:ng^3
	nyo^3 ta^3
	seu:k^3 sa^4
	dtang^2 bpa:^{3} tet^5
	ta:^{3} laeng^3 kao^2

Ministry of	finance
	public works
	education
	foreign affairs
	information

ໂຮງການ	ໄປສະນີ
	ຕຳຣວດ
	ກອງບັນຊາການ

hong3 gan1	bpai:1 sa:3 ni3
	dta:m1 luat5
	gohng1 ba:n1 sa3 gan1

Office (of the)	Post office
	Police station
	Military headquarters

ນີ້ແມ່ນ	ຕລາດເຊົ້າ
	ຕລາດແລງ
	ສະພາແຫ່ງຊາດ
	ໂຮງໝໍວຽງຈັນ
	ໂຮງໝໍມະໂຫສົດ
	ອະນຸສາວະຣີ
	ໂຮງແຮມລ້ານຊ້າງ
	ຖນົນສາມແສນໄທ
	ຖນົນເສດຖາທິຣາດ
	ພຣະຣາຊວັງ
	ຖນົນລ້ານຊ້າງ

ni5 maen2	dta:3 lat6 sao:5
	dta:3 lat6 laeng3
	sa:3 pa3 haeng2 sat5
	hong3 moh4 wiang3 cha:n1
	hong3 moh4 ma2 ho4 so:t3
	a:3 nu:2 sa4 wa2 li3
	hong3 haem3 lan5 sang5
	ta:3 no:n3 sam4 saen4 tai:3
	ta:3 no:n3 set6 ta4 ti:2 lat5
	pa:2 lat5 sa:2 wa:ng3
	ta:3 no:n3 lan5 sang5

This is	the morning market.
	the evening market.
	the National Assembly.
	Vientiane hospital.
	Mahosot hospital.
	the monument.
	the Lane Xang Hotel.
	Samsenthai street.
	the Royal Palace.
	Lane Xang Avenue

ເມື່ອໃດລາວກັບ	ໄປ	ວຽງຈັນ
	ມາ	ບ້ານ
		ເມືອງຝຣັ່ງ

meua2 dai:1 lao3 ga:p3	bpai:1	wiang3 cha:n1
	ma3	ban5
		meuang3 fa:2 la:ng2

When will he	go back to	Vientiane?
	come back	home?
		France?

ເມື່ອໃດບໍ່ໄດ້ໄປເບິ່ງຊີເນມາ ເຮົາ	ຢູ່ບ້ານ
	ກິນເຂົ້ານອກ
	ຍາມໝູ່ເຮົາ
	ໄປຫາພີ່ນ້ອງ

meua^2 dai:^{1} boh^2 dai:^{5} bpai:^{1} beu:ng^2 si^3 ne^3 ma^3 hao:^{3}	yu^2 ban^5
	gi:n^1 kao:^{6} nohk^5
	yam^1 mu^2 hao:^{3}
	bpai:^{1} ha^4 pi^2 nohng^5

When we don't go to the cinema, we	stay at home.
	eat outside.
	meet our friends.
	visit relatives.

ເພາະ	ຂ້ອຍ	ຢາກພັກຜ່ອນ
	ລາວ	ມີວຽກຢູ່ບ້ານ
	ຂະເຈົ້າ	ຕ້ອງຊ່ອຍເຂົາເຮັດວຽກ
	ເພິ່ນ	ບໍ່ຢາກໄປ
		ກິນເຂົ້າຢູ່ບ້ານ
		ບໍ່ຮູ້ຈັກທາງໄປ
		ຕ້ອງເຮັດກິນ

poh:^{2}	kohy^6	yak^6 pa:k^2 pohn^2
	lao^3	mi^3 wiak^5 yu^2 ban^5
	ka:^{3} chao:^{5}	dtohng^5 sohy^2 kao:^{4} he:t^2 wiak
	per:n^2	boh^2 yak^6 bpai:^{1}
		gi:n^1 kao:^{6} yu^2 ban^5
		boh^2 hu^5 cha:k^3 tang^3 bpai:^{1}
		dtohng^5 he:t^2 gi:n^1

Father	mine	wants to rest.
	his	has work at home.
	their	must help them to work.
	their	doesn't want to go.
		eats at home.
		doesn't know the way to go.
		must prepare the food.

Vocabulary Exercise

	Lao	Transliteration	English
10-1	<u>ທ່ຽວ</u>	<u>tiaw</u>^{2}	<u>To take a walk, to spend time (to enjoy), to tour, to visit for fun</u>
	ທຸກໆວັນອາທິດ ເຮົາໄປທ່ຽວຕລາດເຊົ້າ	tu:k^{2} tu:k^{2} wa:n^{3} a'ti:t^{2} hao:^{3} bpai:^{1} tiaw^{2} dta:^{3} lat^{6} sao:^{5}	We go to spend our time at the Morning Market every Sunday.
	ບໍ່ມີວຽກ ມາທ່ຽວຊື່ໆ	boh^{2} mi^{3} wiak^{5}, ma^{3} tiaw^{2} seu^{2} seu^{2}	I'm not on business, I just came to enjoy myself.
	ຂະເຈົ້າມັກຂັບຣົດໄປທ່ຽວບ້ານນອກ	ka:^{3} chao:^{5} ma:k^{2} ka:p^{3} lo:t^{2} bpai:^{1} tiaw^{2} ban^{5} nohk^{5}	They like to drive a car and tour the country-side.
10-2	<u>ເອີ້ນວ່າ</u>	<u>ern^{5} wa^{2}</u>	<u>To call, to name</u>
	ພາສາລາວອັນນີ້ເອີ້ນວ່າຫຍັງ	pa^{3} sa^{4} lao^{3} a:n^{1} ni^{5} ern^{5} wa^{2} nya:ng^{4}	What do you call it in Lao?
	ພາສາລາວອັນນີ້ເອີ້ນວ່າທາດ	pa^{3} sa^{4} lao^{3} a:n^{1} ni^{5} ern^{5} wa^{2} tat^{5}	It is called a "That" in Lao.
	ບ່ອນນີ້ເອີ້ນວ່າຫຍັງ	bohn^{2} ni^{5} ern^{5} wa^{2} nya:ng^{4}	What is the name of this place?
	ວັດນັ້ນ ເອີ້ນວ່າວັດທາດຫລວງ	wa:t^{2} na:n^{5} ern^{5} wa^{2} wa:t^{2} tat^{5} luang^{4}	That wat is called "Wat That Luang."
10-3	<u>ລ້ຽວ</u>	<u>liaw</u>^{5}	<u>To turn</u>
	ລ້ຽວຂວາແດ່	liaw^{5} kwa^{4} dae^{2}	Turn to right, please.
	ລ້ຽວຊ້າຍເຂົ້າເສັ້ນນັ້ນ	liaw^{5} sai^{5} kao:^{6} se:n^{6} na:n^{5}	Turn left and enter that road.
	ລ້ຽວຢູ່ນີ້ບໍ່ ຫຼືເສັ້ນຕໍ່ໄປ	liaw^{5} yu^{2} ni^{5} boh^{2} leu^{4} se:n^{6} dtoh^{2} bpai:^{1}	Do we turn here or go straight?

10-4	<u>ກຳລັງ</u>	<u>ga:m^{1} la:ng^{3}</u>	<u>To be (do)ing now (progressive tense form)</u>
	ລູກສິດກຳລັງຮຽນໜັງສື	luk^{5} si:t^{3} ga:m^{1} la:ng^{3} hian^{3} na:ng^{4} seu^{4}	Students are learning (in class).
	ລາວກຳລັງຊັກເຄື່ອງນຸ່ງ	lao^{3} ga:m^{1} la:ng^{3} sa:k^{2} keuang^{2} nu:ng^{2}	She is washing clothes now.
	ຂະເຈົ້າກຳລັງກໍ່ສ້າງໂຮງຮຽນ	ka:^{3} chao:^{5} ga:m^{1} la:ng^{3} goh^{2} sang^{6} hong^{3} hian^{3}	They are building a school.
	ແມ່ກຳລັງເຮັດກິນ	mae^{2} ga:m^{1} la:ng^{3} he:t^{2} gi:n^{1}	Mother is cooking now.
10-5	<u>ເຫັນ</u>	<u>he:n^{4}</u>	<u>To see, to be seen or found</u>
	ເຈົ້າເຫັນຕຶກສູງນັ້ນບໍ່	chao:^{5} he:n^{4} dteu:k^{3} sung^{4} sung^{4} na:n^{5} boh^{2}	You see that tall building?
	ຂ້ອຍເຫັນຄົນລາວຫຼາຍຄົນຢູ່ວັດ	kohy^{6} he:n^{4} ko:n^{3} lao^{3} lai^{4} ko:n^{3} yu^{2} wa:t^{2}	I saw many Lao people at the temple.
	ລາວຢູ່ໃສ ລາວບໍ່ເຫັນ	lao^{3} yu^{2} sai:^{4} lao^{3} boh^{2} he:n^{4}	Where is he? He is not around here.
	ຈາກນີ້ບໍ່ເຫັນທາດຫຼວງ	chak^{6} ni^{5} boh^{2} he:n^{4} tat^{5} luang^{4}	We can't see That Luang from here.
10-6	<u>ຢຸດ</u>	<u>yu:t^{3}</u>	<u>To stop</u>
	ຢຸດນີ້ແດ່	yu:t^{3} ni^{5} dae^{2}	Stop here!
	ລາວຢຸດຣົດເພາະວ່າໄຟສີແດງແລ້ວ	lao^{3} yu:t^{3} lo:t^{2} poh:^{2} wa^{2} fai:^{3} si^{4} daeng^{1} laew^{5}	He stops his car because the light has turned red.
	ລາວຢຸດຮຽນໜັງສື	lao^{3} yu:t^{3} hian^{3} na:ng^{4} seu^{4}	He has stopped studying.

	Lao	Transcription	English
10-7	<u>ສາກ່ອນ</u>	<u>sa^{4} gohn^{2}</u>	<u>First, (of all), before</u>
	ນັ່ງລົງສາກ່ອນ	na:ng^{2} lo:ng^{3} sa^{4} gohn^{2}	Please sit down first.
	ກິນເຂົ້າສາກ່ອນ ແລ້ວໄປເບິ່ງ	gi:n^{1} kao:^{6} sa^{4} gohn^{2} laew^{5} bpai:^{1} beu:ng^{2}	Eat something first, then go out sightseeing.
	ເຮົາຊິໄປໂຮງໝໍສາກ່ອນ	hao:^{3} si:^{2} bpai:^{1} hong^{3} moh^{4} sa^{4} gohn^{2}	We'll go to the hospital first.
10-8	<u>ນ້ອຍນຶ່ງ</u>	<u>nohy^{5} ne:ung^{2}</u>	<u>A little, a few, a moment</u>
	ມີແຕ່ນ້ອຍນຶ່ງບໍ່ຫຼາຍ	mi^{3} dtae^{2} nohy^{5} neu:ng^{2} boh^{2} lai^{4}	There are a few, not many.
	ຖ້ານ້ອຍນຶ່ງຂ້ອຍຊິເອີ້ນຂະເຈົ້າ	ta^{6} nohy^{5} ne:ung^{2}; kohy^{6} si:^{2} ern^{5} ka:^{3} chao:^{5}	Wait a moment, I'll call them.
	ບໍ່ຮູ້ຈັກດີແຕ່ປາກໄດ້ນ້ອຍນຶ່ງ	boh^{2} hu^{5} cha:k^{3} di^{1} dtae^{2} bpak^{6} dai:^{5} nohy^{5} neu:ng^{2}	(I) don't know it well, but (I) can speak a little.
10-9	<u>ສຳຄັນ</u>	<u>sa:m^{4} ka:n^{3}</u>	<u>Important</u>
	ເພິ່ນເປັນຄົນສຳຄັນ	per:n^{2} bpe:n^{1} ko:n^{3} sa:m^{4} ka:n^{3}	He is a V.I.P.
	ອັນນີ້ສຳຄັນຫຼາຍ ຂ້ອຍຈຶ່ງຊິເວົ້າອີກເທື່ອນຶ່ງ	a:n^{1} ni^{5} sa:m^{4} ka:n^{3} lai^{4} kohy^{6} cheu:ng^{2} si:^{2} wao:^{5} ik^{6} teua^{2} ne:ung^{2}	This is very important I'll repeat it again.
	ມີວຽກສຳຄັນຕ້ອງເຮັດແລ້ວໃນມື້ນີ້	mi^{3} wiak^{5} sa:m^{4} ka:n^{3} dtohng^{5} he:t^{2} laew^{5} nai:^{3} meu^{5} ni^{5}	I have an important job which I have to finish today.
10-10	<u>ເວລາ</u>	<u>we^{3} la^{3}</u>	<u>When, time</u>
	ເວລາເຈົ້າຢູ່ຫຼວງພຣະບາງ ໄປທ່ຽວທາງແຄມນ້ຳຂອງບໍ່	we^{3} la^{3} chao:^{5} yu^{2} luang^{4} pa:^{2} bang^{1} bpai:^{1} tiaw^{2} tang^{3} kaem^{3} na:m^{5} kohng^{4} boh^{2}	When you were in Luang Prabang, did you take a walk along the Mekong?

	Lao	Transcription	English
	ເວລາຂ້ອຍບໍ່ຢູ່ບ້ານ ມີຄົນມາຫາບໍ່	we^{3} la^{3} kohy^{6} boh^{2} yu^{2} ban^{5} mi^{3} ko:n^{3} ma^{3} ha^{4} boh^{2}	When I was not home, did anyone come to see me ?
	ເວລາລູກບໍ່ໄປໂຮງຮຽນ ເຂົາມັກລຸກສວຍ	we^{3} la^{3} luk^{5} boh^{2} bpai:^{1} hong^{3} hian^{3} kao:^{3} ma:k^{2} lu:k^{2} suay^{4}	When the children do not go to school, they often get up late in the morning.
	ເວລາມີບຸນຢູ່ວັດ ມີຄົນຫຼາຍຄົນໄປ	we^{3} la^{3} mi^{3} bu:n^{1} yu^{2} wa:t^{2} mi^{3} ko:n^{3} lai^{4} ko:n^{3} bpai:^{1}	When they have a festival at the temple, many people go.
10-11	<u>ພັກ</u>	<u>pa:k^{2}</u>	<u>To rest, to stay</u>
	ລາວພັກຢູ່ໂຮງແຮມ	lao^{3} pa:k^{2} yu^{2} hong^{3} haem^{3}	He stays at a hotel.
	ມື້ນີ້ຂ້ອຍພັກ ບໍ່ໄປການ	meu^{5} ni^{5} kohy^{6} pa:k^{2} boh^{2} bpai:^{1} gan^{1}	Today I'm off duty. I don't go to work.
	ເຈົ້າພັກຢູ່ໃສ ເວລາຢູ່ປະເທດໄທ	chao:^{5} pa:k^{2} yu^{2} sai:^{4} we^{3} la^{3} yu^{2} bpa:^{3} tet^{5} tai:^{3}	Where did you stay when you were in Thailand?
	ລາວບໍ່ເຄີຍພັກ ມັກເຮັດວຽກເລື້ອຍ ໆ	lao^{3} boh^{2} kery^{3} pa:k^{2} ma:k^{2} he:t^{2} wiak^{5} leuay^{5} leuay^{5}	He never takes a holiday. He is always fond of working.
10-12	<u>ກິນລ້ຽງ</u>	<u>gi:n^{1} liang^{5}</u>	<u>To have a party</u>
	ຂະເຈົ້າກິນລ້ຽງເພາະລູກແຕ່ງງານ	ka:^{3} chao:^{5} gi:n^{1} liang^{5} poh:^{2} luk^{5} dtaeng^{2} ngan^{3}	They have a party because their child is to get married.
	ຂ້ອຍຕ້ອງໄປກິນລ້ຽງຢູ່ບ້ານໝູ່	kohy^{6} dtohng^{5} bpai:^{1} gi:n^{1} liang^{5} yu^{2} ban^{5} mu^{2}	I must go to a party at a friend's house.
	ຕອນແລງມື້ນີ້ບໍ່ເຮັດການເພາະໄປກິນລ້ຽງ	dtohn^{1} laeng^{3} meu^{5} ni^{5} boh^{2} he:t^{1} gi:n^{1} poh:^{2} bpai:^{1} gi:n^{1} liang^{5}	We don't work this evening because we will go to a party.

to the Military Headquarters
VIENTIANE, LAOS
(showing the route taken
in Lesson 10 text)
That Luang
Vientiane
Hospital
Ministry
of Finance
National
Assembly
Monument
Vientiane
High School
Lane Xang Ave
Police
Department
Morning
Market
Post Office
Samsenthai
Ministry of
Foreign Affairs
Evening
Market
Shops
Fountain
Royal
Palace
Mahosot
Hospital
Setthathirath
Lane
Xang
Hotel
Wat
Ong Tu
to Tha Deua
MEKONG RIVER
N
to the airport

Text

ບົດ ຮຽນ ທີ່ ສິບ

1. ຂ້ອຍຊິພາເຈົ້າໄປທ່ຽວໃນເມືອງ

2. ຂອບໃຈຫຼາຍ

3. ເຮົາຊິໄປທາງເສັ້ນນີ້ນໍ ບ່ອນນີ້ຂະເຈົ້າເອີ້ນວ່າເດີ່ນທາດຫຼວງ
ທາດນັ້ນແມ່ນທາດຫຼວງ.....ລ້ຽວຂວາຢູ່ສີ່ແຍກລິງໄປ...ຢູ່ເບື້ອງຂວານັ້ນແມ່ນໂຮງໝໍ ວຽງຈັນ

4. ອັນນັ້ນແມ່ນຕຶກຫຣັງ

5. ເຂົາກຳລັງກໍ່ສ້າງ ກອງບັນຊາການ ດຽວນີ້ເຮົາລ້ຽວຊ້າຍໄປຖນົນລ້ານຊ້າງ ທາງໜ້າ
ເຈົ້າເຫັນບໍ່ ຕຶກໃຫ່ຽໆ **ອັນນັ້ນແມ່ນອະນຸສາວະຣີ**

6. ແຖວນີ້ມີສຖານທູດຫຼາຍນໍ

7. ແມ່ນ, ມີສຖານທູດໄທ, ຂເມນ , ອິນໂດເນເຊັຽ ແລະສຖານທູດວຽດນາມ, ອັງກິດ
ຍີ່ປຸ່ນກໍມີໃກ້ນີ້ ໂຮງການກະຊວງໂຍທາຢູ່ຫັ້ນ ເບື້ອງນີ້ແມ່ນສາພາແຫ່ງຊາດ
ຕຶກສູງນັ້ນແມ່ນກະຊວງການຄັງ.

8. ອັນນັ້ນແມ່ນໂຮງຮຽນບໍ່ ເຫັນລູກສິດອອກມາຫຼາຍຄົນ.

9. ແມ່ນວິທຍາລັຍວຽງຈັນ ໂອ! ໄຟສີແດງແລ້ວ ຢຸດກ່ອນນ້ອຍນຶ່ງ....ຢູ່ວຽງຈັນມີຕລາດ
ໃຫ່ຽສອງບ່ອນ ຄືຕລາດເຊົ້າ ແລະຕລາດແລງ
ອັນນັ້ນແມ່ນໂຮງການຕຳຣວດ ຕລາດເຊົ້າຢູ່ນີ້ຫຼະ ຫັ້ນເດ໋ໂຮງໄປສະນີ ນີ້ແມ່ນຖນົນ
ສາມແສນໄທ ມີຮ້ານຫຼາຍຮ້ານ ທາງເສັ້ນນີ້ໄປເດີ່ນບິນ ເສັ້ນນັ້ນໄປຕລາດແລງ.

10. ວັດນີ້ງາມນໍ.

11. ວັດນີ້ເອີ້ນວ່າວັດອິງຕື້ ເປັນວັດສຳຄັນ ເພີ່ນເຮັດພິທີເວລາມີບຸນໃຫ່ຽ ບ່ອນນີ້ເອີ້ນວ່ານ້ຳພຸ
ມີໂຮງການກະຊວງຖແລງຂ່າວ ກະຊວງການຕ່າງປະເທດ ກະຊວງສຶກສາ ດຽວນີ້ໄປເບິ່ງ
ທາງແຄມນ້ຳຂອງນ້ອຍນຶ່ງນໍ ນີ້ແມ່ນໂຮງແຮມລ້ານຊ້າງ ຕໍ່ໄປແມ່ນພຣະຣາຊວັງຢູ່ວຽງຈັນ
ບ່ອນນີ້ແມ່ນໂຮງໝໍມະໂຫສົດ ທາງເສັ້ນນີ້ກໍງາມ

12. ເຮົາຍັງມີເວລານຶ່ງຊົ່ວໂມງປາຍກ່ອນຊິໄປກິນລ້ຽງ

13. ເຮົາໄປທ່ຽວທ່າເດື່ອກໍໄດ້.

BO:T3 HIAN3 TI2 SI:P3

1. C : Kohy6 si:2 pa3 chao:5 bpai:1 tiaw2 nai:3 meuang3.

2. X : Kohp6 chai:1 lai4.

3. C : Hao:3 si:2 bpai:1 tang3 se:n6 ni5 noh3. Bohn2 ni5 ka:3 chao:5 ern5 wa2 dern2 tat5 luang4. Tat5 na:n5 maen2 tat5 luang4 ...... liaw5 kwa4 yu2 si2 nyaek5 lo:ng3 bpai:1....... yu2 beuang5 kwa4 na:n5 maen2 hong3 moh4 wiang3 cha:n1.

4. X : A:n1 na:n5 maen2 dteu:k3 nya:ng4?

5. C : Kao4 ga:m1 la:ng3 goh2 sang6 gohng1 ba:n1 sa3 gan1. Diaw1 ni5 hao:3 liaw5 sai5 bpai:1 ta:3 no:n4 lan5 sang5. Tang3 na6 chao:5 he:n4 boh2 dteu:k3 nyai:2 nyai:2 a:n1 na:n5 maen2 a:3 nu:2 sa4 wa:2 li3.

6. X : Taew4 ni5 mi3 sa:3 tan4 tut5 lai4 noh3. ?

7. C : Maen2. Mi3 sa:3 tan4 tut5 tai:3, ka:3 men4, i:n1 do1 ne3 sia3 lae:2 sa:3 tan4 tut5 wiat5 nam3, a:ng1gi:t3, nyi2 bpu:n2 goh1 mi3 gai:5 ni5. Hong3 gan1 ga:3 suang3 nyo3 ta3 yu2 han6. Beuang5 ni5 maen2 sa4 pa3 haeng2 sat5. Dteuk3 sung4 na:n5 maen2 ga:3 suang3 gan1 ka:ng3.

8. X : A:n1 na:n5 maen2 hong3 hian3 boh2? He:n4 luk5 sit6 ohk6 ma3 lai4 ko:n3.

9. C : Mean2 wi:2 ta:2 nya3 lai:3 wiang3 cha:n1. O1 fai:3 si4 daeng1 laew5. yu:t3 gohn2 nohy5 neu:ng2..... yu2 wiang3 cha:n1 mi3 dta:3 lat6 nyai:2 sohng4 bohn2 keu3 dta3 lat6 sao:5 lae:2 dta:3 lat6 laeng3. A:n1 na:n5 maen2 hong3 gan1 dta:m1 luat5. Dta:3 lat6 sao:5 yu2 ni5 la3. Han6 de2 hong3 bpai:1 sa:3 ni3. Ni5 maen2 ta:3 no:n4 sam4 saen4 tai:3. Mi3 lan5 lai4 lan5. Tang3 se:n6 ni5 bpai:1 dern2 nyo:n3 se:n6 na:n5 bpai:1 dta:3 lat6 laeng3.

10. X : Wa:t2 ni5 ngam3 noh3.

11. C : Wa:t2 ni5 ern5 wa2 wa:t2 o:ng1 dteu5. Bpe:n1 wa:t2 sam4 kan3 per:n2 he:t2 pi:2 ti3 we3 la3 mi3 bu:n1 nyai:2. Bohn2 ni1 ern5 wa2 na:m5 pu:2. Mi3 hong3 gan1 ga:3 suang3 ta:3 laeng kao2, ga:3 suang3 gan1 dtang2 bpa:3 tet5 ga:3 suang3 seu:k3 sa4. Diaw1 ni5 bpai:1 berng2 tang3 kaem3 na:m5 kohng4 nohy5 neu:ng2 noh3. Ni5 maen2 hong3 haem3 lan5 sang5. Dtoh2 bpai:1 maen2 pa:2 lat5 sa2 wa:ng3 yu2 wiang3 cha:n1. Bohn2 ni5 maen2 hong3 moh4 ma:2 ho4 so:t3. Tang3 se:n6 ni5 goh1 ngam3

12. X : Hao:3 nyang3 mi3 we3 la3 neu:ng2 sua2 mong3 bpai1 gohn2 si:2 bpai:1 gi:n1 liang5.

13. C : Hao:3 bpai:1 tiaw2 ta2 deua2 goh1 dai:5.

LESSON 10: TOURING VIENTIANE

1. C: I'll take you to tour the city.

2. X: Thank you very much.

3. C: We'll go on this road! This place, they call That Luang plaza. That stupa is That Luang.... We'll turn right at crossroad to go downhill....On the righthand side, that is Vientiane hospital.

4. X: What building is that?

5. C: They are now building offices for the Military Headquarters. Now we turn left to go Lane Xang Avenue. In front, do you see the big construction? That is the Monument.

6. X: There are many embassies in this area!

7. C: Yes. There are Thai, Kampuchea, Indonesian embassies and Vietnamese, British, Japanese embassies are also near here. The Ministry of Public Works offices are there. This side is the National Assembly. That high building is the Finance Ministry.

8. X: Is that a school? (I) see many students coming out.

9. C: Yes. Vientiane high school. Oh! The light has turned red. Let's stop a moment....In Vientiane, there are two big markets: the Morning Market and the Evening Market. That is the Police Department. The Morning Market is here! Over there is the post office. This is Samsenthai Street. There are many shops. This road goes to the airport. That one leads to the Evening Market.

10. X: This Temple (Wat) is beautiful!

11. C: This Wat is called Wat Ong Tu. It is an important Wat. People hold celebrations when we have big festivals. This place is called the Fountain (place). There are the Ministries of Information, Foreign Affairs and Education. Now let's go to see the road along the Mekong for a while.

    This is the Lane Xang Hotel. The next one is the Royal Palace in Vientiane. This place is Mahosot Hospital. This street is beautiful.

12. X: We still have more than one hour time before going to the party.

13. C: We can go to tour Tha Deua.

LESSON 11: CHATTING

Substitution Exercise

ຂອບໃຈຫຼາຍໆທີ່	ພາມາ
	ພາເດັກນ້ອຍມາ
	ມາຊ່ວຍ
	ມາສອນໜັງສື
	ເຊີນເຮົາມື້ນີ້
	ເຊີນພວກຂ້ອຍ
	ສົ່ງຂ້ອຍມາ

kohp^6 chai:^{1} lai^4 lai^4 ti^2	pa^3 ma^3
	pa^3 de:k^3 nohy^5 ma^3
	ma^3 sohy^2
	ma^3 sohn^4 na:ng^4 seu^4
	sern^3 hao:^{3} meu^5 ni^5
	sern^3 puak^5 kohy^6
	so:ng^2 kohy^6 ma^3

Thank you very much for	taking me.
	taking the child.
	coming to teach.
	asking us today.
	asking us.
	sending for me.

ມື້ນີ້ຂ້ອຍຕ້ອງການ	ໝາກເລັ່ນແລະຫົວຜັກທຽມ
	ຊີ້ນແລະໝາກໄມ້
	ເຄື່ອງເຮືອນຫຼາຍຢ່າງ
	ຊີ້ນໝູຫ້າກິໂລ
	ນ້ຳອົບແລະສະບູ

meu^5 ni^5 kohy^6 dtohng^5 gan^1	mak^6 le:n^2 lae:^{2} hua^4 pa:k^3 tiam^3
	sin^5 lae:^{2} mak^6 mai:^{5}
	keuang^2 heuan^3 lai^4 yang^2
	sin^5 mu^4 ha^6 gi^1 lo^3
	na:m^5 o:p^3 lae:^{2} sa:^{3} bu^1

Today I want	tomatoes and garlic.
	meat and fruit.
	many kinds of appliances.
	pork 5 kilos.
	perfume and soap.

ຕ້ອງການຫຍັງແດ່ເພື່ອຈະ ເຮັດ	ຂອງກິນນັ້ນ
	ນາ
	ກິນ
	ບຸນ

dtohng[5] gan[1] nya:ng[4] dae[2] peua[2] cha:[3] he:t[2]	kohng[4] gi:n[1] na:n[5]
	na[3]
	gi:n[1]
	bu:n[1]

What do you want in order to make	that food?
	a field?
	a meal?
	a festival?

ໝາກຫຸ່ງ	ແມ່ນ	ໝາກໄມ້	ທີ່ຂ້ອຍມັກຫຼາຍ
ພາສາລາວ		ພາສາ	
ຫຼວງພຣະບາງ		ບ່ອນ	
ນ້ຳຂອງ		ແມ່ນ້ຳ	
ເຮືອນແບບນີ້		ເຮືອນ	

mak[6] hu:ng[2]	maen[2]	mak[6] mai:[5]	ti[2] kohy[6] ma:k[2] lai[4]
pa[3] sa[4] lao[3]		pa[3] sa[4]	
luang[4] pa:[2] bang[1]		bohn[2]	
na:m[5] kohng[4]		mae[2] na:m[5]	
heuan[3] baep[6] ni[5]		heuan[3]	

Papaya	is	the fruit	that I like a lot.
Lao		the language	
Luang Prabang		the place	
The Mekong		the river	
A house like this		the house	

	Lao	Romanization	English
11-1	<u>ຂຶ້ນ</u>	<u>keun6</u>	<u>(Go) up, (come) up, to get in (a car)</u>
	ເຊີນຂຶ້ນມາເຮືອນຕີ໊	sern3 keun6 ma3 heuan3 dti1	Please come up to our house (on stilts).
	ຂຶ້ນຣົດຂ້ອຍ ໄປໂຮງຮຽນນຳກັນນໍ	keun6 lo:t2 kohy6 bpai:1 hong3 hian3 na:m3 ga:n1 noh3	Get in my car; let's go to school together.
	ຣາຄາຂຶ້ນອີກ ຫ້າສິບກີບ	la3 ka3 keun6 ik6 ha6 si:p3 gip6	The price is going up 50 kip again.
	ດຽວນີ້ນ້ຳຂອງຂຶ້ນແລ້ວ ມີນ້ຳຫຼາຍ	diaw1 ni5 na:m5 kohng4 keun6 laew5 mi3 na:m5 lai4	Now the Mekong river water is up; there is a lot of water.
11-2	<u>ໄດ້ຍິນ</u>	<u>dai:5 nyi:n3</u>	<u>To hear</u>
	ເຈົ້າໄດ້ຍິນບໍ່ ຂ້ອຍບໍ່ໄດ້ຍິນ	chao:5 dai:5 nyi:n3 boh2 kohy6 boh2 dai:5 nyi:n3	Can you hear it? I don't here it.
	ລາວໄດ້ຍິນຄົນເວົ້າກັນ ຢູ່ຊັ້ນເທິງ	lao3 dai:5 nyi:n3 ko:n3 wao:5 ga:n1 yu2 sa:n5 ter:ng2	He heard people talking upstairs.
	ຂ້ອຍບໍ່ໄດ້ຍິນເຈົ້າເຂົ້າມາຫ້ອງ	kohy6 boh2 dai:5 nyi:n3 chao:5 kao:6 ma3 hohng6	I didn't hear you coming into the room.
	ຂ້ອຍໄດ້ຍິນຣົດຢຸດ ຢູ່ທາງໜ້າບ້ານຂ້ອຍ	kohy6 dai:5 nyi:n3 lo:t2 yu:t3 yu2 tang3 na6 ban5 kohy6	I hear a car stopping in front of my house.
11-3	<u>ສົ່ງ</u>	<u>so:ng2</u>	<u>To send, to take (bring) a person</u>
	ທຸກໆມື້ເມັຽໄປສົ່ງຜົວໄປການ	tu:k2 tu:k2 meu5 mia3 bpai:1 so:ng2 pua4 bpai:1 gan1	The wife goes to take her husband to work every day.
	ຂ້ອຍມາສົ່ງເດັກນ້ອຍ	kohy6 ma3 so:ng2 de:k3 nohy5	He went to get the things that were sent from abroad.
	ລາວໄປຮັບເຄື່ອງທີ່ສົ່ງມາຈາກຕ່າງປະເທດ	lao3 bpai:1 ha:p2 keuang2 ti2 so:ng2 ma3 chak6 dtang2 bpa:3 tet5	You can send these things through the post office without any difficulty or having to pay much money.
	ສົ່ງເຄື່ອງແບບນີ້ຢູ່ໂຮງໄປສະນີ ບໍ່ຍາກແລະບໍ່ແພງ	so:ng2 keuang2 baep6 ni5 yu2 hong3 bpai:1 sa:3 ni3 boh2 nyak5 lae:2 boh2 paeng3	

11-4	ຄິດ	ki:t^{2}	To think
	ຍັງເວົ້າບໍ່ໄດ້ ຂ້ອຍກຳລັງຄິດ	nya:ng^{3} wao:^{5} boh^{2} dai:^{5} kohy^{6} ga:m^{1} la:ng^{3} ki:t^{2}	I still can't say anything about it. I'm thinking about it.
	ເລື່ອງນີ້ຄິດຍາກຫຼາຍ	leuang^{2} ni^{5} ki:t^{2} nyak^{5} lai^{4}	It is very hard to think about this matter.
	ຂ້ອຍຄິດວ່າເຈົ້າຕ້ອງການເງິນຫຼາຍພັນ	kohy^{6} ki:t^{2} wa^{2} chao:^{5} dtohng^{5} gan^{1} nger:n^{3} lai^{4} pa:n^{3}	I thought you needed several thousand kip.
11-5	ຂອງ , ເຄື່ອງ	kohng^{4}, keuang^{2}	Things (to eat) things (to wear)
	ເຈົ້າມັກກິນຂອງກິນຝຣັ່ງບໍ່	chao:^{5} ma:k^{2} gi:n^{1} kohng^{4} gi:n^{1} fa:^{3} la:ng^{2} boh^{2}	Do you want to eat French food?
	ເຄື່ອງນຸ່ງແບບລາວງາມ	keuang^{2} nu:ng^{2} baep^{6} lao^{3} ngam^{3}	Lao clothes are beautiful.
	ຂ້ອຍມາຢູ່ເມືອງລາວບໍ່ດົນ ຕ້ອງຊື້ເຄື່ອງເຮືອນ ຫຼາຍຢ່າງ	kohy^{6} ma^{3} yu^{2} meuang^{3} lao^{3} boh^{2} do:n^{1} dtohng^{5} seu^{5} keuang^{2} heuan^{3} lai^{4} yang^{2}	I just arrived in Laos not long ago. I have to buy a lot of furniture.
	ລາວມັກກິນແຕ່ຂອງກິນຈີນ	lao^{3} ma:k^{2} gi:n^{1} dtae^{2} kohng^{4} gi:n^{1} chin^{1}	He only likes Chinese food.
11-6	ຕ້ອງການ	dtohng^{5} gan^{1}	To need, to want
	ລາວບໍ່ຕ້ອງການຫຍັງດອກ	lao^{3} boh^{2} dtohng^{5} gan^{1} nyang^{4} dohk^{6}	He doesn't want anything.
	ເຮົາຕ້ອງການຫຍັງແດ່ ເພື່ອຈະເດີນທາງໄປຕ່າງ ປະເທດ	hao:^{3} dtohng^{5} gan^{1} nya:ng^{4} dae^{2} peua^{2} cha:^{3} dern^{1} tang^{3} bpai:^{1} dtang^{2} bpa:^{3} tet^{5}	What do we need to travel to foreign countries?
	ຂະເຈົ້າຕ້ອງການເງິນເທົ່າໃດ ເພື່ອຈະກໍ່ສ້າງຕຶກ ຊັ້ນສາມ	ka:^{3} chao:^{5} dtohng^{5} gan^{1} nger:n^{3} tao:^{2} dai:^{1} peua^{2} cha:^{3} goh^{2} sang^{6} dteu:k^{3} sa:n^{5} sam^{4}	How much money do they need to construct a 3-storey building?
	ທັມມະດາເຮົາຕ້ອງການຣົດເພື່ອເຮັດວຽກ	ta:m^{3} ma:^{2} da^{1} hao:^{3} dtohng^{5} gan^{1} lo:t^{2} peua^{2} he:t^{1} wiak^{5}	As a rule we need cars to do our job.

11-7	ເພື່ອ	peua2	For, (in order) to
	ລາວໄປອະເມຣິກາເພື່ອເຮັດຫຍັງ	lao3 bpai:1 a:3 me3 li3 ga1 peua2 he:t2 nya:ng4	What does he go to America for?
	ລູກສິດຄົນລາວຫຼາຍຄົນໄປຝຣັ່ງເພື່ອຮຽນໜັງສື	luk5 si:t3 ko:n3 lao3 lai4 ko:n3 bpai:1 fa:3 la:ng2 peua2 hian3 na:ng4 seu4	Many students go to France for study.
	ເຮົາໄດ້ຄິດຫຼາຍຢ່າງ ຫຼາຍເທື່ອເພື່ອຈະຫາທາງດີ	hao:3 dai:5 ki:t2 lai4 yang2 lai4 teua2 peua2 cha:3 ha4 tang3 di1	We considered many methods over and over again to find a good one.
	ລາວຂໍເງິນນຳພໍ່ເພື່ອຈະຊື້ລົດ	lao3 koh4 nger:n3 na:m3 poh2 peua2 cha:3 seu5 lo:t2	He asked his father for money to buy a car.
11-8	ສຳລັບ	sa:m4 la:p2	For, as for
	ວຽກເຮັດແລ້ວ ສຳລັບມື້ນີ້	wiak5 he:t2 laew5 sa:m4 la:p2 meu5 ni5	The work is done for today.
	ສຳລັບໂຮງການເຮົານີ້ ເຮົາຕ້ອງການອີກຄົນນຶ່ງ ມາເຮັດວຽກນຳເຮົາ	sa:m4 la:p5 hong3 gan1 hao:3 ni5 hao:3 dtohng5 gan1 ik6 ko:n3 neu:ng2 ma3 he:t2 wiak5 na:m3 hao:3	For our office we need one more man who will work with us.
	ອັນນີ້ດີທີ່ສຸດສຳລັບການສຶກສາ	a:n1 ni5 di1 ti2 su:t3 sa:m4 la:p2 gan1 seu:k3 sa4	This is the best for education.
11-9	ພົບ	po:p2	To meet
	ຂ້ອຍເຄີຍພົບເພິ່ນເທື່ອນຶ່ງແລ້ວ ເວລາມີກິນລ້ຽງຢູ່ສະຖານທູດໄທ	kohy6 kery3 po:p2 teua2 neu:ng2 laew5 we3 la3 mi3 gi:n1 liang5 yu2 sa:3 tan4 tut5 tai:3	I met him once when they had a party at the Thai Embassy.
	ຂ້ອຍຍິນດີທີ່ໄດ້ພົບທ່ານ	kohy6 nyi:n3 di1 ti2 dai:5 po:p2 tan2	I am glad to meet you, sir.
	ຂ້ອຍພົບລາວຢູ່ທຸກໆບ່ອນ	kohy6 po:p2 lao3 yu2 tu:k2 tu:k2 bohn2	I meet him everywhere.
	ພົບກັນຢູ່ເດີ່ນຍົນນໍ	po:p2 ga:n1 yu2 dern2 nyo:n3 noh3	See you at the airport.

Text

ບົດ ຮຽນ ທີ່ ສິບ ເອັດ

1. ມາດາມ : ເຈົ້າກໍຈະໄປຕລາດບໍ

2. ນາງແພງ: ແມ່ນແລ້ວຂ້ອຍຈະໄປຕລາດ

3. ມາດາມ : ເຊີນຂຶ້ນຣົດໄປນຳກັນຕີ້

4. ນາງແພງ: ຂອບໃຈ ຂ້ອຍໄດ້ຍິນຣົດເຈົ້າອອກໄປເທື່ອນຶ່ງແລ້ວ ເຈົ້າໄປສົ່ງສາມີເຈົ້າໄປການບໍ່.

5. ມາດາມ : ແມ່ນແລ້ວ ມື້ນີ້ເຈົ້າຈະເຮັດຫຽັງກິນ

6. ນາງແພງ: ຂ້ອຍຈະຊື້ຊີ້ນໝູກ່ອນ ເພາະມື້ນີ້ຂ້ອຍຄິດຢາກກິນສົ້ມຊີ້ນໝູ

7. ມາດາມ : ສົ້ມໝູແມ່ນຂອງກິນລາວທີ່ຂ້ອຍມັກຫຼາຍ
   ມື້ນີ້ຂ້ອຍຕ້ອງການເຄື່ອງເຮືອນເລັກໆ ນ້ອຍໆ

8. ນາງແພງ: ເຄື່ອງທີ່ເຈົ້າຕ້ອງການຢູ່ທາງນີ້ ຂອບໃຈຫຼາຍໆທີ່ພາມາ ພົບກັນຢູ່ບ້ານນໍ

9. ມາດາມ : ບໍ່ເປັນຫຽັງ

BO:T^{3} HIAN^{3} TI^{2} SI:P^{3} E:T^{3}

1. Ma^{3} dam^{1} x : Chao:^{5} goh^{1} cha:^{3} bpai:^{1} dta:^{3} lat^{6} boh^{2} ?

2. Nang^{3} Paeng^{3}: Maen^{2} laew^{5}. Kohy^{6} cha:^{3} bpai:^{1} dta:^{3} lat^{6}.

3. Ma^{3} dam^{1} x : Sern^{3} keun^{6} lo:t^{2} bpai:^{1} nam^{3} ga:n^{1} dti^{5}.

4. Nang^{3} Paeng^{3}: Kohp^{6} chai:^{1}. Kohy^{6} dai:^{5} nyi:n^{3} lo:t^{2} chao:^{5} ohk^{6} bpai:^{1} teua^{2} neu:ng^{2} laew^{5}. Chao:^{5} bpai:^{1} so:ng^{2} sa^{4} mi^{3} chao:^{5} bpai:^{1} gan^{1} boh^{2}?

5. Ma^{3} dam^{1} x : Maen^{2} laew^{5}. Meu^{5} ni^{1} chao:^{5} cha:^{3} he:t^{2} nya:ng^{4} gi:n^{1}?

6. Nang^{3} Paeng^{3}: Kohy^{6} cha:^{3} seu^{5} sin^{5} mu^{4} gohn^{2} poh:^{2} meu^{5} ni^{5} kohy^{6} ki:t^{2} yak^{6} gi:n^{1} so:m^{6} sin^{5} mu^{4}.

7. Ma^{3} dam^{1} x : So:m^{6} mu^{4} maen^{2} kohng^{4} gi:n^{1} lao^{3} ti^{2} kohy^{6} mak^{2} lai^{4}. Meu^{5} ni^{1} kohy^{6} dtohng^{5} gan^{1} keuang^{2} heuan^{3} le:k^{2} le:k^{2} nohy^{5} nohy^{5}.

8. Nang^{3} Paeng^{3}: Keuang^{2} ti^{2} chao:^{5} dtohng^{5} gan^{1} yu^{2} tang^{3} ni^{5}. Kohp^{6} chai:^{1} lai^{4} lai^{4} ti^{2} pa^{3} ma^{3} Po:p^{2} ga:n^{1} yu^{2} ban^{5} noh^{3}.

9. Ma^{3} dam^{1} x : Boh^{2} bpe:n^{1} nya:ng^{4}.

LESSON 11: CHATTING

1. Madame X: Will you go to market, too?

2. Nang Pheng: Yes, I'm going to market.

3. Madame X: Please get in the car, let's go together!

4. Nang Pheng: Thank you. I heard your car going out once. Did you take your husband to go to work?

5. Madame X: Yes. Today what are you cooking?

6. Nang Pheng: I'll buy pork first because today I want to eat sausage.

7. Madame X: Pork sausage is a Lao food that I like a lot.

8. Nang Pheng: The things you want are here. Thank you for taking (me) here. See you at home!

9. Madame X: You're welcome.

LESSON 12: LAO CLASS (A letter)

Substitution Exercise

ເຈົ້າຮຽນລາວ	ຢູ່ໃສ
	ຈັກມື້ໃນອາທິດນຶ່ງ
	ມື້ນຶ່ງຈັກຊົ່ວໂມງ
ເຈົ້າຮຽນບົດຮຽນທີ່ເທົ່າໃດມື້ນີ້	
ເຈົ້າຮຽນລາວນຳໃຜ	
ເຈົ້າຮຽນຫຍັງໃນບົດຮຽນນີ້	

ຂ້ອຍຮຽນຢູ່ຫ້ອງຮຽນ
ໃນອາທິດນຶ່ງຫ້າມື້
ມື້ນຶ່ງຫ້າສິບນາທີ
ມື້ນີ້ຮຽນບົດຮຽນທີ່ຊາວ
ຮຽນນຳນາຍຄຣູທີ່ສອນດີໆ
ໃນບົດຮຽນນີ້ ຂ້ອຍຮຽນວັນທີ່ແລະມື້ໃນອາທິດ

chao:^{5} hian^3 lao^3	yu^2 sai:^{4}	kohy^6 hian^3 yu^2 hong^3 hian^3
	cha:k^3 meu^5 nai:^{3} a^1 ti:t^2 neu:ng^2	nai:^{3} a^1 ti:t^2 neu:ng^2 ha^6 meu^5
	meu^5 neu:ng^2 cha:k^3 sua^2 mong^3	hian^3 meu^5 neu:ng^2 ha^6 si:p^3 na^3 ti^3
chao:^{5} hian^3 bo:t^3 hian^3 ti^2 tao:^{2} dai:^{1} meu^5 ni^5		meu^5 ni^5 hian^3 bo:t^3 hian^3 ti^2 sao^3
chao:^{5} hian^3 lao^3 na:m^3 pai:^{4}		hian^3 na:m^3 nai^3 ku^3 ti^2 sohn^4 di^1 di^1
chao:^{5} hian^3 nya:ng^4 nai:^{3} bo:t^3 hian^3 ni^5		nai:^{3} bo:t^3 hian^3 ni^3 kohy^6 hian^3 wa:n^3 ti^2 lae:^{2} meu^5 nai:^{3} a^1 ti:t^2

You study Lao	where?	I study at the school.
	how many days/week?	Five days per week.
	how many hours/day?	Fifty minutes per day.
You study the lesson which number today?		Today I studied lesson 20.
You study Lao with who?		I studied with the teacher who teaches very well.
What are you studying in this lesson?		In this lesson I study about dates and the days of the week.

ນາຍຄຣູຖາມ	ຢ່າງໃດ
ລູກສິດຕອບ	
ເພິ່ນສອນຕົວໜັງສືລາວ	
ວິທີສອນຂອງເພິ່ນເປັນ	
ລູກສິດຮຽນ	

nai³ ku³ tam⁴	yang² dai:¹
luk⁵ si:t³ dtohp⁶	
per:n² sohn⁴ dtua¹ na:ng⁴ seu⁴ lao³	
wi:² ti³ sohn⁴ kohng⁴ per:n² bpe:n¹	
luk⁵ si:t³ hian³	

The teacher asks	how?
The student answers	
He teaches the Lao alphabet	
His teaching method is	
The student studies	

ເພິ່ນຖາມວ່າມື້ນີ້ແມ່ນວັນຫຍັງ
ລາວຕອບວ່າແມ່ນວັນຈັນ
ຂຽນໃສ່ປຶ້ມຂຽນຕາມນາຍຄຣູເວົ້າ
ວິທີຂອງເພິ່ນດີກວ່າໝູ່
ຂະເຈົ້າຕັ້ງໃຈຮຽນນຳນາຍຄຣູ

per:n² tam⁴ wa² meu⁵ ni⁵ maen² wa:n³ nya:ng⁴
lao³ dtohp⁶ wa² maen² wa:n³ cha:n¹
kian⁴ sai:² bpeu:m⁵ kian⁴ dtam¹ nai³ ku³ wao:⁵
wi:² ti³ kohng⁴ per:n² di¹ gwa² mu²
ka:³ chao:⁵ dta:ng⁵ chai:¹ hian³ na:m³ nai³ ku³

He asked, what day is it today.
He answered that it's Monday.
(By) writing in the notebook as the teacher speaks.
His method is better than (my) friend's.
They are eager to study with the teacher

	ແມ່ນ	ວັນອາທິດ	ວັນທີ	ຊາວ
ມນີ້		ວັນຈັນ		ຊາວເອັດ
		ວັນອັງຄານ		ຊາວສອງ
		ວັນພຸດ		ຊາວສາມ
		ວັນພະຫັດ		ຊາວສີ່
		ວັນສຸກ		ຊາວຫ້າ
		ວັນເສົາ		ຊາວຫົກ

meu⁵ ni⁵	maen²	wa:n³ a¹ ti:t²	wa:n³ ti²	sao³
meu⁵ wa:n³ ni⁵		wa:n³ cha:n¹		sao³ e:t³
meu⁵ eun²		wa:n³ a:ng¹ kan³		sao³ sohng⁴
		wa:n³ pu:t²		sao³ sam⁴
		wa:n³ pa:² ha:t³		sao³ si²
		wa:n³ su:k³		sao³ ha⁶
		wa:n³ sao:⁴		sao³ ho:k³

Today	is	Sunday	the 20th.
Yesterday		Monday	the 21st.
Tomorrow		Tuesday	the 22nd.
		Wednesday	the 23rd.
		Thursday	the 24th.
		Friday	the 25th.
		Saturday	the 26th.

ດຽວນີ້ຫົກໂມງ	ຫ້ານາທີ
ເຈັດໂມງ	ຍັງສິບນາທີ

diaw^{1} ni^{5} ho:k^{3} mong^{3}	ha^{6} na^{3} ti^{3}
che:t^{3} mong^{3}	nya:ng^{4} si:p^{3}
Now it's 6 o'clock	(plus) 5 minutes.
7 o'clock	less 10.

ຂ້ອຍຢາກໃຫ້	ເຈົ້າ	ມານີ້ສາມໂມງ
	ລາວ	ອ່ານບົດຣຽນທີ່ຊາວ
	ຂະເຈົ້າ	ຂຽນຕົວໜັງສືລາວໃສ່ກະດານດຳ
		ຕັ້ງໃຈເຮັດວຽກ
		ຊ່ອຍກວາດເຮືອນ
		ຊ່ອຍເຮັດນາ
		ພາໄປວຽງຈັນ

kohy^{6} yak^{6} hai:^{6}	chao:^{5}	ma^{3} ni^{5} sam^{4} mong^{3}
	lao^{3}	an^{2} bo:t^{3} hian^{3} ti^{2} sao^{3}
	ka:^{3} chao:^{5}	kian^{4} dtua^{1} na:ng^{4} seu^{4} lao^{3} sai:^{2} ga:^{3} dan^{1} da:m^{1}
		dta:ng^{5} chai:^{1} he:t^{2} wiak^{5}
		sohy^{2} gwat^{6} heuan^{3}
		sohy^{2} he:t^{2} na^{3}
		pa^{3} bpai:^{1} wiang^{3} cha:n^{1}

I want for	you	to come here at 3 o'clock.
	him	to read lesson 20.
	them	to write Lao letters on the blackboard.
		to be eager to work.
		to help sweep the house.
		to help work the fields.
		to take (him) to go to Vientiane.

Vocabulary Exercise

	Lao	Romanization	English
12-1	<u>ພຽງແຕ່</u>	<u>piang^3 dtae^2</u>	<u>Only</u>
	ຂ້ອຍຈິພັກຢູ່ຫັ້ນພຽງແຕ່ສາມມື້	kohy^6 si:^{2} pa:k^2 yu^2 ha:n^6 piang^3 dtae^2 sam^4 meu^5	I will stay there only three days.
	ຢູ່ບ້ານເຮົາມີຄົນພຽງແຕ່ສອງຄົນ	yu^2 ban^5 hao:^{3} mi^3 ko:n^3 piang^3 dtae^2 sohng^4 ko:n^3	In our house, there are only two of us.
	ໂຮງຮຽນນັ້ນນ້ອຍມີນາຍຄູພຽງແຕ່ສີ່ຄົນ	hong^3 hian^3 na:n^5 nohy^5 mi^3 nai^3 ku^3 piang^3 dtae^2 si^2 ko:n^3	The school is small; there are only four teachers.
	ໄປນຳແທັກຊີບໍ່ແພງ ເຂົາເອົາພຽງແຕ່ຫ້າສິບກີບ	bpai:^{1} na:m^3 tae:k^5 si^3 boh^2 paeng^3 kao:^{4} ao:^{1} piang^3 dtae^2 ha^6 si:p^3 gip^6	Going by taxi is not expensive; they charge only 50 kip.
12-2	<u>ໝົດທຸກ</u>	<u>mo:t^3 tu:k^2</u>	<u>Every</u>
	ດຽວນີ້ໝົດທຸກບ່ອນຢູ່ໃນເມືອງຂາຍປຶ້ມຂຽນ	diaw^1 ni^5 mo:t^3 tu:k^2 bohn^2 yu^1 nai^3 meuang^3 kai^4 bpeu:m^5 kian^4	Now every place in town sells notebooks.
	ລູກສິດໝົດທຸກຄົນອ່ານຕົວໜັງສືລາວໄດ້	luk^5 si:t^3 mo:t^3 tu:k^2 ko:n^3 an^1 dtua^1 na:ng^4 seu^4 lao^3 dai:^{5}	Every student can read Lao characters.
	ຢູ່ຕລາດເຊົ້າວຽງຈັນມີເຄື່ອງໝົດທຸກຢ່າງ	yu^1 dta:^{3} lat^6 sao:^{5} wiang^3 cha:n^1 mi^3 keuang^2 mo:t^3 tu:k^2 yang^2	Everything can be found in Vientiane's morning market.
	ຂ້ອຍມັກພາກໄມ້ໝົດທຸກແນວ		I like all kinds of fruits.
12-3	<u>ວິທີ</u>	<u>wi:^{2} ti^3</u>	<u>How to do, method</u>
	ເຮົາຮຽນວິທີອ່ານແລະຂຽນຢູ່ໂຮງຮຽນ	hao:^{3} hian^3 wi:^{2} ti^3 an^1 lae:^{2} kian^4 yu^2 hong^3 hian^3	We learn how to read and write in school.
	ວິທີອ່ານພາສາລາວບໍ່ຍາກ	wi:^{2} ti^3 an^1 pa^3 sa^4 lao^3 boh^2 nyak^5	Reading Lao is not difficult.
	ເພິ່ນໄປຕ່າງປະເທດເພື່ອຮຽນວິທີສອນໜັງສື	per:n^2 bpai:^{1} dtang^2 bpa:^{3} tet^5 peua^2 hian^3 wi:^{2} ti^3 sohn^4 na:ng^4 seu^4	She (he) goes abroad to learn teaching methods.
	ຂ້ອຍບໍ່ຮູ້ຈັກວິທີເຮັດບໍ່ໄດ້	kohy^6 boh^2 hu^5 cha:k^3 wi:^{2} ti^3 he:t^2 boh^2 dai:^{5}	I don't know why I can't do it.

	Lao	Transliteration	English
12-4	**ກ່ວາ**	gwa^{2}	More.... than...
	ອັນນີ້ໃຫຍ່ກວ່າອັນນັ້ນ	an^{1} ni^{5} nyai:^{2} gwa^{2} a:n^{1} na:n^{5}	This one is bigger than that one.
	ຕຶກນີ້ສູງກ່ວາຕຶກນັ້ນ ແຕ່ຕຶກນັ້ນງາມກວ່າ	dteu:k^{3} ni^{5} sung^{4} gwa^{2} dteu:k^{3} na:n^{5} dtae^{2} dteu:k^{3} na:n^{5} ngam^{3} gwa^{2}	This building is taller than that building, but that one is more beautiful.
	ສຳລັບຂ້ອຍພາສາລາວງ່າຍກວ່າພາສາຈີນ	sa:m^{4} la:p^{2} kohy^{6} pa^{3} sa^{4} lao^{3} ngai^{2} gwa^{2} pa^{3} sa^{4} chin^{1}	For me Lao is easier than Chinese.
	ມື້ນີ້ເຢັນກ່ວາມື້ວານນີ້	meu^{5} ni^{5} ye:n^{1} gwa^{2} meu^{5} wan^{3} ni^{5}	Today is cooler than yesterday.
12-5	**ທີ່**	ti^{2}	-th (for cardinal numbers)
	ປີນີ້ແມ່ນປີທີ່ສອງ	bpi^{1} ni^{5} maen^{2} bpi^{1} ti^{2} sohng^{4}	This year is the second year.
	ເທື່ອທີ່ນຶ່ງລາວໄປປະເທດໄທ ເທື່ອທີ່ສອງໄປເມືອງຝຣັ່ງ	teua^{2} ti^{2} neu:ng^{2} lao^{3} bpai:^{1} bpa:^{3} tet^{5} tai:^{3} teua^{2} ti^{2} sohng^{4} bpai:^{1} meuang^{3} fa:^{3} la:ng^{2}	The first time he went to Thailand; the second time he went to France.
	ຫ້ອງການຂ້ອຍຢູ່ຊັ້ນທີ່ສີ່	hohng^{6} gan^{1} kohy^{6} yu^{2} sa:n^{5} ti^{2} si^{2}	My office is on the fourth floor.
	ວັນທີ່ນຶ່ງແມ່ນວັນພະຫັດ	wa:n^{3} ti^{2} neu:ng^{2} maen^{2} wa:n^{3} pa:^{2} ha:t^{3}	The first day is Thursday.
12-6	**ກ່ຽວ**	giaw^{2}	About, concerning, to have something to do with
	ຂ້ອຍອ່ານເຣື່ອງກ່ຽວກັບເມືອງລາວ	kohy^{6} an^{1} leuang^{2} giaw^{2} ga:p^{3} meuang^{3} lao^{3}	I read (a story) about Laos.
	ຂ້ອຍບໍ່ກ່ຽວກັບອັນນັ້ນ	kohy^{6} boh^{2} giaw^{2} ga:p^{3} a:n^{1} na:n^{5}	I do not have anything to do with it.
	ເຈົ້າບໍ່ກ່ຽວກໍໄດ້	chao:^{5} boh^{2} giaw^{2} goh^{1} dai:^{5}	You can stay away from it.

	Lao	Romanization	English
12-7	**ໃຫ້**	hai:6	To have (allow) someone do ..
	ລາວໃຫ້ເຈົ້າຂັບຣົດລາວບໍ່	lao3 hai:6 chao:5 ka:p3 lo:t2 lao3 boh2	Does he let you drive his car?
	ນາຍໝໍບໍ່ໃຫ້ລາວກິນເຂົ້າສອງມື້	nai3 moh4 boh2 hai:6 lao3 gi:n1 kao:6 sohng4 meu5	The doctor won't let him eat for two days.
	ຂະເຈົ້າຍັງບໍ່ໃຫ້ຄົນເຂົ້າ	ka:3 chao:5 nya:ng3 boh2 hai6 ko:n3 kao:6	They don't allow people to enter yet.
	ແມ່ໃຫ້ລູກໄປຊື້ຂອງ	mae2 hai:6 luk5 bpai:1 seu5 kohng4	Mother has the children go buy things.
	ນາຍລາວໃຫ້ລາວພັກອາທິດນຶ່ງ	nai3 lao3 hai:6 lao3 pa:k2 a'ti:t2 neu:ng2	His boss gives him a one week holiday.
12-8	**ໃສ່** (See also p.155/6.5)	sai:2	In, into, on
	ຂຽນຊື່ເຈົ້າໃສ່ກະດານ	kian4 seu2 chao:5 sai:2 ga:3 dan1	Write your name on the board.
	ລາວຂຽນໃສ່ປື້ມນ້ອຍ ເວລາພົບກັບໝູ່	lao3 kian4 sai:2 bpeu:m5 nohy5 we3 la3 po:p2 ga:p3 mu2	She writes in a small book when she meets her friends.
	ເອົານໍ້າໃສ່ແກ້ວສາກ່ອນ	ao:1 na:m5 sai:2 gaew5 sa4 gohn2	Put water in the glass first.
	ເອົາອັນນີ້ໃສ່ຣົດແດ່	ao:1 a:n1 ni5 sai:2 lo:t2 dae2	Put this into the car.
12-9	**ໄວ**	wai:3	Fast, quickly, early
	ມາໄວດຸ ບໍ່ມີເວລາຫຼາຍ	ma3 wai:3 du:3 boh2 mi3 we3 la3 lai4	Come quickly, you don't have much time.
	ເຮົາຕ້ອງໄປໄວໆ	hao:3 dtohng5 bpai:1 wai:3 wai:3	We have to go very fast (or very early).
	ເຈົ້າຂັບຣົດໄວພໍ	chao:5 ka:p3 lo:t2 wai:3 poh3	You are driving fast enough.
	ລາວເວົ້າໄວຂ້ອຍບໍ່ເຂົ້າໃຈ	lao3 wao:5 wai:3 kohy6 boh2 kao:6 chai:1	He speaks fast. I don't understand.

	Lao	Transliteration	English
12-10	ຄັກ	ka:k^{2}	Clear(ly)
	ລາວເວົ້າຫຍັງ ຂ້ອຍບໍ່ເຂົ້າໃຈຄັກ	lao^{3} wao:^{5} nya:ng^{4} kohy^{6} boh^{2} kao:^{6} chai:^{1} ka:k^{2}	What is he saying? I don't understand it clearly.
	ເວລາຄົນວຽດນາມເວົ້າພາສາລາວ ຂ້ອຍຟັງບໍ່ຄັກ	we^{3} la^{3} ko:n^{3}wiat^{5} nam^{3} wao:^{5} pa^{3} sa^{4} lao^{3} kohy^{6} fa:ng^{3} boh^{2} ka:k^{2}	When Vietnamese speak Lao, I can't understand (them) clearly.
	ເພິ່ນເວົ້າພາສາລາວບໍ່ຄັກ	per:n^{2} wao:^{5} pa^{3} sa^{4} lao^{3} boh^{2} ka:k^{2}	He does not speak Lao clearly.
	ຕົວໜັງສືຂຽນບໍ່ຄັກ ອ່ານຍາກຫຼາຍ	dtua:^{1} na:ng^{4} seu^{4} kian^{4} boh^{2} ka:k^{2} an^{2} nyak^{5} lai^{4}	The characters are not written clearly. It is very difficult to read.
12-11	ຜິດ	pi:t^{3}	To make a mistake
	ຂ້ອຍຂຽນຜິດ ອັນນີ້ຕ້ອງເປັນໃກ້ ບໍ່ແມ່ນໄກ	kohy^{6} kian^{4} pi:t.^{3} a:n^{1} ni^{5} dtohng^{5} bpe:n^{1} gai:^{5} boh^{2} maen^{2} gai:^{1}	I misspelt it. This must be "near" not "far".
	ຂະເຈົ້າເຂົ້າໃຈຜິດ	ka:^{2} chao:^{5} kao:^{6} chai:^{1} pi:t^{3}	They misunderstand.
	ຕ້ອງຮຽນ ດີ ດີ ເພື່ອບໍ່ໃຫ້ຜິດຫຼາຍ	dtohng^{5} hian^{3} di^{1} di^{1} peua^{2} boh^{2} hai:^{6} pi:t^{3} lai^{4}	You must learn very well not to make a lot of mistakes.
12-12	ຖາມ	tam^{4}	To ask
	ຂ້ອຍຖາມລາວວ່າ ລາວຢາກກິນສົ້ມໝູບໍ່	kohy^{6} tam^{4} lao^{3} wa^{2} lao^{3} yak^{6} gi:n^{1} so:m^{6} mu^{4} boh^{2}	I asked him if he wanted to eat Lao pork sausage.
	ລາວຖາມຂ້ອຍວ່າ ລາວຂໍພັກອາທິດນຶ່ງໄດ້ບໍ່	lao^{3} tam^{4} kohy^{6} wa^{2} lao^{3} koh^{4} pa:k^{2} a^{1} ti:t^{2} neu:ng^{2} dai:^{5} boh^{2}	He askes me if he can have a week's holiday.
	ຂະເຈົ້າຖາມວ່າ ເຈົ້າຂອງເຮືອນໃຫ້ເຊົ່າຫຼັງນີ້ແມ່ນໃຜ	ka:^{3} chao:^{5} tam^{4} wa^{2} chao:^{5} kohng^{4} heaun^{3} hai:^{6} sao:^{2} la:ng^{4} ni^{5} maen^{2} pai:^{4}	They asked who was the owner of this house for rent.
	ລູກສິດບໍ່ເຂົ້າໃຈ ເຂົາຖາມນາຍຄູ	luk^{5} si:t^{3} boh^{2} kao:^{6} chai:^{1} kao:^{4} tam^{4} nai^{3} ku^{3}	(When) students do not understand, they ask the teacher.

Text

ບົດ ຮຽນ ທີ່ ສິບ ສອງ

1. ຂ້ອຍຮຽນພາສາລາວຢູ່ຫ້ອງຮຽນຫ້າມື້ໃນອາທິດນຶ່ງ ມື້ນຶ່ງຮຽນຫ້າສິບນາທີ
2. ຢູ່ໃນຫ້ອງ ຮຽນຂອງຂ້ອຍມີລູກສິດພຽງແຕ່ເຈັດຄົນ ໝົດທຸກຄົນຕັ້ງໃຈຮຽນນຳນາຍຄຣູ
3. ວິທີສອນຂອງເພິ່ນກໍດີກວ່າໝູ່
4. ມື້ວານນີ້ພວກເຮົາຮຽນບົດຮຽນທີ່ສິບເອັດກ່ຽວກັບວັນທີ່ແລະມື້ໃນອາທິດ
5. ນາຍຄຣູຖາມວ່າ ມື້ນີ້ແມ່ນວັນຫຍັງ ລູກສິດຄົນນຶ່ງຕອບວ່າວັນຈັນ.
6. ນາຍຄຣູຖາມອີກວ່າ ມື້ອື່ນເດ໊ແມ່ນວັນຫຍັງແລະວັນທີ່ເທົ່າໃດ
7. ລູກສິດຕອບວ່າວັນອັງຄານວັນທີ່ຊາວ
8. ແລ້ວເພິ່ນໃຫ້ລູກສິດໝົດທຸກຄົນເວົ້າຊື່ມື້ໃນອາທິດ

   ວັນຈັນ ວັນອັງຄານ ວັນພຸດ ວັນພະຫັດ ວັນສຸກ ວັນເສົາ ວັນອາທິດ
9. ພວກເຮົາຮຽນວິທີຂຽນຕົວໜັງສືລາວ
10. ເພິ່ນຂຽນຄວາມລາວໃສ່ກະດານດຳ ແລະໃຫ້ລູກສິດອ່ານ
11. ເວົ້າຄວາມລາວໃຫ້ລູກສິດຟັງ ແລ້ວໃຫ້ຂຽນຢູ່ໃນປຶ້ມຂຽນ
12. ບາງເທື່ອເພິ່ນເວົ້າໄວ ພວກເຮົາບໍ່ເຂົ້າໃຈຄັກ ເວລາຂຽນຈຶ່ງຜິດຈາກນາຍຄຣູເວົ້າ.

BO:T^{3} HIAN^{3} TI^{2} SI:P^{3} SOHNG^{4}

1. Kohy^{6} hian^{3} pa^{3} sa^{4} lao^{3} yu^{2} hohng^{6} hian^{3} ha^{6} meu^{3} nai:^{3} a^{1} ti:t^{2} neu:ng^{2}. Meu^{5} neu:ng^{2} hian^{3} ha^{6} si:p^{3} na^{3} ti^{1}.
2. Yu^{2} nai:^{3} hohng^{6} hian^{3} kohng^{4} kohy^{6} mi^{3} luk^{5} si:t^{3} piang^{3} dtae^{2} che:t^{3} ko:n^{3}. Mo:t^{3} tu:k^{2} ko:n^{3} dta:ng^{5} chai:^{1} hian^{3} na:m^{3} nai^{3} ku^{3}.
3. Wi^{2} ti^{3} sohn^{4} kohng^{4} per:n^{2} goh^{1} di^{1} gwa^{2} mu^{2}.
4. Meu^{5} wan^{3} ni^{5} puak^{5} hao:^{3} hian^{3} bo:t^{3} hian^{3} ti^{2} si:p^{3} e:t^{3} giaw^{2} ga:p^{3} wa:n^{3} ti^{2} lae^{2} meu^{5} nai:^{3} a^{1} ti:t^{2}.
5. Nai^{3} ku^{3} tam^{4} wa^{2} meu^{5} ni^{5} maen^{2} wa:n^{3} nya:ng^{4}? Luk^{5} si:t^{3}ko:n^{3} neu:ng^{2} dtohp^{6} wa^{2} wa:n^{3} cha:n^{1}.

6. Nai^{3} ku^{3} tam^{4} ik^{6} wa^{2} meu^{3} ni^{5} de^{1} maen^{2} wa:n^{3} nya:ng^{4} lae:^{2} wa:n^{3} ti^{2} tao:^{2} dai:^{1} ?

7. Luk^{5} si:t^{3} dtohp^{6} wa^{2} wa:n^{3} a:ng^{1} kan^{3} wa:n^{3} ti^{2} sao^{3}.

8. Laew^{5} per:n^{2} hai^{6} luk^{5} si:t^{3} mo:t^{3} tu:k^{2} ko:n^{3} wao:^{5} seu^{5} meu^{5} nai:^{3} a^{1} ti:t wa:n^{3} cha:n,^{1} wa:n^{3} a:ng^{1} kan,^{3} wa:n^{3} pu:t,^{2} wa:n^{3} pa:^{2} ha:t,^{3} wa:n^{3} su:k,^{3} wa:n^{3} sao:,^{4} wa:n^{4} a^{1} ti:t^{2}.

9. Puak^{5} hao:^{3} hian^{3} wi^{2} ti^{3} kian^{4} dtua^{1} na:ng^{4} seu^{4} lao^{3}.

10. Per:n^{2} kian^{4} kwam^{3} lao^{3} sai:^{2} ga:^{3} dan^{1} da:m^{1} lae:^{2} hai^{6} luk^{5} si:t^{3} an^{1}.

11. Wao:^{5} kwam^{3} lao^{3} hai:^{6} luk^{5} si:t^{3} fa:ng^{3} laew^{5} hai:^{6} kian^{4} yu^{2} nai:^{3} bpeu:m kian^{4}.

12. Bang^{1} teua^{2} per:n^{2} wao:^{5} wai:^{3} puak^{5} hao:^{3} boh^{2} kao:^{6} chai:^{1} ka:k^{2} we^{5} la^{3} kian^{4} cheu:ng^{2} pi:t^{3} chak^{6} nai^{3} ku^{3} wao:^{5}.

LESSON 12: LAO CLASS (A letter)

1. I study Lao in school five days a week. Each day I study 50 minutes.

2. In my class there are only 7 students. Everybody studies eagerly with the teacher.

3. His teaching method is better than any other's.

4. Yesterday we studied Lesson 11 which is about dates and the days of the week.

5. The teacher asked what day it is today. A student answered that it was Monday.

6. The teacher asked again how about tomorrow. What day of the week and what day of the month will it be tomorrow?

7. The student answered that it will be Tuesday and the 20th.

8. Then the teacher had all the students say the days of the week: Monday, Tuesday, Wednesday, Thursday, Friday, Saturday, Sunday.

9. We learned how to write Lao letters.

10. The teacher (he) writes Lao on the blackboard and the students read it.

11. (He) speaks Lao to let the students listen and write in (their) notebooks.

12. Sometimes he speaks fast (and) we don't understand clearly, so when we write, we make mistakes which are different from what the teacher said.

PART 2: GRAMMAR REVIEW

Section 1: Question Words and Short Answers

1.1 Question words

Typically, question words come at the end of a Lao sentence.

nya:ng^{4}	What?
sai:^{4}	Where?
kohng^{4} pai:^{4}	Whose?
pai:^{4}	Who?
meua^{2} dai:^{1}	When?
a:n^{1} dai:^{1}	Which?
yang^{2} dai:^{1}	How? (in what way)
tao:^{2} dai:^{1}	How much?
cha:k^{3}	How many (units)?
do:n^{1} bpan^{1} dai:^{1}	How long ago? How soon?

a:n^{1}ni^{5}maen^{2} nya:ng^{4}	What is that?
chao:^{5} ma^{3} dtae^{2} sai:^{4}	Where do you come from?
a:n^{1} na:n^{5} maen^{2} bpeu:m^{5} kohng^{4} pai:^{4}	Whose book is that?
pu^{6}na:n^{5} maen^{2} pai:^{4}	Who is that?
meua^{2} dai:^{1} lao^{3} si:^{2} ga:p^{3}	When will he return to Vientiane?
chao:^{5} si:^{2} ao:^{1} a:n^{1} dai:^{1}	Which one do you want?
seu^{2} chao:^{5} wa^{2} yang^{2} dai:^{1}	How do people say your name?
la^{3} ka^{3} tao:^{2} dai:^{1}	How much does it cost?
cha:k^{6} gi^{1}lo^{3}diaw^{1}ni^{5}	How many kilos now?
chao:^{5} ma^{3}do:n^{1} bpan^{1}dai:^{1}	Will you come soon?

1.2 Question particles

boh^2	? (common)
noh^3	Okay?
de^2	Isn't it?
wa:^{2}	And...?
maen^2 boh^2	Huh? (informal)
	Right?
	True?

chao:^{5} si:^{2} bpai:^{1} boh^2	Will you go?
bpai:^{1} noh^3	Go, okay?
ngam^3 noh^3	Beautiful, isn't it?
kohy^6 sa:^{3} bai^4 di^1 chao:^{5} de^2	I'm fine, and you?
lo:t^2 chao:^{5} pe^3 wa:^{2}	Is your car broken?
lao^3 ma^3 laew^5 maen^2 boh^2	He came already, right?

1.3 Responses and negative answers

1.3.1 How to say "YES"

a) Repeat the verb in the question (see Section 5.4 below.)

b) er^1 — Yes (conversational).

c) maen^2 laew^5 — Yes it is.

d) chao:^{5} — (polite)

e) doy^1 (ka:^{3} nohy^5) — (self-humbling, respectful)

f) dai:^{5} — Okay, you can.

1.3.2 How to say "NO"

a) Negate the verb in the question with "boh^2." (see Section 5.4 below)

b) boh^2 da:ng^2 na:n^5 — It's not like that.

c) boh^2 maen^2 — No, it isn't.

Section 2: Nouns and Pronouns

2.1 Nouns

2.1.1 Nouns have only one form whether singular or plural. 1/

ka:n^{6} dai:^{1}	Stair, stairs
heuan^{3}	House, houses
gerp^{6}	Shoe, shoes

Note: Plurality (which is frequently omitted in Lao) can be indicated by using the adjective "many = lai^{4}" or a classifier plus a numeral (see Section 4 below on classifiers).

2.1.2 Adjectives and Verbs may be transformed into nouns with use of the prefixes "gan^{1}" and "kwam^{3}". Generally speaking "gan^{1}" is for words indicating action, whereas "kwam^{3}" is for passive concepts.

<u>gan^{1}</u>	<u>Actions</u>
gan^{1} bpai:^{1} ma^{3}	Traffic
gan^{1} sohn^{4}	Teaching
gan^{1} a:t^{3} siang^{4}	Recording

<u>kwam^{3}</u>	<u>Concepts</u>
kwam^{3} hu^{5}	Knowledge
kwam^{3} bpuay^{2}	Sickness
kwam^{3} bpe:n^{1} ma^{3}	Origin

2.1.3 <u>Noun</u> prefixes for Verbs

Many verbs have noun forms when used in combination with certain prefixes. Some of the common nouns made in such a way are listed below.

<u>sang^{2}</u>	<u>Craftsman</u>
sang^{2} dta:t^{3} po:m^{4}	Barber
sang^{2} fai:^{3} fa^{5}	Electrician
sang^{2} dta:t^{3} seua^{6}	Tailor
sang^{2} dti^{1} nger:n^{3}	Silversmith

1/ See also p.109/9-17

na:k^{2}	Professionals
na:k^{2} bi:n^{1}	Pilot
na:k^{2} gi^{3} la^{3}	Athlete
na:k^{2} gan^{1} tut^{5}	Diplomat
na:k^{2} hian^{3}	Student
pu^{6}	Doers
pu^{6} cha:t^{3} gan^{1}	Manager
pu^{6} nyai:^{2}	Adult
pu^{6} dtaeng^{2}	Author
pu^{6} kai^{4}	Vendor
luk^{5} (poh^{2}, mae^{2})	Familial types
mae^{2} ban^{5}	Housewife
luk^{5} fa^{4} faet^{6}	Twin
poh^{2} ka^{5}	Vendor
luk^{2} si:t^{3}	Student
ko:n^{3}	Persons in general
ko:n^{3} ki^{6} dtua:^{3}	Liar
ko:n^{3} ngan^{3}	Worker
ko:n^{3} chao:^{5} su^{5}	Lover
ko:n^{3} ha^{4} bpa^{1}	Fisherman

2.2 Pronouns

2.2.1 Pronouns do not indicate gender. For example, the word "lao^{3}" is used for both "he" and "she".

2.2.2 Pronouns have only one form no matter what part of speech they indicate. For example, there is only one word for "she, hers" and that is "lao^{3}"; however, the position of the pronoun changes depending upon its function either as a noun (before the verb) or as an adjective (following the noun) as shown below.

a:n^1 ni^5 maen^2 kohng^4 <u>chao:</u>^{5}	This is <u>yours</u>.
poh^2 <u>chao:</u>^{5} bpai^1 sai:^{4}	Where is <u>your</u> father going?
<u>chao:</u>^{5} bpai:^{1} sai:^{4}	Where are <u>you</u> going?

2.2.3 English pronouns only indicate the number of persons (ie, singular or plural) and their position from the speaker (1st, 2nd, 3rd person); however, Lao pronouns and additionally indicate the ranks of both the listener and the speaker. Four main groups of listeners are listed below:

a. Monks
b. Elders
c. Groups or in writing
d. Equals

Depending on who is speaking to whom, a different pronoun is used. On the following page is a chart showing which pronoun to use to address people properly in terms of their rank from the average person's point of view as speaker.(Note: the plural prefix "puak^5" is often used to form a plural pronoun form. Refer also to page 109/9-17.)

2.2.4 Titles of address

(a) Mr., Mrs., Sir
There are many different titles of address which should be used when talking to a person to show respect for his position in life. Such a title is used as a prefix with the first name, or alone as a pronoun. If it is used as a pronoun, it functions as either second or third person pronoun (singular on plural).

tan^2	Respectful title (Sir)
nang^3	Miss, Mrs.
tao^5	Mr.

PRONOUN CHARTS: to address listeners of different ranks from the average person's point of view

Legend:

I	We
you	you(pl.)
he, she	they

To Elders	
ka^{6} nohy^{5}	puak^{5} ka^{6} nohy^{5}
tan^{2}	puak^{5} tan^{2} tan^{2} ta:ng^{3} lai^{4}
per:n^{2}	puak^{5} per:n^{2} per:n^{2} ta:ng^{3} lai^{4} puak^{5} tan^{2}

To Monks	
ka^{6} pa:^{2} bat^{6}	puak^{5} ka^{6} pa:^{2} bat^{6}
a^{1} chan^{1} nya^{3} poh^{2}	puak^{5} a^{1} chan^{1}
pa:^{2}	puak^{5} a^{1} chan^{1}

In Speeches and Writing	
ka^{6} pa:^{2} chao:^{5}	puak^{5} ka^{6} pa:^{2} chao:^{5}
tan^{2}	puak^{5} tan^{2}
lao^{3}	puak^{5} kao:^{4} kao:^{4} chao:^{5}

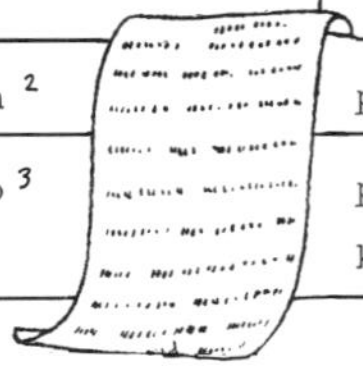

MAIN CHART (To Equals)	
kohy^{6} hao:^{3}	hao:^{3} puak^{5} khoy^{6}
chao:^{5}	mu^{2} chao:^{5} puak^{5} chao:^{5}
lao^{3} kao:^{4}	ka:^{3} chao:^{5} puak^{5} kao:^{4} puak^{5} lao^{3}

(b) General

In order to show respect towards relatives of parental age or older, the honorific prefix "nya^3" is placed before the appropriate familial term. (For a list of family names, see the table below.) In order to show respect for non-relatives whom you respect as much as you respect your own relatives, familial terms, both with and without the honorific prefix are used. For example:

nya^3 poh^2	Father
nya^3 mae^2	Mother
ay^5	Big brother
nohng^5 sao^4	Little sister

LIST OF FAMILY NAMES

	PATERNAL RELATIVES		MATERNAL RELATIVES	
GRANDPARENTS' GENERATION	poh^2 bpu^2	Grandfather	poh^2 tao:^{6}	Grandfather
	mae^2 nya^2	Grandmother	mae^2 tao:^{6}	Grandmother
PARENTS' GENERATION	poh^2	Father	mae^2	Mother
	lu:ng^3	Older uncle	eu:ng^3	Older uncle
	ao^1	Younger uncle	na^5 bao^2	Younger uncle
	bpa^5	Older aunt	bpa^5	Older aunt
	a^1	Younger aunt	na^5 sao^4	Younger aunt
CHILDREN'S GENERATION	ay^5	Older brother	luk^5	Child
	nohng^5 sai^3	Younger brother	lan^4	Grand child
	euay^5	Older sister	le:n^4	Great grandchild
	nohng^5 sao^4	Younger sister	lohn^6	Great great grandchild

2.3 Time, Day and Date, Nouns

we^{3} la^{3}	Times	
meu^{5} sao:^{5}	morning	(6am-12am)
dtohn^{1} tiang^{2}	noon, mid-day	(12am)
dtohn^{1} bai^{2}	afternoon	(1pm-6pm)
meu^{5} laeng^{3}	evening	(3pm onward)
gang^{1} keun^{3}	night	(after dark)
wa:n^{3}	Days	
wa:n^{3} cha:n^{1}	Monday	
wa:n^{3} a:ng^{1} kan^{3}	Tuesday	
wa:n^{3} pu:t^{2}	Wednesday	
wa:n^{3} pa:^{2} ha:t^{3}	Thursday	
wa:n^{3} su:k^{3}	Friday	
wa:n^{3} sao:^{4}	Saturday	
wa:n^{3} a^{1} ti:t^{2}	Sunday	
deuan^{1}	Months	
ma:^{2} ga:^{3} la^{3}	January	
gu:m^{1} pa^{3}	February	
mi^{3} na^{3}	March	
me^{3} sa^{4}	April	
peu:t^{2} sa:^{3} pa^{3}	May	
mi:^{2} tu:^{3} na^{3}	June	
goh^{1}la:^{2} ga:^{3} da^{1}	July	
si:ng^{4} ha^{4}	August	
ga:n^{1} nya^{3}	September	
dtu:^{3} la^{3}	October	
peu:t^{2} sa:^{3} chi:^{3} ga^{1}	November	
ta:n^{3} wa^{3}	December	
bpi^{1}	12-year cycle	
bpi^{1} suat^{5}	Rat	(1960)
bpi^{1} sa:^{3} lu:^{2}	Ox	
bpi^{1} kan^{4}	Tiger	(1950)
bpi^{1} toh:^{3}	Rabbit	
bpi^{1} ma:^{2} long^{3}	Dragon	(2000)
bpi^{1} ma:^{2} se:ng^{4}	Snake	
bpi^{1} ma:^{2} mia^{3}	Horse	(1990)
bpi^{1} ma:^{2} mae^{3}	Goat	
bpi^{1} wohk^{5}	Monkey	(1980)
bpi^{1} la:^{2} ga^{1}	Cock	
bpi^{1} choh^{1}	Dog	(1970)
bpi^{1} gu:n^{1}	Pig	

Section 3: Adjectives

3.1 Lao has no articles (the, a, an).

3.2 Unlike English, Lao adjectives follow the noun they modify:

dto:3 ni5	This table
dtao5 dohk6 mai:5	Flower vase

3.3 Most predicate adjectives function as verbs and therefore do not require a verb as in English.

nohng5 sao4 ngam3 lai4	Younger sister is beautiful.
a:n1 ni5 di1	It is good.

3.4 Repeating an adjective in Lao is a common way of intensifying the quality of the adjective. Although the two words are the same, they are pronounced on different tones with the first of the pair of adjectives pronounced on a higher level tone, higher than tone #3.

chao:5 ngam3' ngam3'	You are very beautiful.
na6 kohy6 daeng3' daeng3'	My face is really red.

Another way of intensifying the quality of an adjective is to use the word "very = lai4".

3.5 Comparative adjectives 1/

gwa2	more than, -er
ti2 sut3	most, -est
gwa2 mu2	more than others/ most
tao:2 dai:1 haeng3 di1	the --- the better

di1 gwa2	better
di1 ti2 su:t3	best
di1 gwa2 mu2	better than others/best
lai4 tao:2 dai1 haeng3 di1	the more the better

3.6 Common value suffixes + Prefixes for adjectives:

di1	positive value suffix
ki6	negative value prefix

1/ See also pp.95/8-24 and 136/12-4

ngiap⁵ di¹	quiet enough
gwang ⁵ di¹	wide enough
ki⁶ lai⁵	ugly
ki⁶ heung⁴	jealous
ki⁶ kan⁵	lazy

Section 4: Classifiers

4.1 In English, there are two types of nouns: countable nouns like "book" and uncountable ones like "water". English quantifies the uncountable nouns by measuring them in terms of countable objects; for example a loaf of bread, a drop of water, a roll of paper, a bunch of bananas, a herd of cattle, etc. On the other hand, Lao quantifies all its nouns in terms of countable objects, or more precisely, in terms of classes of objects. Consequently, the count words are known as "classifiers". The main classifiers in Lao are listed on the following page.

4.2 In practice, all numerals that indicate the quantity of a noun (like one elephant or two trees) are always used with classifiers. These classifiers are similar to adjectives in that they follow the noun they classify. The typical word order is Noun-Number-Classifier as shown in the following examples:

nohng⁵ sai⁵ sohng⁴ ko:n³	Younger brother two people (ie, two younger brothers)
sang⁵ si:p³ dtua¹	Elephant ten animals (ie, ten elephants)
mai:⁵ cha:n¹ sam⁴ go:k³	Sandlewood three trees (ie, three sandlewood trees)

However, the position of the number "one" is an exception. It's location in the sentence differs from all other numbers in that it follows the classifier (Noun-Classifier-"One" instead of preceeding it.

heuan³ la:ng⁴ neu:ng²	House building one (one house)
chia⁵ bai:¹ neu:ng²	Paper sheet one (one sheet of paper)

LIST OF COMMON CLASSIFIERS

a:n^{1}. Thing (for general objects)

baep^{6}. Style, way

bai:^{1}. Leaf, sheet

bohn^{2}. Place

dohk^{6}. Flower

dto:n^{5}. Plant, tree

dto^{1}. Animal

dtua^{1}. Body, animal

ga:p^{3}. Box

gaew^{5}. Bottle

go:k^{3}. Tree

gohk^{6}. Cigarette

gohn^{5}. Solids, soap, cake

gohng^{1}. A group

hohng^{6}. Room

hua^{4}. Vegetables, head, round objects

hup^{5}. Picture

ka:n^{3}. Machines, vehicles

kap^{5}. Meal

ko:n^{3}. Person

ku^{2}. A pair

la:m^{3}. Boat, plane

muat^{6}. Combined units

naew^{3}. Kind, sort

nuay^{2}. Fruit, Small round objects

o:ng^{1}. Holy person

peun^{4}. Cloth, rolls

sa:^{3} ba:p^{3}. Copy

sa:n^{5}. Floor

se:n^{4}. Line road, long objects

sohng^{3}. Envelope

taew^{4}. Row

teua^{2}. Times

ti^{3}. Times, -th

tiaw^{2}. Journey, trip

wi^{4}. Banana, comb

yang^{2}. Example

la:ng^{4}. Building, homes

le:m^{3}. Book

loh:t^{6}. Tube

luk^{5}. Bullet, ball

ma:t^{2}. Bound bunch, bundle

me:t^{2}. Grain

mu^{2}. Group

Section 5: Verbs and Tenses

5.1 Verbs have only one form no matter who or what their subject is.

kohy 6	ma 3	I	come
chao: 5	ma 3	You	come
lao 3	ma 3	He	comes
hao: 3	ma 3	We	come
chao: 5	ma 3	You (pl.)	come
kao: 4 chao: 5	ma 3	They	come

5.2 Verbs have only one form no matter what tense they indicate. Tenses are indicated by additional word particles (discussed one by one in the paragraphs which follow)[1/] which are either placed before or after the verb.

a. The <u>past</u> tense particle "laew 5" follows the verb and the past tense particle "dai: 5" comes before the verb:

laew 5	Already	2/
dai: 5	Did, already	

lao 3 ma 5 <u>laew 5</u>	He came
lao 3 yu 2 ni 5 <u>laew 5</u>	He was here
kohy 6 boh 2 <u>dai: 5</u> bpai: 1	I didn't go

b. The <u>future</u> tense particle comes before the verb or the negative if there is one. The future tense can be formed with either of two words "si: 2 or cha: 3") since they are interchangeable.

si: 2	Will
cha: 3	Will

chao: 5 <u>si: 2</u> ma 3 boh 2	Will you come?
kohy 6 <u>si: 2</u> boh 2 ma 3	I will not come.
lao 3 <u>cha: 3</u> bpai: 1 wiang 3 cha:n 1	He will go to Vientiane.

1/ Refer also to page 107/9-12 (<u>imperative</u> (must, should, have to) and page 118/10-4 <u>progressive</u> (to be (do)ing now).

2/ See also p.37/3-9

c. Perfect tenses in Lao are formed by placing the particle "kery3" in front of the verb.

kery3	Have, has

kohy6 kery3 bpai:1 bpak6 se3	I have gone to Pakse.

d. The passive voice is formed by placing the particle "teuk6"

teuk6	Was ... - ed

ki6 la:k2 teuk6 cha:p3	The robber was captured
kohng4 ni5 teuk6 so:ng2 ma3 chak6 wiang3 cha:n1	These things were brought from Vientiane.

The subject or actor can be inserted between "teuk6" the verb and the passive voice still maintained, as follows:

ki6 la:k2 teuk6 dta:m1 luat5 cha:p3	The robber was caught by the police.

5.3 In Lao many verbs can be placed one after another in a chain without intervening words. The verbs are assummed to be arranged in the order in which the action took place. 1/

lao3 bpai:1 hian3 yu2 bpa3 tet5 lao3	He went to study in Laos.
lao3 hian3 bpai:1 yu2 bpa3 tet6 lao3	He studied to go live in Laos.

5.4 "Yes" answers are commonly given in Lao by simply repeating the verb(s). Similarly, "No" answers are made by negating and repeating the verb(s).

chao:5 mi3 ay5 boh2. mi3	Do you have brothers? Yes.
chao:5 kery3 bpai:1 dta:3 lat6 boh2. boh2 kery3 bpai:1	Have you ever gone to market? No.

5.5 The verb "TO BE" in English has three main forms in Lao: 2/

maen2	To link subject and predicate.
bpe:n1	To indicate class, group, condition.
yu2	To indicate location.

a:n1 ni5 maen2 nya:ng4	What is this?
kian4 bpe:n1 dtua1 peu:m5	The writing is to be in capital letters
ban5 kohy6 yu2 ni5	My house is here

5.6 The verb "CAN" in English has two main forms in Lao.

dai:5	For permission, possibility
bpe:n1	For skill, learned activity

chao:5 ma3 dai:5 boh2	Can you come?
ka:p3 lo:t2 bpe:n1 boh2	Can you drive a car?

1/ See also pp.28/2-6 and 69/6-13
2/ See also pp.20/1-3 and 36/3-5

5.7 a. "Bpai:1 and ma3" as auxillary verbs usually indicate the direction of the action from the speakers point of view: 1/

bpai:1	The action is going away from the speaker.
ma3	The action is coming towards the speaker.

lo:t2 ohk6 <u>bpai:1</u> laew5 — The car left already.

nai3 ku3 ohk6 <u>ma3</u> dtae2 hohng6 hian — The teacher is coming from the classroom.

kohy6 si:2 pa3 chao:5 <u>bpai:1</u> dta3 lat6 sao:5 — I'll take you to the Morning market.

lao3 dai:5 pa3 kohy6 <u>ma3</u> ni5 — He brought me here.

b. As an anxillary verb "go and come" can also be used to describe a thought.

o5 kohy6 leum3 <u>bpai:1</u> — Oh! I forgot that completely (that has gone completely out of my mind).

Section 6: Adverbs

6.1 1. As in English, adverbs of time can come at the beginning or end of a sentence, or before or after the predicate.

<u>diaw1 ni5</u> hao:3 si:2 bpai:1 sai:4 — <u>Now</u> where shall we go?

hao:3 yu2 sai:4 <u>diaw1 ni5</u> — Where are we <u>now</u>?

6.2 Adjectives can function as adverbs, in which case they have an adverbial meaning. 2/

	Adj.	Adv.
ge:ng2	Clever, good	Well
mai:2	New	Again

lao3 <u>ge:ng2</u> — He is <u>clever</u>.

tan2 bpak6 pa3 sa4 lao3 <u>ge:ng2</u> — You speak Lao <u>well</u>.

la:ng4 ni5 maen2 heuan3 <u>mai:2</u> — This building is a <u>new</u> house.

kohy6 cha:3 ma3 yiam5 yam1 <u>mai:2</u> — I'll come visit <u>again</u>.

6.3 In Lao, one way to give emphasis to an adverb is by repeating it. 3/

bpai:1 <u>wai:3 wai:3</u> — Go <u>very fast</u>!

mi3 <u>lai4 lai4</u> — There are <u>so many</u>!

1/ See also p.20/1-1 and 1-2
2/ See also p.54/5-7
3/ See also p.44/4-4 and 4-5

6.4 "Wai:5" - As a simple adverb, "wai:5" means "down" or "keep" (and implies for a future reason).

kian4 seu2 wai:5 ni5	Write down your name.
wang3 wai:5 ni5	Put it down here, keep it here.

6.5 "Sai:2" - As a simple adverb "sai:2" means "in". 1/

ao:1 na:m5 dtan1 sai:2 ga1 fe3	Put sugar in the coffee.

However, as a verb sai:2 means "to put on".

sai:2 seua6 pa6	Put on your clothes.

Section 7: Connecting Particles

7.1 "Wa2" Typically this word introduces a secondary thought. Occasionally it is used as a verb to mean "say".

kohy6 ki:t2 wa2	I think that .....
kohy6 wa2 chao:5 bpai:1 goh1 dai:5	I say you can go.
dtae2 wa5	But....
ta6 wa2	If ....

7.2 "Cheu:ng2" ("then", "so", "because") indicates a causal relationship between two thoughts (pattern: cause - effect). 2/

liaw5 sai5 cheu:ng2 boh2 mi3 ki6 fu:n2	Turn right so you can avoid the dust.
bpaet6 si:p3 cheu:ng2 cha:3 bpai:1	80 kip, then I'll go.
bpe:n1 nya:ng4 cheu:ng2 paeng3 tae5	Why is it so expensive?
lo:t2 chao:5 pe3 boh2 cheu:ng2 boh2 ki2 ma3	Has your car broken down? Then you didn't come by car.

7.3 "Goh1" ("then", "because") introduces a secondary thought (pattern: statement - reason). 3/

hian3 lai4 teua2 goh1 leum3 lery3	I study all the time, then I forget it right away.
kao:4 chao:5 goh1 bpai:1 dta:3 lat6	They then will go to the market.
kohy6 goh1 yak6 hian3 keu3 ga:n1	I then want to study too.
yak6 bpai:1 ber:ng2 si:2 ne3 ka:3 chao:5 goh1 sai:5 yu2 wa:t2	I want to see a movie because they're showing one at the temple.

1/ See also p.137/12-8
2/ See also p.53/5-6
3/ See also p.93/8-18

7.4 "Ti^{2}" ("that, which, what, for") introduces a secondary claus or thought.

so:m^{6} mu^{4} maen^{2} kohng^{4} gi:n^{1} lao^{3} ti^{2} kohy^{6} ma:k^{2} lai^{4}	Sour meat is the Lao food which I like very much.
keuang^{2} ti^{2} chao:^{5} dtohng^{5} gan^{1} yu^{2} tang^{3} ni^{5}	The things that you need are over there.
kohp^{6} chai:^{5} lai^{4} lai^{4} ti^{2} pa^{3} ma^{3}	Thank you very much for taking me
kohy^{6} nyi:n^{3} di^{1} ti^{2} dai:^{5} po:p^{2} chao:^{5}	I am happy that I met you.

7.5 "Dta:ng^{5}" ("so" many, so much) shows the number of items mentioned is unusual.

he:n^{4} chao:^{5} sen^{5} bpi^{5} dta:ng^{5} lai:^{4} bai:^{1}	I see you bought so many tickets.
dta:ng^{5} sam^{3} si^{2} hohy^{5} ko:n^{3} ma^{3} gi:n^{1} liang^{5}	3 or 4 hundred people came to the party.

Section 8: Symbols and Punctuation

Symbol	Name	Function
ໆ	goh:^{3} la:^{2}	repeat the previous word
ໆ	goh:^{3} la:^{2}	ditto mark
ໆລໆ	nya:ng^{3} mi^{3} ik^{6} dtoh^{2} bpai:^{1}	et cetera (etc.)
.	me:t^{2}	period
,	chu:t^{3}	comma
:	sohng^{4} me:t^{2}	colon
-	kit^{6} ka:n^{6}	hyphen
————	kit^{6} mai^{4}	underlining
....	me:t^{2} la:^{2}	omission
?	tam^{4}	question mark
!	a:t^{3} sa:^{3} cha:n^{1}	exclamation mark
" "	le:p^{2} sohn^{5}	quotation marks
( )	wo:ng^{3} le:p^{2}	parentheses
໑ ໒ ໓ ໔ ໕ ໖ ໗ ໘ ໙	lek^{5}	numbers (1 to 9)

PART 3: HOW TO READ LAO

THE LESSON PLAN

	CONSONANTS							VOWELS				TONE MARKS		TONES						
	Kang	Nasal finals (n, ng, m)	Tam	Sung	Aspirants	Stops (p, t, k)	Consonant clusters (-w-) and the missing "a:"	Long	Short	Diphthongs (ia, ua, eua)	Semi-vowels (-w, -y)	Mai ek	Mai to	1 Low	2 Mid	3 High	4 Rising	5 High falling	6 Low falling	Page
SON 1	(X)							X						X						162
SON 2	X											X			X					164
SON 3	(X)								X							X				167
SON 4		X	(X)																	169
SON 5										X										172
SON 6			(X)								X									174
SON 7			X												X	X				176
SON 8				X												X	X			179
SON 9					X															183
SON 10													X					X	X	185
SON 11						X												X	X	188
SON 12							X													191

Introduction on Tones and Letters

The reading mastery of Lao words can be achieved step by step with the exercises in this section. Reading mastery covers two elements: the learning of an alphabet originating from an ancient Indian script, and the development of the ability to read tones.

1. TONES

The role of tones in the Lao Language is large since each word has a tone which is coded as part of its spelling. In fact, the tones are often the only way to distinguish between words; some examples of words with the same sound but different tones are shown below.

Sound of word	Case A		Case B	
	Tone	Meaning	Tone	Meaning
gai:	1	far	5	near
ha	4	meet	6	five
kao:	4	they	6	rice
poh	3	father	2	enough
mu	4	pig	2	friend
sao:	2	rent	5	morning
si	2	four	4	color

In Lao there are six tones which are relative in pitch to each other. They are summarized in the following table and referred to by number: 1, 2 and 3 are level tones, 4 is a rising tone, 5 and 6 are falling tones.

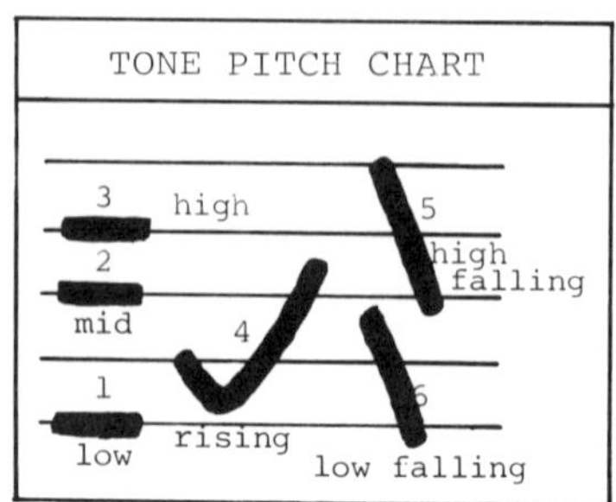

The way to read the tone of a Lao word is from its spelling which is a code combination of four possible letters:

1. an initial consonant: 3 types (kang, tan and sung)
2. a vowel : 2 types (long and short)
3. a final consonant : 3 types (stops, nasals and others)
4. a tone mark : 2 common types (mai ek and mai to)

The code for tone determination is summarized below and then introduced in a progressive learning sequence in the lessons which follow.

TONE DETERMINATION CODE

The spelling of Lao words determines their tone.

Consonant group \ Vowel and tone mark	Long or Long+ nasal or Short+ nasal	Short or Short+ stop	Long+stop	Tone mark	
				mai ek	mai to
Kang Group	1	3	6	2	5
Tam Group	3	2	5	2	5
Sung Group	4	3	6	2	6

2. LETTERS

Lao letters are not written one after another in a string, as in English. Rather, each of four types of Lao letters (initial consonant, vowel, final consonant and tone marks) are written in different positions in a syllable. The seven possible positions in the Lao syllable for each of the four types of letters are shown below.

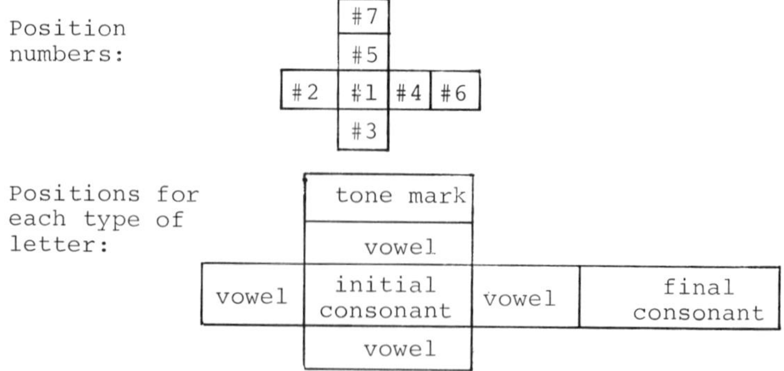

The four types of Lao letters are further summarized in the paragraphs which follow.

1) INITIAL CONSONANTS - first letter, position #1. Every Lao word must have an initial consonant which is in the position #1. There are three groups of Lao consonants or "akson":

   a. kang

   b. tam

   c. sung

Note: Do not attempt to translate the Lao names of the consonant groups into English as these names relate to their old tone which is no longer used and will only confuse you.

2) VOWELS - second letter, position #2, #3, #4 and/or #5. Every Lao word (syllable) must have a vowel. Depending on which vowel, it might be written in any one or combination of positions #2 to #5. There are two types of vowels:

   a. long vowels

   b. short vowels

Unlike English, long vowels and short vowels in Lao have the same sound; they differ only with respect to the duration over which they are pronounced.

3) FINAL CONSONANTS - third letter, position #6.
Only some Lao words have a final consonant which if it exists, is written in the #6 position. There are only two significant groups of final consonants:

a. nasal finals (n, ng, m)

b. unreleased stops (k, p, t)

4) TONE MARKS - fourth letter, position #7.
Only some Lao words have a tone mark which, if it exists, is written in the #7 position. Although there are four tone marks in Lao, two of the marks (mai chadtawa and mai dti) are rarely used. The 4 tone marks are as follows:

Common:	x່	mai[5] ek[1]	fixes the tone of all syllables as mid-tone.
	x້	mai[5] to[4]	fixes the tone of all syllables as a falling tone.
Rare:	x໊	mai[5] dti[1]	raises the tone of a syllable.
	x໋	mai[5] cha:[3] dta:[3] wa[3]	

Although the focus of PART 3 is on teaching reading, large-size letters are introduced to clearly show how the written letters are formed. The loop is always the starting point for writing a letter. Most consonants contain a loop; however, this starting loop is not essential and it is often omitted when writing in cursive script. Nonetheless, the reason it is usually included is that this loop makes writing look more attractive.

Note: The phonetic equivalents of all exercises are listed at the end of PART 3 after Lesson 12 (page 194).

LESSON 1: kang + long = tone 1

3
2
1 ▬ low tone

The first tone, tone 1, is a low tone. It is coded by an akson kang consonant (low tone consonant) and a long vowel. In this lesson, one of the akson kang consonants and the basic long vowels are covered.

In an initial position the consonant ອ (pronounced "oh'") is an akson kang consonant (ie, it belongs to the group of consonants to be introduced in Lesson 2). When the consonant is the initial letter of a word, it has no consonant sound unlike the other consonants such as "boh'" which have sounds ("b", etc.). Thus, a syllable with the initial consonant "oh'" plus a vowel ("a") is simply pronounced as the vowel ("a'"). When this akson kang consonant is followed by a long vowel sound, the resulting syllable is spoken on tone 1. Because it has no consonant sound, this letter is the silent first letter of all syllables beginning with a vowel sound which is needed in writing since all written words must start with a consonant letter.

In Lao there are nine basic long vowels. Each vowel is written in a fixed position relative to the initial consonant; this position is called its picture. Although each vowel has only one picture, the pictures of all vowels are not the same: some vowels are written above the consonant, some below, some before, some after, and some have a combination of positions. The basic vowel pictures relative to the initial consonant ອ are shown below; all are pronounced on tone 1.

CHART OF BASIC VOWEL POSITIONS

	Above i' eu' oh'		
	ອີ ອື ອໍ		
Before e' ae' o'	**Initial consonant**	**After** a'	**Combination** er'
ເອ ແອ ໂອ	ອ	ອາ	ເອີ
	Below u'		
	ອູ		

Contrast Exercise

1.1	ອາ	ອີ	ແອ	ເອ
1.2	ອໍ	ໂອ	ອູ	ອື
1.3	ເອີ	ອື	ອູ	ໂອ

Reading Exercise

1.4	ອີ	ອາ	ອີ	ເອ	ອູ
1.5	ໂອ	ແອ	ອື	ເອີ	ອໍ
1.6	ເອ	ອາ	ເອີ	ແອ	ອີ
1.7	ອູ	ອໍ	ອື	ໂອ	ເອ

Letter Writing Style : Basic Long Vowels

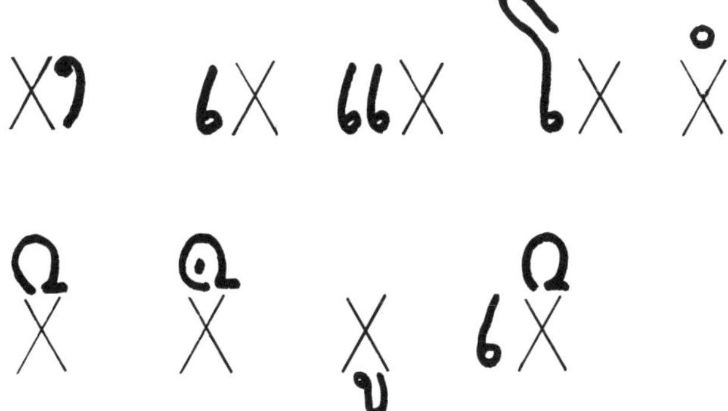

LESSON 2: mai ek + any syllable = tone 2

There are eight akson kang letters; one you know already (oh'). The following chart presents all the akson kang consonants which, when spoken as letters, are pronounced on tone 1 since the letter name includes a long vowel.

No initial consonant sound	Voiced			Voiceless			
oh'	boh'	doh'	yoh'	bpoh'	dtoh'	goh'	choh'
ອ	ບ	ດ	ຢ	ປ	ຕ	ກ	ຈ

Note: Aspiration is a little puff of air that you can feel with your hand when you say the English letters "k" or "p" or "t". Each of these aspirated letters has an unaspirated counterpart which, when spoken, has no significant puff of air; for example, when you say the English letter "g". (Try the hand test.) The unaspirated letters "bp" and "dt" in Lao occur as initial sounds, whereas in English they occur only as medial sounds, as in the words "happy" and "bottle". These sounds seem to be halfway between the letters "b and p" and between "d and t" respectively; hence the phonetic transcripts "bp" and "dt".

The new tone introduced in this lesson is tone 2, which is a level mid tone.

3
2 ▬ mid tone
1

Tone 2 is coded by a mai ek tone mark on any syllable. A mai ek looks like the number 1. It is written above the first consonant of a syllable (x̍). The drills in this lesson are designed to help you learn to hear the new kang sounds and the new tone introduced here (tone 2).

Contrast Exercise

2.1	ບາ	ປາ	ດາ	ຕາ
2.2	ບີ	ປີ	ເດ	ເຕ
2.3	ແບ	ແປ	ດູ	ຕູ
2.4	ໂບ	ໂປ	ດໍ	ຕໍ
2.5	ເບີ	ເປີ		

Tone Exercise

2.6	ບໍ	ບໍ່	ດາ	ດ່າ
2.7	ປູ	ປູ່	ເກົາ	ເກົ່າ
2.8	ປາ	ປ່າ	ຈີ	ຈີ່
2.9	ຕໍ	ຕໍ່	ໂກ	ໂກ່

Reading Exercise

2.10	ອາ	ດາ	ປາ
2.11	ຕີ	ຈີ	ກີ
2.12	ເບ	ເປ	ເດ
2.13	ບື	ກື	ຈື
2.14	ປູ	ຕູ	ອູ
2.15	ແຈ	ແດ	ແກ
2.16	ເອີ	ເບີ	ເຕີ
2.17	ໂປ	ໂດ	ໂກ
2.18	ປໍ	ບໍ	ຈໍ

Letter Writing Style: Kang Consonants

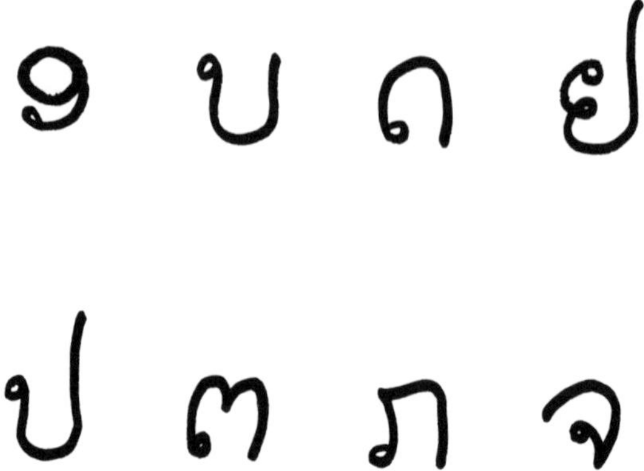

LESSON 3: kang + short = tone 3

3 ▬ high tone
2
1

This lesson introduces a new tone, tone 3, which is a level high tone. It is coded by an akson kang consonant combined with a short vowel. The short vowels are spoken with the same sound as the long vowels, only their duration is shorter and they end with a sudden stop which is phoneticized as a colon(:). A syllable composed of an akson kang consonant with a short vowel is spoken on tone 3. The following chart compares the short and long vowel written forms of the nine basic vowels.

BASIC SHORT AND LONG VOWELS

Short vowels	a:^{3}	e:^{3}	ae:^{3}	o:^{3}	oh:^{3}	i:^{3}	eu:^{3}	u:^{3}	er:^{3}
	ອະ	ເອະ	ແອະ	ໂອະ	ເອາະ	ອິ	ອຶ	ອຸ	ເອິ
Long vowels	a'	e'	ae'	o'	oh'	i'	eu'	u'	er'
	ອາ	ເອ	ແອ	ໂອ	ອໍ	ອີ	ອື	ອູ	ເອີ

NOTE A NOTE B NOTE C

Notice three changes for writing short vowels:

A. The symbol xະ is often used as part of the vowel picture to indicate a short vowel.

B. The symbol ເອາະ is quite different from its long vowel form ອໍ.

C. Many long vowels merely subtract a tail to form their short vowel form.

Duration Exercise

3.1 ອະ ອາ ບີ ບິ

3.2 ເຕະ ເຕ ແກ ແກະ

3.3 ເຕາະ ຕໍ ປູ ປຸ

3.4 ເກິ ເກີ

Tone Exercise

3.5 ຈີ ຈີ້ ຈິ ຕາ ຕ່າ ຕະ

3.6 ບໍ ບໍ້ ເບາະ ໂດ ໂດ່ ໂດະ

3.7 ອູ ອູ່ ອຸ ອື ອື້ ອຶ

3.8 ແປ ແປ່ ແປະ ເອ ເອ່ ເອະ

3.9 ເກີ ເກີ້ ເກິ

Reading Exercise

3.10 ອະ ບິ ເບະ ແປະ ດຸ

3.11 ອຶ ໂດະ ເຕາະ ເກິ ຈະ

3.12 ໂຢະ ກຸ ດະ ຕິ ເຈິ

3.13 ເອາະ ເຕະ ກະ ຈຸ ຕຶ

Letter Writing Style: Basic Short Vowels

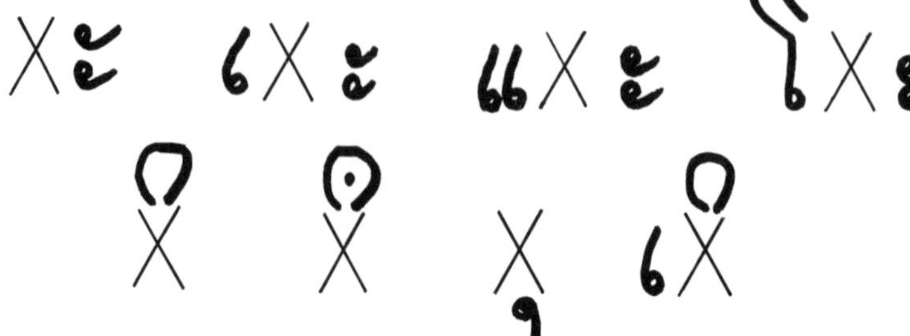

LESSON 4: Nasal finals (-n, -ng, -m)

There are three nasal consonants (n, ng and m). When used as final consonants, nasal consonants code only the tone of syllables with short vowels. For example, an akson kang plus only a short vowel is a code for tone 3, but with a nasal final it is a code for tone 1. An akson kang with a long vowel, with or without a nasal final, is a code for tone 1. An akson kang with a long vowel, with or without a nasal final, is a code for tone 1. The nasal finals are tam consonants. They are written as follows and spoken on tone 3.

	Long vowel syllable			Short vowels syllable		
Without final	a'	e'	i'	a:^{3}	e:^{3}	i:^{3}
With nasal final	an'	eng'	im'	a:n'	e:ng'	i:m'

In certain cases a final consonant changes the written picture of the vowel in a syllable. The following table indicates these changes:

	a	e	ae	o	oh	i	eu	u	er
List of long vowels	×າ	ເ×	ແ×	ໂ×	×ໍ	×ີ	×ື	×ູ	ເ×ີ
Long which have new forms with final consonants	-	-	-	-	×ອ×	-	-	-	-
	a:	e:	ae:	o:	oh:	i:	eu:	u:	er:
List of short vowels	×ະ	ເ×ະ	ແ×ະ	ໂ×ະ	ເ×າະ	×ິ	×ຶ	×ຸ	ເ×ິ
Short which have new forms with final consonants	×ັ×	ເ×ັ×	ແ×ັ×	×ົ×	×ັອ×	-	-	-	-
		NOTE A		NOTE B	NOTE C				

There are three types of changes in writing vowels in syllables with final letters:

A. In most cases when words end in a final letter, the symbol for a short vowel ×ະ changes to a symbol known as a mai^5 ga:n^1 (×ັ×) which is written above the initial consonant.

B. The one exception is the vowel ໂ×ະ which changes completely to a new symbol known as a mai^5 go:n^1 (×ົ×) when followed by a final consonant; it is written above the initial consonant.

C. The vowel ×ໍ changes to the letter ×ອ× in syllables with final letters; its short form ເ×າະ changes to a similar vowel symbol which is distinguishable by the addition of a mai ga:n (×ັອ×). (Note: This vowel symbol is the same symbol as the akson kang consonant ອ, but used after an initial consonant instead of being the initial consonant itself.

The final sound -a:m has two different pictures: (×ັມ) and (×ຳ). Both follow the tone rules for a short vowel ending with a nasal final, although the latter form is preferred in writing.

CUMULATIVE TONE CODES	
Tone 1	kang + long kang + short + nasal
Tone 2	any syllable + mai ek
Tone 3	kang + short

TONE PITCH CHART	
3	high
2	mid
1	low

Contrast Exercise

4.1 ຕາງ ຕາມ ດາມ ດາມ

4.2 ກາງ ກາມ ຈາມ ຈາມ

4.3 ຢາງ ຢາມ ປາມ ປາມ

Duration Exercise

4.4 ຂາງ ຂັມ ຈາງ ຈັມ

4.5 ອາມ ອັມ ກາມ ກັມ

4.6 ຕາມ ຕຳ ຈາມ ຈຳ

Reading Exercise

4.7 ໂອງ ແອມ ອອມ ອຶງ ອິມ ອົມ

4.8 ອ່າງ ເອ່ມ ອ່ອມ ອຶ່ງ ອຸ່ມ ອ່ຳ

4.9 ຂາງ ຂາມ ໂຂມ ເຂັງ ຂິມ ຂຳ

4.10 ແຂ່ງ ຂ່ອມ ເຂ່ມ ຂຶ່ງ ຂິ່ມ ຂ່ຳ

4.11	ປອງ	ປານ	ໂປນ	ປຸງ	ເປັນ	ປິນ
4.12	ເປ່ງ	ເປີ້ນ	ປ່ານ	ປົ້ງ	ປີ້ນ	ປຸ່ນ
4.13	ແດງ	ເດີນ	ດອນ	ດຶງ	ດິນ	ດຳ
4.14	ດ່າງ	ເດີ້ນ	ດ່ານ	ດົ້ງ	ດັ້ນ	ດື້ນ
4.15	ຕອງ	ຕອນ	ຕານ	ເຕັງ	ຕິນ	ຕຳ
4.16	ຕ່າງ	ຕື້ນ	ຕ່ອນ	ຕັ້ງ	ຕຸ່ນ	ຕ່ຳ
4.17	ກອງ	ເກນ	ແກນ	ກຸງ	ກັນ	ກືນ
4.18	ແກ່ງ	ກ່ອນ	ໂກ່ນ	ກັ້ງ	ກິ້ນ	ກ່ຳ
4.19	ໂຢງ	ຢືນ	ຢືນ	ຢັງ	ຢັນ	ຢຳ
4.20	ຢ່າງ	ຢ່ອນ	ຢື້ນ	ຢັ້ງ	ຢັ້ນ	ຢ່ຳ
4.21	ເຈີງ	ຈືນ	ຈອນ	ເຈັງ	ຈຸນ	ຈຳ
4.22	ແຈ່ງ	ເຈີ້ນ	ຈ່ານ	ຈື້ງ	ຈົ້ນ	ຈ່ຳ

Letter Writing Style : Nasal Finals

LESSON 5: Diphthongs (ia, ua, eua)

Diphthongs are combinations of two vowel sounds (i or u or eu plus a). They follow the same tone code rules as long and short simple vowels. Their written picture involves a combination of several positions. Some of the pictures even change form when they are in a syllable with a final consonant. The following table lists all the dipthongs and their variant forms.

	ia	ua	eua
List of long diphthongs	ເxັຍ	xົວ	ເxືອ
Long which change with final consonants	xຽx	xວx	-
	ia:	ua:	eua:
List of short diphthongs	ເxັຍະ	xົວະ	ເxືອ
Short which have new forms with final consonants	xັຽx	xັວx	-

CUMULATIVE TONE CODES	
Tone 1	kang + long kang + short + nasal
Tone 2	any syllable + mai ek
Tone 3	kang + short

TONE PITCH CHART	
3	high
2	mid
1	low

Duration Exercise

5.1 ເປັຽ ເປັຽະ ເດືອ ເດືອ

5.2 ຕົວ ຕົວະ

Tone Exercise

5.3 ເບືອ ເບື້ອ ຈົວ ຈ໊ວ

5.4 ອຽນ ອ່ຽນ ກຽງ ກ່ຽງ

Reading Exercise

5.5 ອຽນ ບ່ຽງ ເປັຽ ດຽນ

5.6 ຕຽນ ກ່ຽງ ເຈັ້ຽ ຈຽນ

5.7 ອ໊ວ ບ໊ວ ປອງ ດ່ອນ

5.8 ຕອງ ກອນ ຢ່ອງ ຈົວ

5.9 ເອືອນ ເບື້ອ ເປືອງ ເດືອນ

5.10 ເກືອ ເຈື້ອງ ເກື້ອນ ເອືອນ

5.11 ເບັຽ ເປັຽ ເດັຽ ເຈັຽ ເຈັ້ຽ

5.12 ອ໊ວ ຕົວ ຈ໊ວ ບົວ ປົວ

5.13 ເກືອ ເດື່ອ ເຈືອ ເບືອ ເບື້ອ

Letter Writing Style

LESSON 6: Semi-vowels (-w, -y)

Semi-vowels are final letter combinations of a vowel and either w or y (ວ or ຍ). Semi-vowels are either long or short depending upon the long or short vowels in them. Semi-vowels function as final letters; hence, there can be no other letters following them. Tables listing all the semi-vowels are shown below.

Semi-vowel		ao	ew	aew	iw	iaw
-w	Long form	×າວ	ເ×ວ	ແ×ວ	×ີວ	×ຽວ
	Short form	ເ×ົາ	-	-	×ິວ	-

Semi-vowel		ai	oy	ohy	iy	uy	ery	uay	euay
-y	Long form	×າຍ	ໂ×ຍ	×ອຍ	×ີຍ	×ູຍ	ເ×ີຍ	×ວຍ	ເ×ືອຍ
	Short form	ໄ× , ໃ×	ໂ×ັຍ	-	×ິຍ	×ຸຍ	-	-	-

Note: As in English, the pronunciation of an initial consonant becomes softer when it is used in a final position. Consequently, the pronunciation of the semi-vowel ວ (as in ກຽວ) is not exactly the same as the tam consonant ວ (as in ວາ) although its picture is the same. Also the pronunciation of the semi-vowel ຍ (as in ລາຍ) is not exactly the same as the tam consonant ຍ (as in ແຍງ) although its picture is also the same.

CUMULATIVE TONE CODES	
Tone 1	kang + long vowel kang + short vowel + nasal
Tone 2	any syllable + mai ek
Tone 3	kang + short

TONE PITCH CHART	
3	high
2	mid
1	low

Tone Exercise

6.1	ອາວ	ອ່າວ	ເອີຍ	ເອີ່ຍ
6.2	ແອວ	ແອ່ວ	ອວຍ	ອ່ວຍ
6.3	ປາຍ	ປ່າຍ	ເປືອຍ	ເປື່ອຍ
6.4	ດຽວ	ດ່ຽວ	ຕິວ	ຕິ່ວ
6.5	ໃບ	ໃບ່	ເຕົາ	ເຕົ່າ
6.6	ໄກ	ໄກ່		

Duration Exercise

6.7	ຕາຍ	ໄຕ	ປ່າຍ	ໄປ່
6.8	ບາຍ	ໃບ	ບ່າຍ	ໃບ່
6.9	ປາວ	ເປົາ	ປ່າວ	ເປົ່າ
6.10	ຕາວ	ເຕົາ	ຕ່າວ	ເຕົ່າ

Reading Exercise

6.11	ບາຍ	ໂດຍ	ອອຍ	ຕູຍ	ຈອຍ	ເດືອຍ
6.12	ອຸຍ	ກຸຍ	ໃບ	ໄປ	ໃຕ	ໄກ
6.13	ດາວ	ແອວ	ກິວ	ດຽວ	ຢຽວ	ແຈວ
6.14	ຍິວ	ເອົາ	ເບົາ	ເຍົາ	ເຕົາ	ເກົາ

Letter Writing Style

LESSON 7: tam + long = tone 3

tam + short = tone 2

This lesson introduces the akson tam consonants (high tone consonants). You already are acquainted with five of these consonants: the three tam consonants which also function as the nasal finals ໝ,ໜ,ງ and the two tam consonants ວ and ຍ which also function as semi-vowels. Although there are new tone rules for these consonants, there are no new tones since akson tam consonants are spoken on tone 3 when followed by a long vowel, and on tone 2 when followed by a short vowel. The following table lists the akson tam consonants.

AKSON TAM CONSONANTS

noh^3	ngoh^3	moh^3	yoh^3	woh^3	foh^3	loh^3	loh^3	soh^3	hoh^3	poh^3	toh^3	koh^3
ໜ	ງ	ໝ	ຫຍ	ຫວ	ຝ	ຫຼ	ຫລ	ສ	ຫ	ຜ	ຖ	ຂ
NASALS		NOTE A				NOTE B				VOICED		

Note: A. The letter ໝ has two pictures of which ໝ is the more modern one, used mostly in handwriting, but not yet in printing.

B. Although there are two "loh" letters, the first is called "loh^3 lo:t^2" and the second "loh^3 ling^3".

CUMULATIVE TONE CODES	
Tone 1	tam + short + nasal kang + short tam + long
Tone 2	any syllable + mai ek tam + short
Tone 3	kang + long kang + short + nasal

TONE PITCH CHART	
3	high
2	mid
1	low

Duration Exercise

7.1 ຟາ ຟະ ອີ ອິ

7.2 ແງ ແງະ ອື ອຶ

7.3 ມູ ມຸ ໂຍ ໂຍະ

7.4 ຊໍ ເຊາະ ເຍັງ ເຍັງະ

7.5 ລິວ ລິວະ ເຊີ ເຊິ

Tone Exercise

7.6 ຟອນ ຟ່ອນ ຟັງ ຟັ່ງ

7.7 ແວນ ແວ່ນ ວັງ ວັ້ງ

7.8 ນາງ ນ່າງ ຍານ ຍ່ານ

7.9 ງານ ງ່ານ ງິນ ງິ້ນ

7.10 ແຮງ ແຮ່ງ ຮອນ ຮ່ອນ

7.11 ແລງ ແລ່ງ ລິນ ລິ້ນ

7.12 ຊິນ ຊິ້ນ ຊອງ ຊ່ອງ

Reading Exercise

7.13 ໄຟ ວຽງ ມ່ອນ ເມົາ ແມວ

7.14 ໃນ ນາຍ ເມືອງ ຍອນ ຍູຍ

7.15 ຍາວ ງ່າຍ ໄງ່ ຮຽນ ຮ່ວມ

7.16 ລາວ ລິວ ຊາຍ ຊ່ວຍ ຟອຍ

7.17 ຟາ ຟູ ເຟືອ ວີ ແວ

7.18 ວື ມາ ມີ ແມ ເມັຽ

7.19 ເມືອ ມາ ເມ ໂມ ເມີ

7.20 ນິວ ຍາ ຍໍ ເຍັຽ ງາ

7.21 ງູ ງິວ ແຣ ເຣືອ ຣູ

7.22 ຣາ ໂຣ ເຣ ລາ ລື

7.23 ລິວ ເລືອ ເລັຽ ຊາ ເຊ

7.24 ແຊ ຊື

Letter Writing Style: Tam Consonants

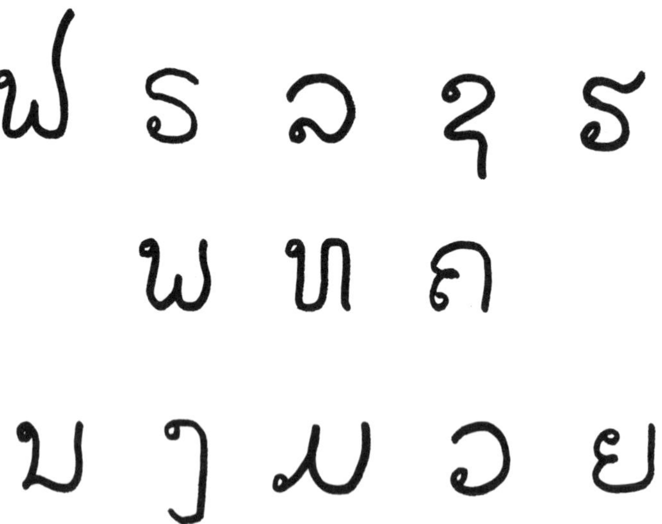

LESSON 8: sung + long = tone 4

sung + short = tone 3

3 2 1 ✓4 rising tone

The new tone introduced in this lesson tone 4, is a low rising tone. It is coded when an akson sung consonant (or rising tone consonant introduced below) is combined with a long vowel. The akson sung consonants have the same sounds as the akson tam consonants; however, akson sung consonants are spoken on tone 4, whereas the akson tam are spoken on tone 3. Each is lowered one tone when used with a short vowel.

When combined with short vowels, akson sung syllables are spoken on tone 3. Most of the akson sung consonants are prefixed or combined with the sung consonant ຫ as shown in the table below.

AKSON SUNG CONSONANTS

	hoh^4	woh^4	ngoh^4	loh^4	lch^4	moh^4	noh^4	nyoh^4	foh^4	soh^4	poh^4	toh^4	koh^4
Sung consonants	ຫ	ຫວ	ຫງ	ຫລ ຫຼ	ຫຣ	ໝ	ໜ	ຫຍ ຫຽ	ຝ	ສ	ຜ	ຖ	ຂ
				NOTE A				NOTE B					
Similar tam letter	ຣ	ວ	ງ	ລ	ຣ	ມ	ນ	ຍ	ຟ	ຊ	ພ	ທ	ຄ

Note: A. ຫຼ is the preferred picture today over its old picture ຫລ.

B. ຫຍ is the preferred picture today, but its old picture ຫຽ also still used.

Having studied all the consonants now, the following tone code generalization can be made about short vowels: they raise the tone of syllables with low consonants (kang and sung) to high tone 3, and they lower the tone of high consonants (tam) to mid tone 2.

CUMULATIVE TONE CODES	
Tone 1	kang + long kang + short + nasal
Tone 2	any syllable + mai ek tam + short kang + short
Tone 3	tam + long tam + short + nasal sung + short
Tone 4	sung + long sung + short + nasal

TONE PITCH CHART	
3 high	
2 mid	4 rising
1 low	

Duration Exercise

8.1 ທາ ທະ ແທງ ແທງະ

8.2 ສໍ ເສາະ ສູ ສຸ

8.3 ສື ສຶ ທີ ທິ

Tone Exercise

8.4 ຟາ ຜ້າ ເຟືອ ເຜືອ

8.5 ວານ ຫວານ ວິ ຫວິ

8.6 ນີ ໜີ ພອນ ນອນ

8.7 ຍັງ ຫຍັງ ເງົາ ເຫງົາ

8.8 ຣູ ຫຼູ ໄທ ໄຣ

8.9 ລາວ ຫຼາວ ສາຍ ຊາຍ

8.10 ເສົາ ເຊົາ ເສີນ ເຊີນ

8.11	ເນາະ	ເກາະ	ແສະ	ແຂະ
8.12	ວະ	ຫວະ	ສະ	ຂະ
8.13	ຫວານ	ຫວ່ານ	ໃໝ	ໃໝ່
8.14	ໝໍ	ໝໍ່	ໝຽງ	ໝ່ຽງ
8.15	ຫງຸນ	ຫງຸ່ນ	ຫາ	ຫ່າ
8.16	ຫໍ	ຫໍ່	ເຫົາ	ເຫົ່າ
8.17	ຫຼັງ	ຫຼັ່ງ	ຫຼໍ	ຫຼໍ່
8.18	ໃສ	ໃສ່	ສອງ	ສ່ອງ
8.19	ສີວ	ສີ່ວ	ເສົາ	ເສົ່າ

Reading Exercise

8.20	ຜາ	ຫວີ	ໝູ	ແໝ	ແຫງ
8.21	ຫງີ	ຫື	ຫຼໍ	ເສັງ	ສໍ
8.22	ເຜີ	ໝາ	ເໝືອ	ຫໍ	ເຫຼືອ
8.23	ສາ	ສີ	ຫຼາ	ໝີ	ຫິວ

Letter Writing Style : Sung Consonants

ຝ ສ ຜ ຖ ຂ

ຫ ຫວ ຫງ ຫຣ

ຫຼ ໜ ໝ ຫຍ

LESSON 9: Aspirants (k, t, p) and non-aspirants (g, dt, bp)

In each of the akson tam and akson sung consonant groups there are three aspirated consonants (p, t and k) which are spoken on tone 3 and tone 4 respectively. They differ from akson kang consonants because kang consonants are spoken on tone 1 and because kang consonants are not aspirated. Be sure to avoid aspiration when saying akson kang consonants, and be sure to pronounce aspiration clearly when saying tam or sung consonants. The following table lists the main aspirated and unaspirated consonants.

Aspirated letters						Unaspirated letters		
Tam			Sung			Kang		
koh^3	toh^3	poh^3	koh^4	toh^4	poh^4	goh^1	dtoh^1	bpoh^1
ค	ท	พ	ข	ถ	ผ	ก	ต	ป

Note: For a discussion of aspiration, see page 164 .

CUMULATIVE TONE CODES	
Tone 1	kang + long kang + short + nasal
Tone 2	any syllable + mai ek tam + short
Tone 3	kang + short tam + long tam + short + nasal sung + short
Tone 4	sung + long sung + short + nasal

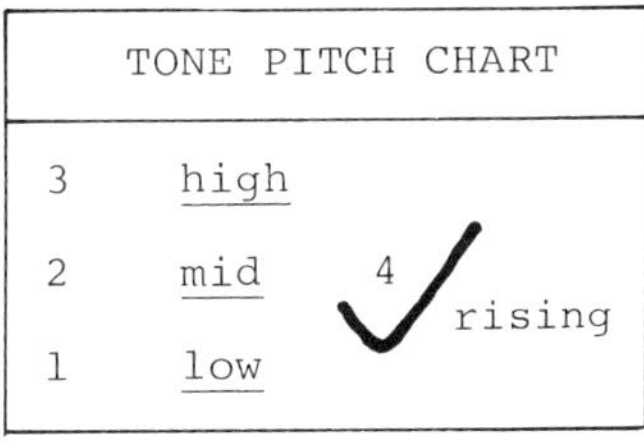

Tone Exercise

9.1 ຄາ ຂາ ຄຽງ ຂຽງ ໄຄ ໄຂ

9.2 ຄິວ ຂິວ ຄິ ຂິ ເຄາະ ເຂາະ

9.3 ທູ ຖູ ທອງ ຖອງ ໄທ ໄຖ

9.4 ທາມ ຖາມ ເທົາ ເຖົາ ທະ ຖະ

9.5 ພີ ຜີ ພິມ ຜິມ ໄພ ໃຜ

9.6 ແພງ ແຜງ ພຸ ຜຸ ພິວ ຜິວ

Contrast Exercise

9.7 ແກ ແຄ ກໍ ຄໍ ກຽວ ຄຽວ

9.8 ໂກະ ໂຄະ ກ່ອນ ຄ່ອນ ໄກ່ ໄຄ່

9.9 ຕາ ທາ ໄຕ ໄທ ຕາຍ ທາຍ

9.10 ເຕີ ເທີ ຕີ່ ທີ່ ຕ່ຽວ ທ່ຽວ

9.11 ປູ ພູ ໄປ ໄພ ປາຍ ພາຍ

9.12 ປະ ພະ ແປ່ ແພ່ ປ່ອງ ພ່ອງ

9.13 ຄື ຄຸ ໂຄະ ໂກະ ຄິ ກິ

9.14 ກັດ ກຸກ ກິດ ກີດ ຂັກ ຂັດ

9.15 ຂຸກ ຄັດ ຄັກ ຄີດ ຄືກ ຄິດ

LESSON 10: mai to + kang = tone 5
mai to + tam
mai to + sung = tone 6

3 5 high falling
2
1 6 low falling

The last two new tones are falling tones: tone 5 is high falling, and tone 6 is low falling. Tone 5 is coded by a mai to on any syllable beginning with an akson kang or akson tam consonant. Tone 6 is coded by a mai to on any akson sung syllable.

A mai to is a tone mark which looks like the number 2 with a long tail (x). It is written above the initial consonant of a syllable. The drills in this lesson are designed to help you learn to hear the new tones introduced here (tone 5 and tone 6).

CUMULATIVE TONE CODES	
Tone 1	kang + long kang + short + nasal
Tone 2	any syllable + mai ek tam + short
Tone 3	kang + short tam + long tam + short + nasal sung + short
Tone 4	sung + long sung + short + nasal
Tone 5	kang + mai to tam + mai to
Tone 6	sung + mai to

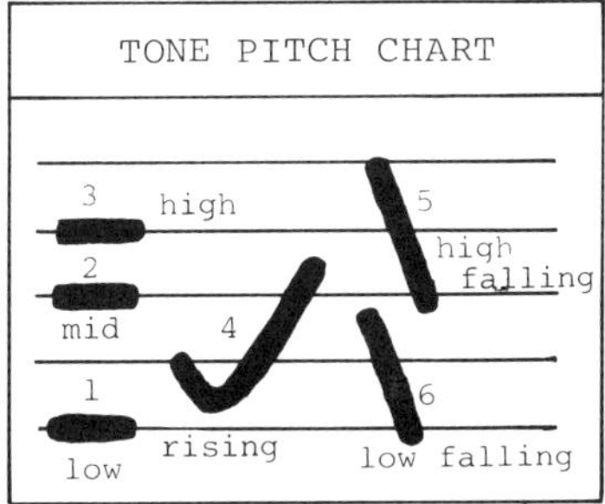

Tone Exercise

10.1 ຄ້າງ ຂ້າງ ຊ້າງ ສ້າງ

10.2 ທ້ອນ ຖ້ອນ ມິ້ນ ໝິ້ນ

10.3 ເທີ້ງ ເຖີ້ງ ຊ້ອນ ສ້ອນ

10.4 ຄ້ານ ຂ້ານ ເລື້ອາ ເຫຼື້ອງ

10.5 ຄ້ອນ ຂ້ອນ ຍຸ້ນ ຫງຸ້ນ

Reading Exercise

10.6 ອ້າ ແອ້ ອື້ ເອື້ອ ອື້

10.7 ເບ້ ບໍ້ ເບັ້ຍ ປູ້ ໂປ້

10.8 ດີ້ ດົ້ວ ແຕ້ ເຕັ້ຽ ກ້າ

10.9 ເກີ້ ໂປ້ ປີ້ ໂຈ້ ເຈັ້ຽ

10.10 ຄ້າ ຄໍ້ ທ້າ ແທ້ ພ້າ

10.11 ແພ້ ພໍ້ ຟ້າ ແວ້ ວໍ້

10.12 ມີ້ ມໍ້ ນ້າ ແນ້ ຍໍ້

10.13 ຢູ້ ງ້າ ງົ້ວ ຮູ້ ເຮື້ອ

10.14 ລ້າ ລໍ້ ຊົ້ ເຊົ້ ຊົ້

10.15 ຂໍ້ ຂີ້ ຖ່າ ຜ່າ ຜູ່

10.16 ຝ່າ ຫວ້າ ຫຼ້າ ເສື້ອ ຫໍ້

10.17 ໝ່າ ຫ່າ ຫິ້ວ ສໍ້ ໜ່າ

10.18 ເຫື້ອ ຫຣໍ້ ເຫ້ຽ ແຂ້ ສ່າ

10.19 ທ່າວ ຂ່ອຍ ເສົ້າ ໄຕ້ ເຈົ້າ

10.20 ເວົ້າ ໄຂ້ ເໝົ້າ ຕ່າຍ ໃຫ້

10.21 ໃຊ້ ເອື້ອຍ ພ່າວ ໄມ້ ຍ່າວ

10.22 ໃກ້ ຢ່າວ ທ່າຍ ຖ່ອຍ ເດົ້າ

10.23 ແງ້ວ ຫຼ່ອຍ ປ້ຽວ ຟ່າວ ແຂ້ວ

LESSON 11: Stops (-k, -t, -p)

kang + long + stop sung + long + stop	= tone 6
tam + long + stop	= tone 5

Stops are unreleased final consonants. There are only three final final sounds: k, t and p. Although there are many Lao consonants which can be written as final letters, they are all pronounced as one of the three final sounds. The following table lists the common and variant written forms of stops:

Pronunciation	Common written form	Variant written forms
k	ກ	ຄ ຂ
t	ດ	ຈ ສ ຊ ຕ ຖ ທ
p	ບ	ປ ຜ ພ

Stops only influence the tone codes of syllables with long vowels so that they are spoken with falling tone instead of level tones. Syllables coded with tam consonants and long vowels are spoken with a high falling tone (tone 5); syllables with kang or sung consonants and long vowels are spoken with a low falling tone (tone 6). The tones of syllables with short vowels are unaffected by the presence of a final stop.

<table>
<tr><th colspan="6">COMPLETE TONE DETERMINATION CODE</th></tr>
<tr><th rowspan="2">Vowel and tone mark / Consonant group</th><th rowspan="2">Long or Long+ nasal or Short nasal</th><th rowspan="2">Short or Short+ stop</th><th rowspan="2">Long +stop</th><th colspan="2">Tone mark</th></tr>
<tr><th>mai ek</th><th>mai to</th></tr>
<tr><td>Kang group</td><td>1</td><td>3</td><td>6</td><td>2</td><td>5</td></tr>
<tr><td>Tam group</td><td>3</td><td>2</td><td>5</td><td>2</td><td>5</td></tr>
<tr><td>Sung group</td><td>4</td><td>3</td><td>6</td><td>2</td><td>6</td></tr>
</table>

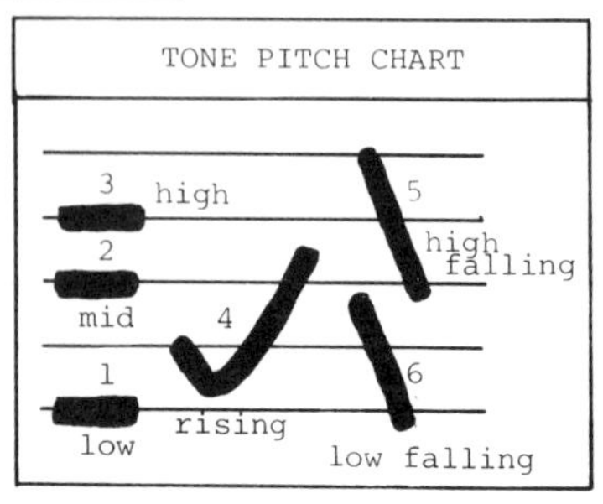

Tone Exercise

11.1	ຄອບ	ຂອບ	ທາດ	ຖາດ
11.2	ແພດ	ແຜດ	ຟາກ	ຝາກ
11.3	ໂວກ	ໂຫວກ	ມອບ	ໝອບ
11.4	ນາດ	ໜາດ	ຍາບ	ຫຍາບ
11.5	ໂງກ	ໂຫງກ	ຣິບ	ຫິບ
11.6	ລູບ	ຫລູບ	ແຊບ	ແສບ
11.7	ຊາບ	ສາບ	ລາບ	ຫຼາບ
11.8	ຄິດ	ຂິດ	ຄັບ	ຂັບ
11.9	ທຶກ	ຖຶກ	ພິດ	ຜິດ
11.10	ຟິດ	ຝິດ	ວັດ	ຫວັດ
11.11	ນັດ	ໜັດ	ນິດ	ໜິດ
11.12	ນັກ	ໜັກ	ຢຸດ	ຫຍຸດ
11.13	ງຸບ	ຫງຸບ	ຣິກ	ຫິກ
11.14	ເຣັດ	ເຫັດ	ເລັກ	ເຫຼັກ
11.15	ຊັກ	ສັກ	ຊິດ	ສິດ

Contrast Exercise

11.16	ອາດ	ອາກ	ອາບ	ແບດ	ແບກ	ແບບ
11.17	ເສິດ	ເສິກ	ເສິບ	ສາດ	ສາກ	ສາບ
11.18	ຣາດ	ຣາກ	ຣາບ	ໂງດ	ໂງກ	ໂງບ
11.19	ກັດ	ກັກ	ກັບ	ຂັດ	ຂັກ	ຂັບ
11.20	ຄັດ	ຄັກ	ຄັບ			

Reading Exercise

11.21 ອຶກ ອອກ ອາບ ບອກ ແບບ ປາກ

11.22 ແປດ ດອກ ແດດ ຕາກ ຕອບ ກຶກ

11.23 ກອກ ເກີດ ກີບ ປາກ ປອດ ຈອກ

11.24 ຈາກ ຈອດ ໂປດ ດດ ເອດ ບາດ

11.25 ອັດ ອິດ ບັກ ບິດ ປຸກ ເປັດ

11.26 ເດັກ ດິບ ຕຶກ ຕັດ ຕິກ ກິກ

11.27 ກັບ ປຸດ ຈັດ ເຈັດ ເຈັບ ຈິບ

11.28 ກະ ກີ ກຸ ຂະ ຂຸ ຄະ

11.29 ຄຶ ຄຸ ໂຄະ ໂກະ ຄີ ກີ

11.30 ກັດ ກຸກ ກິດ ກີດ ຂັກ ຂັດ

11.31 ຂຸກ ຄັດ ຄັກ ຄີດ ຄຶກ ຄິດ

LESSON 12: Consonant clusters and the missing "a:"

1. Consonant clusters are initial letters composed of an initial consonant and the tam consonant ວ. They are pronounced as one sound unit and follow the same tone code rules as their initial letters. The following are a list of the most common consonant clusters in Lao:

COMMON CONSONANT CLUSTERS

	w-	gw-	chw-
kang	ອວ	ກວ	ຈວ

	kw-	tw-	ngw-	hw-	lw-	sw-
tam	ຄວ	ທວ	ງວ	ຮວ	ລວ	ຊວ

	kw-	sw-
sung	ຂວ	ສວ

2. Many polysyllabic words in Lao omit writing the vowel ະ from one of their syllables; thus, they give the appearance of beginning with a consonant cluster except that they do not involve the letter "ວ". In addition, they are not pronounced as one sound unit. Instead, they are spoken as if the short vowel were written between the two consonants as shown in the following examples:

	Written form	Pronounced form	First consonant of each syllable
a.	ຄລາ	ka:la (ຄະລາ)	tam tam
b.	ຂຍາຍ	ka:nyai (ຂະຍາຍ)	sung tam
c.	ຕລາດ	dta:lat (ຕະລາດ)	kang tam
d.	ສບາຍ	sa:bai (ສະບາຍ)	sung kang

Note: Some polysyllabic words have a special tone code. If only the second letter is tam, as in examples b and c above, then the second syllable is spoken on the tone as if it began with an akson sung letter as shown with the same examples b and c below.

	Monosyllabic tone coding	Polysyllabic tone coding
b.	ka^3 nya^3	ka^3 $nyao^4$
c.	ta^3 lat^5	dta^3 lat^6

Reading Exercise

12.1 ອວ່າຍ ອວານ ກວາ ກວາງ ຈວາດ

12.2 ຄວ້າ ຄວາມ ຄວັນ ໄຄວ ແຄວກ

12.3 ທວາຍ ງວາກ ຣວາຍ ຣວ້າຍ ລວາ

12.4 ຊວ່ານ ຊວາງ ຂວາ ຂວັ້ນ ໄຂວ

12.5 ຖວາຍ ສວ່າງ ສວາຍ

12.6 ປໂຍດ ຂຍາຍ ຂນາດ ຂເມນ

12.7 ຖນອນ ຖແລງ ຖວິນ ຜຍາ

12.8 ຖນົນ ຜແຍກ ຜລິດ ສງວນ

12.9 ສຍາມ ສນາມ ສລາດ ສມານ

12.10 ສງົບ ສນັກ ສຣະ ສມັຍ

12.11 ຄົມນາ ພົມວິຫານ ກາຍບໍຣິຫານ

12.12 ສິລປະການ ກຸລວົນ ຈຸລພົນ

12.13 ພົລເມືອງ ກະເສຕກັມ ກິຈການ

12.14 ເທສບານ ສາສນາ ປະຖົມເທສນາ

12.15 ພິພິທພັນ ວັຈນານຸກົມ ວິທຍຸ

12.16 ວັທນາ ອຸປກອນ ສັປດາ

12.17	ນ້ຳທາ	ຜົ້ງສາລີ	ຫ້ວຍຊາຍ
12.18	ໄຊຍະບຸຣີ	ຫຼວງພຣະບາງ	ຊຳເໜືອ
12.19	ວຽງຈັນ	ຊຽງຂວາງ	ປາກຊັນ
12.20	ບໍຣິຄັນ	ຄຳມ່ວນ	ທ່າແຂກ
12.21	ສວັນນະເຂດ	ຄົງເຊໂດນ	ສາຣະວັນ
12.22	ປາກເຊ	ຈຳປາສັກ	ອັຕປື
12.23	ໂຂງ	ແມ່ນ້ຳຂອງ	ນ້ຳອູ
12.24	ນ້ຳງື່ມ	ນ້ຳກະດິງ	ເຊບັ້ງໄຟ
12.25	ເຊບັ້ງຫຽງ	ເຊໂດນ	ຕລາດເຊົ້າ
12.26	ຕລາດແລງ	ຖນົນລ້ານຊ້າງ	ຖນົນສາມແສນໄທ
12.27	ຖນົນເຊດຖາທິຣາດ	ຫາດຫຼວງ	ວັດອິນແປງ
12.28	ຫາດຂາວ	ຈີ່ນາຍໂມ້	ທ່າເດື່ອ
12.29	ວັດອົງຕື້	ອະນຸສາວະຣີ	ສນາມກິລາ
12.30	ເດີ່ນບິນ	ສີໄຄ	ວັດໄຕ
12.31	ສີຖານ	ປາກປາສັກ	ສີຫອມ
12.32	ເຈົ້າອານຸ	ສາຍລົມ	ນາໄຮ່ດຽວ
12.33	ສີເມືອງ	ໂພນໄຊ	ໜອງບອນ

Phonetic Equivalents to the Exercises in PART 3

Lesson 1

1.1	a^{1}	i^{1}	ae^{1}	e^{1}	
1.2	oh^{1}	o^{1}	u^{1}	eu^{1}	
1.3	er^{1}	eu^{1}	u^{1}	o^{1}	
1.4	i^{1}	a^{1}	i^{1}	e^{1}	u^{1}
1.5	o^{1}	ae^{1}	eu^{1}	er^{1}	oh^{1}
1.6	e^{1}	a^{1}	er^{1}	ae^{1}	i^{1}
1.7	u^{1}	oh^{1}	eu^{1}	o^{1}	e^{1}

Lesson 2

2.1	ba^{1}	bpa^{1}	da^{1}	dta^{1}
2.2	bi^{1}	bpi^{1}	de^{1}	dte^{1}
2.3	be^{1}	bpe^{1}	dtu^{1}	du^{1}
2.4	bo^{1}	bpo^{1}	doh^{1}	dtoh^{1}
2.5	ber^{1}	bper^{1}		
2.6	boh^{1}	boh^{2}	da^{1}	da^{2}
2.7	bpu^{1}	bpu^{2}	gae^{1}	gae^{2}
2.8	ya^{1}	ya^{2}	cheu^{1}	cheu^{2}
2.9	dtoh^{1}	dtoh^{2}	go^{1}	go^{2}
2.10	a^{1}	da^{1}	bpa^{1}	
2.11	dti^{1}	chi^{1}	gi^{1}	
2.12	be^{1}	bpe^{1}	de^{1}	
2.13	beu^{1}	keu^{1}	cheu^{1}	
2.14	bpu^{1}	dtu^{1}	u^{1}	
2.15	chae^{1}	dae^{1}	gae^{1}	
2.16	er^{1}	ber^{1}	dter^{1}	
2.17	bpo^{1}	do^{1}	go^{1}	
2.18	yoh^{1}	boh^{1}	choh^{1}	

Lesson 3

3.1	a:^{3}	a^{1}	bi^{1}	bi:^{3}		
3.2	dte:^{3}	dte^{1}	gae^{1}	gae:^{3}		
3.3	dtoh:^{3}	dtoh^{1}	bpu^{1}	bpu:^{3}		
3.4	ger:^{3}	ger^{1}				
3.5	chi^{1}	chi^{2}	chi^{3}	dta^{1}	dta^{2}	dta:^{3}
3.6	boh^{1}	boh^{2}	boh:^{3}	do^{1}	do^{2}	do:^{3}
3.7	u^{1}	u^{2}	u:^{3}	eu^{1}	eu^{2}	eu:^{3}
3.8	bpae^{1}	bpae^{2}	bpae:^{3}	e^{1}	e^{2}	e:^{3}
3.9	ger^{1}	ger^{2}	ger:^{3}			
3.10	a:^{3}	bi:^{3}	be:^{3}	bpae:^{3}	du:^{3}	
3.11	eu:^{3}	do:^{3}	dtoh:^{3}	ger:^{3}	cha:^{3}	
3.12	yo:^{3}	yu:^{3}	da:^{3}	dti:^{3}	cher:^{3}	
3.13	oh:^{3}	dte:^{3}	ga:^{3}	chu:^{3}	dteu:^{3}	

Lesson 4

4.1	dtang^1	dtan^1	dan^1	dam^1		
4.2	gang^1	gan^1	chan^1	cham^1		
4.3	yang^1	yan^1	bpan^1	bpam^1		
4.4	bang^1	ba:n^1	chang^1	cha:n^1		
4.5	an^1	a:n^1	gan^1	ga:n^1		
4.6	dtam^1	dta:m^1	cham^1	cha:m^1		
4.7	ong^1	aen^1	ohm^1	eu:ng^1	i:n^1	o:m^1
4.8	ang^2	en^2	ohm^2	o:ng^2	u:n^2	a:m^2
4.9	bang^1	ban^1	bom^1	be:ng^1	bi:n^1	ba:m^1
4.10	baeng^2	bohn^2	bem^2	bo:ng^2	bi:n^2	ba:m^2
4.11	bpohng^1	bpan^1	bpom^1	bpu:ng^1	bpe:n^1	bpo:m^1
4.12	bpeng^2	bpern^2	bpam^2	bpo:ng^2	bpi:n^2	bpu:m^2
4.13	daeng^1	dern^1	dohm^1	deu:ng^1	do:n^1	da:m^1
4.14	dang^2	dern^2	dam^2	do:ng^2	da:n^2	deu:m^2
4.15	dtohng^1	dtohn^1	dtam^1	dte:ng^1	dti:n^1	dta:m^1
4.16	dtang^2	dteun^2	dtohm^2	dta:ng^2	dtu:n^2	dta:m^2
4.17	gohng^1	gen^1	gaem^1	gu:ng^1	ga:n^1	geu:m^1
4.18	gaeng^2	gohn^2	gom^2	ga:ng^2	gi:n^2	ga:m^2
4.19	yong^1	yeun^1	yeum^1	ya:ng^1	ya:n^1	ya:m^1
4.20	yang^2	yohn^2	yeum^2	ya:ng^2	ya:n^2	ya:m^2
4.21	cher:ng^1	chin^1	chohm^1	che:ng^1	chu:n^1	cha:m^1
4.22	chaeng^2	chern^2	cham^2	cheu:ng^2	cho:n^2	cha:m^2

Lesson 5

5.1	bpia^1	bpia:^{3}	deua^1	deua:^{3}	
5.2	dtua^1	dtua:^{3}			
5.3	beua^1	beua^2	chua^1	chua^2	
5.4	ian^1	ian^2	giang^1	giang^2	
5.5	ian^1	biang^2	bpia^1	diam^1	
5.6	dtian^1	giang^2	chia^2	chiam^1	
5.7	ua^2	bua^2	bpuang^1	duan^2	
5.8	dtuang^1	guan^1	yuang^2	chua^1	
5.9	euan^1	beua^2	bpeuang^1	deuan^1	
5.10	geua^1	cheuang^2	geuan^2	euam^1	
5.11	bia^1	bpia^1	dia^1	chia^1	chia^2
5.12	ua^2	dtua^1	chua^2	bua^1	bpua^1
5.13	geua^1	deua^2	cheua^1	beua^1	beua^2

Lesson 6

6.1	ao^{1}	ao^{2}	ery^{1}	ery^{2}		
6.2	aeo^{1}	aeo^{2}	uay^{1}	uay^{2}		
6.3	bpai^{1}	bpai^{2}	bpeuay^{1}	bpeuay^{2}		
6.4	diaw^{1}	diaw^{2}	dtiw^{1}	dtiw^{2}		
6.5	bai:^{1}	bai:^{2}	dtao:^{1}	dtao:^{2}		
6.6	gai:^{1}	gai:^{2}				
6.7	dtai^{1}	dtai:^{1}	bpai^{2}	bpai:^{2}		
6.8	bai^{1}	bai:^{1}	bai^{2}	bai:^{2}		
6.9	bpao^{1}	bpao:^{1}	bpao^{2}	bpao:^{2}		
6.10	dtao^{1}	dtao:^{1}	dtao^{2}	dtao:^{2}		
6.11	bai^{1}	doy^{1}	ohy^{1}	dtui^{1}	chuay^{1}	deuay^{1}
6.12	ui^{1}	gui^{1}	bai:^{1}	bpai:^{1}	dtai:^{1}	gai:^{1}
6.13	dao^{1}	aew^{1}	giw^{1}	diaw^{1}	yiaw^{1}	chaew^{1}
6.14	piw:^{1}	ao:^{1}	bao:^{1}	yao:^{1}	dtao:^{1}	gao:^{1}

Lesson 7

7.1	fa^{3}	fa:^{2}	wi^{3}	wi:^{2}	
7.2	ngae^{3}	ngae:^{2}	weu^{3}	weu:^{2}	
7.3	mu^{3}	mu:^{2}	nyo^{3}	nyo:^{2}	
7.4	soh^{3}	soh:^{2}	nyia^{3}	nyia:^{2}	
7.5	lua^{3}	lua:^{2}	ser^{3}	ser:^{2}	
7.6	fohn^{3}	fohn^{2}	fa:ng^{3}	fa:ng^{2}	
7.7	waen^{3}	waen^{2}	wa:ng^{3}	wa:ng^{2}	
7.8	mang^{3}	mang^{2}	nyan^{3}	nyan^{2}	
7.9	ngam^{3}	ngam^{2}	ngeu:m^{3}	ngeu:m^{2}	
7.10	haeng^{3}	haeng^{2}	hohm^{3}	hoh:m^{2}	
7.11	laeng^{3}	laeng^{2}	li:n^{3}	li:n^{2}	
7.12	seu:m^{3}	seu:m^{2}	soh:ng^{3}	soh:ng^{2}	
7.13	fai:^{3}	wiang^{3}	muan^{2}	mao:^{3}	maeo^{3}
7.14	nai:^{3}	nai^{3}	neuang^{3}	nyuan^{3}	nyui^{3}
7.15	nyao^{3}	ngai^{2}	ngai:^{2}	hian^{3}	huam^{2}
7.16	lao^{3}	li:w^{3}	sai^{3}	suai^{2}	fohi^{3}
7.17	fa^{3}	fu^{3}	feua^{3}	wi^{3}	wae^{3}
7.18	wi^{3}	ma^{3}	mi^{3}	mae^{3}	mia^{3}
7.19	meua^{3}	na^{3}	ne^{3}	no^{3}	ner^{3}
7.20	nua^{3}	nya^{3}	nyoh^{3}	nyia^{3}	nga^{3}
7.21	ngu^{3}	ngua^{3}	hae^{3}	heua^{3}	hu^{3}
7.22	la^{3}	lo^{3}	le^{3}	la^{3}	leu^{3}
7.23	lua^{3}	leua^{3}	lia^{3}	sa^{3}	se^{3}
7.24	sae^{3}	si^{3}			

Lesson 8

8.1	ha^{4}	ha:^{3}	ngae^{4}	ngae:^{3}	
8.2	so^{4}	so:^{3}	su^{4}	su:^{3}	
8.3	si^{4}	si:^{3}	heu^{4}	heu:^{3}	
8.4	fa^{3}	fa^{4}	feua^{3}	feua^{4}	
8.5	wan^{3}	wan^{4}	wi^{3}	wi^{4}	
8.6	mi^{3}	mi^{4}	nohn^{3}	nohn^{4}	
8.7	nya:ng^{3}	nya:ng^{4}	ngao:^{3}	ngao:^{4}	
8.8	hu^{3}	hu^{4}	hai:^{4}	hai:^{3}	
8.9	lao^{3}	lao^{4}	sai^{4}	sai^{3}	
8.10	sao:^{4}	sao:^{3}	sern^{4}	sern^{3}	
8.11	moh:^{2}	moh:^{3}	sae:^{3}	sae:^{2}	
8.12	wa:^{2}	wa:^{3}	sa:^{3}	sa:^{2}	
8.13	wan^{4}	wan^{2}	mai:^{4}	mai:^{2}	
8.14	noh^{4}	noh^{2}	niang^{4}	niang^{2}	
8.15	ngu:m^{4}	ngu:m^{2}	ha^{4}	ha^{2}	
8.16	hoh^{4}	hoh^{2}	hao:^{4}	hao:^{2}	
8.17	la:ng^{4}	la:ng^{2}	loh^{4}	loh^{2}	
8.18	sai:^{4}	sai:^{2}	sohng^{4}	sohng^{2}	
8.19	siw^{4}	siw^{2}	sao:^{4}	sao:^{2}	
8.20	fa^{4}	wi^{4}	mu^{4}	nae^{4}	haeng^{4}
8.21	ngi^{4}	heu^{4}	loh^{4}	se:ng^{4}	soh^{4}
8.22	fer^{4}	na^{4}	neua^{4}	hoh^{4}	leua^{4}
8.23	sa^{4}	si^{4}	la^{4}	ni^{4}	hua^{4}

Lesson 9

9.1	ka^{3}	ka^{4}	kiang^{3}	kiang^{4}	kai:^{3}	kai:^{4}
9.2	kua^{3}	kua^{4}	ki:^{2}	ki:^{3}	koh:^{2}	koh:^{3}
9.3	tu^{3}	tu^{4}	tohng^{3}	tohng^{4}	tai:^{3}	tai:^{4}
9.4	tam^{3}	tam^{4}	tao:^{3}	tao:^{4}	ta:^{2}	ta:^{3}
9.5	pi^{3}	pi^{4}	po:m^{3}	po:m^{4}	pai:^{3}	pai:^{4}
9.6	paeng^{3}	paeng^{4}	pu:^{2}	pu:^{3}	pua^{3}	pua^{4}
9.7	gae^{1}	kae^{3}	goh^{1}	koh^{3}	giaw^{1}	kiaw^{3}
9.8	go:^{1}	ko:^{2}	gohn^{2}	kohn^{2}	gai:^{2}	kai:^{2}
9.9	dta^{1}	ta^{3}	dtai:^{1}	tai:^{3}	dtai^{1}	tai^{3}
9.10	dter:^{1}	ter:^{2}	dti^{2}	ti^{2}	dtiaw^{2}	tiaw^{2}
9.11	bpu^{1}	pu^{3}	bpai:^{1}	pai:^{3}	bpai^{1}	pai^{3}
9.12	bpa:^{3}	pha:^{2}	bpae^{2}	pae^{2}	bpuang^{2}	puang^{2}
9.13	keu:^{2}	ku:^{2}	ko:^{2}	go:^{3}	ki:^{2}	gi:^{3}
9.14	ga:t^{3}	gu:k^{3}	go:t^{3}	gi:t^{3}	ka:k^{3}	ka:t^{3}
9.15	ku:k^{3}	ka:t^{2}	ka:k^{2}	ki:t^{2}	keu:k^{2}	ko:t^{2}

Lesson 10

10.1	kang^{5}	kang^{6}	sang^{5}	sang^{6}	
10.2	tohn^{5}	tohn^{6}	mo:n^{5}	mo:n^{6}	
10.3	terng^{5}	terng^{6}	sohm^{5}	sohm^{6}	
10.4	kam^{5}	kam^{6}	leuang^{5}	leuang^{6}	
10.5	kuan^{5}	kuan^{6}	nyu:m^{5}	nyu:m^{6}	
10.6	a^{5}	ae^{5}	eu^{5}	eua^{5}	eu^{5}
10.7	be^{5}	boh^{5}	bia^{5}	bpu^{5}	bpo^{5}
10.8	di^{5}	dua^{5}	dtae^{5}	dtia^{5}	ga^{5}
10.9	ger^{5}	yo^{5}	yeu^{5}	cho^{5}	chia^{5}
10.10	ka^{5}	koh^{5}	ta^{5}	tae^{5}	pa^{5}
10.11	pae^{5}	poh^{5}	fa^{5}	wae^{5}	woh^{5}
10.12	meu^{5}	moh^{5}	na^{5}	nae^{5}	nyoh^{5}
10.13	nyu^{5}	nga^{5}	ngua^{5}	hu^{5}	heua^{5}
10.14	la^{5}	loh^{5}	si^{5}	ser^{5}	seu^{5}
10.15	koh^{6}	ki^{6}	ta^{6}	pa^{6}	pu^{6}
10.16	fa^{6}	wa^{6}	la^{6}	seua^{6}	hoh^{6}
10.17	na^{6}	ha^{6}	hiw^{6}	soh^{6}	na^{6}
10.18	heua^{6}	nyoh^{6}	nye^{6}	kae^{6}	sa^{6}
10.19	tao^{5}	kohy^{6}	sao:^{6}	dtai:^{5}	chao:^{5}
10.20	wao:^{5}	kai:^{6}	mao:^{6}	dtai^{5}	hai:^{6}
10.21	sai:^{5}	euay^{5}	pao^{5}	mai^{5}	nyaw^{5}
10.22	gai:^{5}	yao^{5}	tai^{5}	tuay^{6}	dao:^{5}
10.23	ngaew^{5}	luay^{6}	bpiaw^{5}	fao^{5}	kaew^{6}

Lesson 11

11.1	kohp^{5}	kohp^{6}	tat^{5}	tat^{6}
11.2	paet^{5}	paet^{6}	fak^{5}	fak^{6}
11.3	wok^{5}	wok^{6}	mohp^{5}	mohp^{6}
11.4	nat^{5}	nat^{6}	nyap^{5}	nyap^{6}
11.5	ngok^{5}	ngok^{6}	hip^{5}	hip^{6}
11.6	lup^{5}	lup^{6}	saep^{5}	saep^{6}
11.7	sap^{5}	sap^{6}	lap^{5}	lap^{6}
11.8	ki:t^{2}	ki:t^{3}	ka:p^{2}	ka:p^{3}
11.9	teu:k^{2}	teu:k^{3}	pi:t^{2}	pi:t^{3}
11.10	fo:t^{2}	fo:t^{3}	wa:t^{2}	wa:t^{3}
11.11	ma:t^{2}	ma:t^{3}	mo:t^{2}	mo:t^{3}
11.12	na:k^{2}	na:k^{3}	yu:t^{2}	yu:t^{3}
11.13	ngu:p^{2}	ngu:p^{3}	ho:k^{2}	ho:k^{3}
11.14	he:t^{2}	he:t^{3}	le:k^{2}	le:k^{3}
11.15	sa:k^{2}	sa:k^{3}	si:t^{2}	si:t^{3}

11.16 at^{6} ak^{6} ap^{6} baet^{6} baek^{6} baep^{6}

11.17 sert^{6} serk^{6} serp^{6} sat^{6} sak^{6} sap^{6}

11.18 hat^{5} hak^{5} hap^{5} ngot^{5} ngok^{5} ngop^{5}

11.19 ga:t^{3} ga:k^{3} ga:p^{3} ka:t^{3} ka:k^{3} ka:p^{3}

11.20 ka:t^{2} ka:k^{2} ka:p^{2}

11.21 ik^{6} ohk^{6} ap^{6} bohk^{6} baep^{6} bpak^{6}

11.22 bpaet^{6} dohk^{6} daet^{6} dtak^{6} dtohp^{6} geuk^{6}

11.23 gohk^{6} gert^{6} gip^{6} yak^{6} yoht^{6} chohk^{6}

11.24 chak^{6} choht^{6} bpot^{6} dut^{6} et^{6} bat^{6}

11.25 a:t^{3} o:t^{3} baik^{3} bo:t^{3} bpu:k^{3} bpe:t^{3}

11.26 de:k^{3} di:p^{3} dteu:k^{3} dta:t^{5} dto:k^{3} go:k^{3}

11.27 ga:p^{3} yu:t^{3} cha:t^{3} che:t^{3} che:p^{3} cho:p^{3}

11.28 ga^{3} gi^{3} gu^{3} ka^{3} ku^{3} ka^{2}

11.29 keu:^{2} ku:^{2} ko:^{2} go:^{3} ki:^{2} gi:^{3}

11.30 ga:t^{3} gu:k^{3} go:t^{3} gi:t^{3} ka:k^{3} ka:t^{3}

11.31 ku:k^{3} ka:t^{2} ka:k^{2} ki:t^{2} keu:k^{2} ko:t^{2}

Lesson 12

12.1 wai^{2} wan^{1} gwa^{1} gwang^{1} chwat^{6}

12.2 kwa^{5} kwam^{3} kwa:n^{3} kwai:^{3} kwaek^{5}

12.3 twai^{3} ngwak^{5} hwai^{3} hwai^{5} lwa^{3}

12.4 swan^{2} swang^{3} kwa^{4} kwa:n^{6} kwai:^{4}

12.5 twai^{4} swang^{2} swai^{4}

12.6 bpa:^{3} nyoht^{6} ka:^{3} nyai^{4} ka:^{3} nat^{6} ka:^{3} men^{4}

12.7 ta:^{3} nohm^{4} ta:^{3} laeng^{4} ta:^{3} wi:n^{4} pa:^{3} nya^{4}

12.8 ta:^{3} no:n^{4} pa:^{3} nyaek^{6} pa:^{3} li:t^{3} sa:^{3} nguan^{4}

12.9 sa:^{3} nyam^{4} sa:^{3} nam^{4} sa:^{3} lat^{6} sa:^{3} man^{4}

12.10 sa:^{3} ngo:p^{3} sa:^{3} na:k^{3} sa:^{3} la:^{3} sa:^{3} mai^{4}

12.11 ko:m^{3} ma:^{2} na^{3} po:m^{3} ma:^{2} wi:^{2} han^{4} gai^{1}nya:^{2} boh^{1} li:^{2} han^{4}

12.12 si:n^{4} la:^{2} pa^{3} gan^{1} gu:n^{1} la:^{2} so:n^{3} chu:n^{1} la:^{2} po:n^{3}

12.13 po:n^{3} la:^{2} meuang^{3} ga:^{3} set^{6} ta:^{3} ga:n^{1} gi:t^{3}cha^{3} gan^{1}

12.14 tet^{5} sa:^{3} ban^{1} sat^{6} sa:^{3} na^{3} bpa^{3} to:m^{4} tet^{6} sa:^{3} na^{3}

12.15 pi:^{2} pi:t^{2} ta:^{2} pa:n^{3} wa:t^{2} cha^{3} nai^{3} nu:^{2} go:m^{3} wi:t^{2} ta^{2} nyu^{2}

12.16 wa:t^{2} ta:^{2} na^{3} u:p^{3} bpa:^{3} kohn^{1} sa:p^{3} bpa:^{3} da^{1}

12.17 na:m^{5} ta^{3} po:ng^{6} sa^{4} li^{3} huay^{6} sai^{3}

12.18 sai:^{3} nya:^{2} bu:^{3} li^{3} luang^{4} pa:^{2} bang^{1} sa:m^{3} neua^{4}

12.19 wiang^{3} cha:n^{1} siang^{3} kwang^{4} bpak^{6} sa:n^{3}

12.20 boh^{1} li:^{2} ka:n^{3} ka:m^{3} muan^{2} ta^{2} kaek^{6}

12.21 sa:^{3} wa:n^{3} na:^{2} ket^{6} ko:ng^{3} se^{3} don^{1} sa^{4} la:^{2} wa:n^{3}

12.22 bpak^{6} se^{3} cha:m^{1} bpa^{1} sa:k^{3} a:t^{3} dta:^{3} bpeu^{1}

12.23	kong4	mae2 na:m5 kohng4	na:m5 u1
12.24	na:m5 ngeu:m2	na:m5 ga:3 di:ng1	se3 bang5 fai:3
12.25	se3 ba:ng5 hiang4	se3 don1	dta:3 lat6 sao5
12.26	dta:3 lat6 laeng3	ta:3 no:n4 lan5 sang5	ta:3 no:n4 sam4 saen4 tai:
12.27	ta:3 no:n4 set5 ta4 ti:2 lat5	tat5 luang4	wa:t2 i:n1 bpaeng1
12.28	tat5 kao4	chi2 nai3 mo5	ta2 deua2
12.29	wa:t2 o:ng1 dteu5	a:3 nu:2 sa4wa:2 li3	sa:3 nam4 gi1 la3
12.30	deun2 nyo:n3	si4 kai:3	wa:t2 dtai:1
12.31	si4 tan4	bpak6 bpa1 sa:k3	si4 hom4
12.32	chao:5 a1 nu:2	sai4 lo:m3	na3 hai:2 diaw1
12.33	si4 meuang3	pon3 sai:3	nohng4 bon1

PART 4: LAO-ENGLISH GLOSSARY FOR BEGINNERS

in English alphabetical order

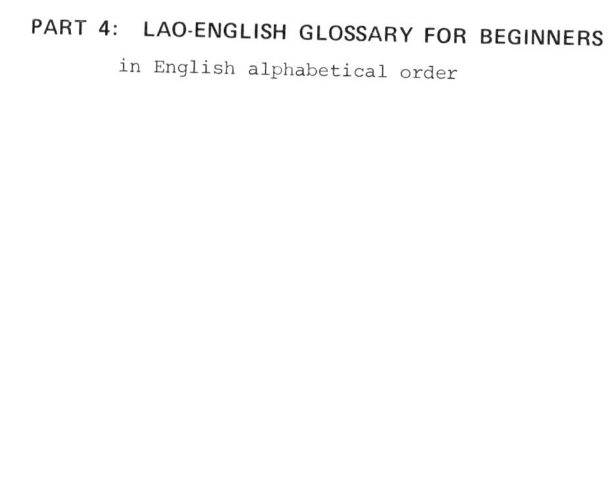

Note: For a more complete word list, please refer to the English-Lao, Lao-English Dictionary compiled by R. Marcus (Tuttle, 1970).

PART 4: LAO-ENGLISH GLOSSARY FOR BEGINNERS

in English alphabetical order

a^{1} han^{4}. Food ອາຫານ

ai:^{1} sa:^{3} ga:^{3} li:m^{3}. Ice cream (Eng.) ໄອສະກຣີມ

a:^{3} me^{3} li^{3}ga^{1}. America ອະເມຣິກາ

an^{2}. To read ອ່ານ

a:n^{1}. Thing (general classifier) ອັນ

a:ng^{1} gi:t^{3}. Britain, English ອັງກິດ

a:^{3} nu:^{2} sawa:^{2} li^{3}. Monument ອະນຸສາວະລີ

a^{1} nyu:^{2}. Age ອາຍຸ

ao:^{1}. To take, to get ເອົາ

a^{1} ti:t^{2}. Week ອາທິດ

ay^{5}. Elder brother ອ້າຍ

baep^{6}. Manner, style, model ແບບ

bai:^{1}. Leaf, sheet, paper (classifier) ໃບ

bai:^{1}dtohng^{1}. Banana leaf ໃບຕອງ

ban^{5}. Home, house ບ້ານ

bang^{1}. Some ບາງ

bang^{1} teua^{2}. Sometime ບາງເທື່ອ

ban^{5} nohk. Country-side, rural area ບ້ານນອກ

bat^{6} na:n^{5}. Then ບາດນັ້ນ

ber^{1}. Butter (Fr.) ເບີ

ber:ng^{2}. To look at, to inspect, to examine ເບິ່ງ

beu:t^{3}. Moment ບຶດ

boh^{1}. Is that so? ບໍ

boh^{2}. ບໍ່ 1. Not, No (negative particle)
2. ? (question particle)

boh^{2} bpe:n^{1} nya:ng^{4}. Never mind, No sweat, You're welcome ບໍ່ເປັນຫຍັງ

bohn^{2}. Place ບ່ອນ

bo:t^{3} hian^{3}. Lesson ບົດຮຽນ

bpa^{1}. Fish ປາ

bpa:^{3} cha:m^{1}. Fixed, permanent ປະຈຳ

bpaet^{6}. Eight ແປດ

bpai^{1}. More than, over, after ປາຍ

bpai:^{1}. To go to ໄປ

bpai:^{1} gon^{2} der^{1}. Good-bye (person leaving) ໄປກ່ອນເດີ

bpai:^{1} hian^{3}. To go study ໄປຮຽນ

bpai:^{1} sa:^{3} ni^{3}. Post-office ໄປສະນີ

bpak^{6}. To speak ປາກ

bpa^{3}man^{3}. About ປະມານ

bpa:n^{5}. To grip ປັ້ນ

bpe:n^{1}. ເປັນ 1. To be (identify class, group, condition)
2. Can (skill, learned activity)

bpe:n^{1} nya:ng^{4}. Why? ເປັນຫຍັງ

bpe:n^{1} yang^{2} dai:^{1}. How's everything? ເປັນຢ່າງໃດ

bpeu:m^{5}. Book ປຶ້ມ

bpeu:m^{5} kian^{4}. Notebook ປຶ້ມຂຽນ

bpi^{1}. Year ປີ

bpuk^{6}. To plant ປູກ

bu:n^{1}. Festival, merit ບຸນ

bu:n^{1}tohng^{3}. Bounthong (name) ບຸນທອງ

cha:^{3}. Will ຈະ

chai:^{1}. Heart ໃຈ

cha:k^{3}. How many? ຈັກ

chak^{6}ni^{5} bpai^{1}. From here to ຈາກນີ້ໄປ

chang^{5}. To hire ຈ້າງ

chao:^{5}. You, your (common) ເຈົ້າ

chao:^{5} kohng^{4}. Owner ເຈົ້າຂອງ

chao:^{5} si^{3} wi:t^{2}. King ເຈົ້າຊີວິດ

che:t^{3}. Seven ເຈັດ

cheun^1. To fry ຈືນ

cheu:ng^2. Then so ຈິ່ງ

chin^1. China, Chinese ຈີນ

chi:t^3. Chit (boy's name) ຈິດ

choht^6. To stop, to park ຈອດ

da:m^1. Black ດຳ

dae^2. (Particle: please) ແດ່

daeng^1. Red ແດງ

dai:^{1}. Which, what? ໃດ

dai:^{5}. Since ໄດ້.....ແລ້ວ

dai^5 nyi:n^3. To hear ໄດ້ຍິນ

de^2. (particle: and ... ?) ເດ່

de:k^3 nohy^5. Baby, child ເດັກນ້ອຍ

der^5. ! (emphatic particle) ເດີ້

dern^2. Ground ເດີ່ນ

dern^{2}nyo:n^3. Airport ເດີ່ນຍົນ

dern^2 tang^3. To travel ເດີນທາງ

di^1. Good, well,(positive value) ດີ

diaw^1. One, only ດຽວ

diaw^1 ni^5. Now ດຽວນີ້

di^1 gwa^2. Better ດີກວ່າ

di:n^1 koh^4. Tiles ດິນຂໍ

di:n^1 chi^2. Bricks ດິນຈີ່

do^1 la^3. Dollar ໂດລາ

dohk^6. !(emphatic particle), flower ດອກ

do:n^1. Long time ດົນ

doy^1 (ka^{6}nohy^5). Yes, (self-humbling or respectful) ໂດຍ(ຂ້ານ້ອຍ)

dtae^2. ແຕ່ 1·(from) 2·(but) 3·(only)

dtae^2 gi^5. Before, once ແຕ່ກີ້

dtae^2 neu:ng^1. Only ແຕ່......ນຶ່ງ

dtaeng^2 ngan^3. To get married ແຕ່ງງານ

dta:k^3. To fetch, to take ຕັກ

dta:^{3} lat^6. Market ຕລາດ

dta:^{3} lat^6 sao:^{5}. Morning market ຕລາດເຊົ້າ

dtam^1. Following, according to ຕາມ

dta:m^1 luat^5. Police ຕຳຣວດ

dtam^{1}ta:m^{3}ma:^{2} da^1. Usually, generally ຕາມທັມມະດາ

dta:ng^2. Chair ຕັ່ງ

dta:ng^5. To stand, so ຕັ້ງ

dtang^2 bpa:^{3} tet^5. Abroad, foreign ຕ່າງປະເທດ

dta:ng^5 chai:^{1}. Eager ຕັ້ງໃຈ

dta:ng^5 dtae^2. From (time) ຕັ້ງແຕ່

dtang^2 kwaeng^4. In the provinces ຕ່າງແຂວງ

dteu:k^3. Building ຕຶກ

dteun^2. To wake up ຕື່ນ

dti:^{3}. (Particle: please) ຕິ

dto:^{3}. Table ໂຕະ

dtoh^2 bpai:^{1}. Next to, the following ຕໍ່ໄປ

dtohng^5. Must, have to ຕ້ອງ

dtohn^1 bai^2. In the afternoon ຕອນບ່າຍ

dtohng^5 gan^1. Necessary, to need ຕ້ອງການ

dtohn^1 laeng^3. In the evening ຕອນແລງ

dtohn^1 tiang^2. At noon ຕອນທ່ຽງ

dtohp^6. To answer ຕອບ

dtua^1. Body, animal (classifier) ຕົວ

dtua:^{3}. To lie ຕົວະ

dtua^1 na:ng^4 seu^4. Letters of the alphabet ຕົວໜັງສື

duay^5. By means of, with ດ້ວຍ

er^1. Yes(conversation agreement) ເອີ

ern^5. To call, to be named ເອີ້ນ

euay^5. Elder sister ເອື້ອຍ

eun^{2}. Other ອື່ນ

fai:^{3}. Light (bulb) ໄຟ

fa:^{3} la:ng^{2}. Foreigner, occidental, westerner ຝຣັ່ງ

fa:ng^{3}. To listen ຟັງ

ga:^{3} dan^{1}. Board ກະດານ

ga:^{3} dta:^{2}. Basket ກະຕ່າ

gaeng^{1}. Soup ແກງ

gaew^{5} Bottle (classifier) ແກ້ວ

ga:^{3} fe^{3}. Coffee (Fr.) ກະເຟ

gai:^{1}. Far ໄກ

gai:^{2}. Chicken ໄກ່

gai:^{5}. Near ໃກ້

ga:^{3} la:m^{3} bpi^{1}. Cabbage ກະລຳປີ

ga:m^{1} la:ng^{3}. To be (do)ing now, (progressive tense) ກຳລັງ

gan^{1}. Actions (noun prefix) ການ

ga:n^{1} Each other, together ກັນ

gan^{1} dtang^{2}bpa:^{3} te:t^{5} Foreign affairs ການຕ່າງປະເທດ

gan^{1} ka:ng^{3} Finance ການຄັງ

gao:^{2} Old, before ເກົ່າ

ga:p.^{3} ກັບ
1. box (classifier)
2. and, with
3. to return

ga:^{3} suang^{3} Ministry ກະຊວງ

ge:ng^{2} Well, skillfully ເກັ່ງ

gert^{6} To be born ເກີດ

giaw^{2} ga:p.^{3} About, concerning ກ່ຽວກັບ

gi^{1} lo^{3}. Kilo (kilogram or kilometer) ກິໂລ

gi:n^{1}kao:^{6} to eat, ກິນເຂົ້າ

gi:n^{1} liang^{5}. Party ກິນລ້ຽງ

goh^{1}. ກໍ
1. then
2. as well, also
3. (changes subject)

goh^{1} dai^{5}:. Can, may, okay ກໍໄດ້

goh^{1} mi^{3}. Also ກໍມີ

gohn^{2}. Before ກ່ອນ

gohn^{5}. Solids, soap cake (classifier) ກ້ອນ

gohng^{5}. Under, below ກ້ອງ

gohng^{1} ba:n^{1} sa^{3}gan^{1}. Military headquarters ກອງບັນຊາການ

goh^{2} sang^{6}. To construct ກໍ່ສ້າງ

gu:ng^{5} Shrimp ກຸ້ງ

gwa^{2}. More than (comparative) ກວ່າ

gwang^{5}. Wide ກວ້າງ

gwat^{6}. To clean ກວດ

ha^{4}. ຫາ
1. to see, meet
2. to, until
3. to look for

ha^{6}. Five ຫ້າ

haeng^{2} sat^{5}. Nation(al) ແຫ່ງຊາດ

hai^{6} ໃຫ
1. (for) in order to be
2. (to)
3. (let, allow)

ha:k^{2}. To love ຮັກ

han^{5}. Shop, store ຮ້ານ

ha:n^{6}. There ຫັ້ນ

hao:^{3}. We (common) ເຮົາ

ha:p^{2}. To receive, meet people ຮັບ

he:n^{4}. To see ເຫັນ

he:t^{2}. To make, to do ເຮັດ

he:t^{2} gan^{1}. To work (in an office) ເຮັດການ

he:t^{2} gi:n^{1}. To cook ເຮັດກິນ

he:t^{2} wiak^{5}. To work (manual labor) ເຮັດວຽກ

heuan^{3}. House ເຮືອນ

heuan^{3} kua^{3}. Kitchen ເຮືອນຄົວ

hian^{3}. To study, learn ຮຽນ

hiw^{4}. To desire ຫິວ

hiw^{4} na:m^{5} Thirsty ຫິວນ້ຳ

hoh^{2}. To wrap ຫໍ່

hohng^{6}. Room (classifier) ຫ້ອງ

hohng^{6} ap^{6} na:m^{5}. Bathroom ຫ້ອງອາບນ້ຳ

hohng^{6} gi:n^{1} kao:^{6}. Dining room ຫ້ອງກິນເຂົ້າ

hohng^{6} hian^{3}. Classroom ຫ້ອງຮຽນ

hohng^{6} ha:p^{2} kaek^{6}. Living room ຫ້ອງຮັບແຂກ

hohng^{6} nohn^{3}. Bedroom ຫ້ອງນອນ

hohy^{5}. Hundred ຮ້ອຍ

hong^{3} gan^{1}. Office ໂຮງການ

hong^{3} haem^{3}. Hotel ໂຮງແຮມ

hong^{3} hian^{3}. School ໂຮງຮຽນ

hong^{3} moh^{4}. Hospital ໂຮງໝໍ

hu^{5}(cha:k^{3}). To know (about) ຮູ້(ຈັກ)

hua^{4}. Head, round things, vegetable (classifier) ຫົວ

ik^{6}. More, again ອີກ

i:n^{1} do^{1} ne^{3} sia^{3}. Indonesia ອິນໂດເນເຊັຽ

ka:^{3} chao:^{5}. They, them, their (common) ຂະເຈົ້າ

kaek^{6}. Indian, Pakistani ແຂກ

kaem^{3}. Along ແຄມ

kai^{4}. To sell ຂາຍ

ka:m^{3}. Kham (boy's name) ຄຳ

ka:k^{2}. Clear(ly) ຄັກ

ka^{6} lat^{5} sa^{2} gan^{1}. Government official ຂ້າຣາຊການ

ka^{3} men^{4}. Kampuchea ຂະເໝນ

ka:n^{3}. ຄັນ 1. Machines, vehicles (classifier)
2. If

kang^{6}. At the side of, beside ຂ້າງ

kang^{6} la:ng^{4}. Behind ຂ້າງຫຼັງ

ka^{3} nohy^{5}. Sir, madam (respectful pronoun) ຂະນ້ອຍ

kao:^{4}. They (common) ເຂົາ

kao:^{6}. ເຂົ້າ 1. Rice
2. To enter

kao^{6} bpaeng^{5}. Powder ເຂົ້າແປ້ງ

kao:^{6} chai:^{1}. To understand ເຂົ້າໃຈ

kao:^{6} nohn^{3}. To fall asleep ເຂົ້ານອນ

ka:p^{3}. To drive (a vehicle) ຂັບ

kat^{6}. To be short of, to lose ຂາດ

kat^{6} teun. To lose money in business ຂາດທຶນ

ker:ng^{2}. Half ເຄິ່ງ

kery^{3}. Used to, have (perfect tense) ເຄີຍ

keu^{3}. ຄື 1. Like, such as
2. Alike, same, equal, similar

keuang^{2}. Motor, things ເຄື່ອງ

keuang^{2} bpuk^{6}. Plants ເຄື່ອງປູກ

keuang^{2} deu:m^{2}. Drinks ເຄື່ອງດື່ມ

keuang^{2} heuan^{3}. Appliances, utensils ເຄື່ອງເຮືອນ

keuang^{2} nu:ng^{2}. Clothes ເຄື່ອງນຸ່ງ

keu^{3} ga:n^{1}. The same, too, also ຄືກັນ

keun^{6}. To get on, to board, to rise ຂຶ້ນ

keu^{3} si:^{2}. To guess, to seem ຄືຊິ

ki^{6}. Bad, (negative value) ຂີ້

kian^{4}. To write ຂຽນ

ki:t^{2}. To think ຄິດ

koh^{4}. Beg ຂໍ

kohng^{4}. Of (possessive), thing ຂອງ

kohng^{4} gi:n^{1}. Food ຂອງກິນ

kohng^{4} wan^{4}. Dessert ຂອງຫວານ

kohp^{6} chai:^{1}. Thank you ຂອບໃຈ

kohp^{5} kua^{3}. Family ຄອບຄົວ

kohy^{6}. I, me, my (common) ຂ້ອຍ

ko:n^{3}. People (race) ຄົນ

ko:n^{3} sai:^{5}. Maid ຄົນໃຊ້

kwa^{4}. Right (direction) ຂວາ

kwam^{3}. Word, concepts (noun prefix) ຄວາມ

la:^{2}. !(emphatic particle) ຫຼະ

la:^{2}. For, per ລະ

lae:^{2}. And ແລະ

laew^{5}. Already, did (past tense) ແລ້ວ

la^{3} gohn^{2}. Good-bye (person staying) ລາກ່ອນ

lai:^{2}. To total, to list ໄລ່

lai^{4}. Very ຫຼາຍ

lai^{3} gan^{1}. List, program ລາຍການ

lai^{3} gan^{1} a^{1} han^{4}. Menu ລາຍການອາຫານ

la^{3} ka^{3}. Price ຣາຄາ

lan^{5}. Million ລ້ານ

lang^{5}. To wash (objects) ລ້າງ

la:ng^{4}. Building, house (classifier) ຫຼັງ

la:ng^{4} chak^{6}. After ຫຼັງຈາກ

la:ng^{4} ka^{3}. Roof ຫຼັງຄາ

lang^{3} tua^{2}. Sometimes ລາງເທື່ອ

lao^{3}. Lao, he, she (common) ລາວ

lao:^{6}. Liquor ເຫຼົ້າ

lao:^{6} waeng^{3}. Wine (Fr.) ເຫຼົ້າແວງ

le:k^{2} le:k^{2} nohy^{5} nohy^{5}. Small (objects) ເລັກໆ ນ້ອຍໆ

leu^{2}. Or ຫຼື

leuang^{2}. Story, subject ເຣື່ອງ

leuay^{5} leuay^{5}. Always, often ເລື້ອຍໆ

leum^{3}. To forget ລືມ

liaw^{5}. To turn ລ້ຽວ

lin^{6}. To play ຫຼິ້ນ

lo^{3} dti^{1}. Roast (Fr.) ໂລຕິ

loh:t^{6}. Tube (classifier) ຫຼອດ

lo:m^{3}. Wind ລົມ

lo:ng^{3}. Down, to get down, alight ລົງ

lo:t^{2}. Car ຣົດ

lo:t^{2} doy^{1} san^{4}. Taxi, bus ຣົດໂດຍສານ

lu:k^{2}. To wake up, get up ລຸກ

luk^{5}. Child ລູກ

luk^{5} si:t^{3}. Student ລູກສິດ

lu:t^{3}. To discount, to lower ຫຼຸດ

luang^{4} pa:^{2} bang^{1}. Luang Prabang (City name) ຫຼວງພຣະບາງ

ma^{3}. To come (action towards speaker) ມາ

ma^{3} dam^{1}. Mrs., Madame, ma'am ມາດາມ

mae^{2}. Mother ແມ່

mae^{2} heuan^{3}. Housewife ແມ່ເຮືອນ

mae^{2} ka^{5}. Sales woman ແມ່ຄ້າ

maen^{2}. To be (equivalence) ແມ່ນ

maen^{2} boh^{2}. Right? ແມ່ນບໍ່

maen^{2} laew^{5}. Right ແມ່ນແລ້ວ

ma:^{2} ho^{4} so:t^{3}. Mahosot (hospital name) ມະໂຫສົດ

mai:^{2}. New, again ໃໝ່

ma:k^{2}. To like, do often ມັກ

mak^{6} giang^{5}. Oranges ໝາກກ້ຽງ

mak^{6} guay^{5}. Banana ໝາກກ້ວຍ

mak^{6} hu:ng^{2}. Papaya ໝາກຫຸ່ງ

mak^{6} le:n^{2}. Tomato ໝາກເລັ່ນ

mak^{6} mai:^{5}. Fruit ໝາກໄມ້

mak^{6} na:t^{2}. Pineapple ໝາກນັດ

mak^{6} sa^{4} li^{3}. Corn ໝາກສາລີ

mak^{6} taeng^{1}. Cucumber, melon ໝາກແຕງ

ma:n^{6}. Solid, strong ໝັ້ນ

ma:t^{2}. Bundles (classifier) ມັດ

meu^{5}. Day ມື້

meua^{2} dai:^{1} ເມື່ອໃດ. 1. When? 2. Whenever

meuang^{3}. Country, city, town ເມືອງ

meuang^{3} lao^{3}. Laos ເມືອງລາວ

meu^{5} eun^{2}. Tomorrow ມື້ອື່ນ

meu^{5} ni^{5}. Today ມື້ນີ້

meu^{5} wan^{3} ni^{5}. Yesterday ມື້ວານນີ້

mi^{3}. To have ມີ

mia^{3}. Wife ເມັຍ

mi:n^{3} la^{3}. Miller (a surname) ມິນລາ

mong^{3}. O'clock, watch, clock ໂມງ

mo:t^{3} tu:k^{2}. Every ໝົດທຸກ

mu^{2}. Friend ໝູ່

mu^{4}. Pig ໝູ

mu:ng^{3}. To roof ມຸງ

na^{3}. Rice-field ນາ

na6. ໜ້າ 1. Face
2. Next

naew3. Kind, sort ແນວ

nai:3. In ໃນ

nai3. Boss ນາຍ

nai3 ku3. Teacher ນາຍຄູ

nai:3 meuang3. Downtown ໃນເມືອງ

na:k.2 Professional ນັກ

na:m3. With ນຳ

na:m5. Water, river ນ້ຳ

na:m3 ga:n1. Together ນຳກັນ

na:m5 kohng4. Mekong River ນ້ຳຂອງ

na:m5 o:p.3 Perfume ນ້ຳອົບ

na:m5 pu:2. Fountain ນ້ຳພຸ

na:m5 sa3. Tea ນ້ຳຊາ

na:n5. That, there ນັ້ນ

nang3. Mrs., Miss ນາງ

na:ng2 (lo:ng3). To sit (down) ນັ່ງ(ລົງ)

na:ng4. Skin ໜັງ

na:ng4 seu4. Letter, writing ໜັງສື

na3 ti3. Minute ນາທີ

neung6. To steam ໜຶ້ງ

neu:ng2. One ນຶ່ງ

ni5. This, here ນີ້

ngai2. Easy ງ່າຍ

ngam3. Beautiful, pretty ງາມ

nger:n3. Money ເງິນ

noh3. Right? ນໍ

nohk5. Outside ນອກ

nohn3 . To sleep ນອນ

nohng4 bohn1. Nong Bone (place name) ໜອງບອນ

nohng5 sai3. Younger brother ນ້ອງຊາຍ

nohng5 sao4. Younger sister ນ້ອງສາວ

nohy5. Small ນ້ອຍ

nohy5 neu:ng2. A bit, a little ໜ້ອຍນຶ່ງ

nuay2. Fruits, small round objects (classifier) ໜ່ວຍ

nyai2. Big, large ໃຫຍ່

nyak5. Difficult ຍາກ

nya:ng3. Still, not yet ຍັງ

nya:ng4. What? ຫຍັງ

nyi:n3 di1. Glad to know you, you're welcome ຍິນດີ

nyi2bpu:n2. Japan ຍີ່ປຸ່ນ

nyo3 ta1. Public works ໂຍທາ

o2. Oh! ໂອ່

ohk6. Out, to get out ອອກ

ohm5. Around ອ້ອມ

oh:ng1 dteu5. Ongtu.(Temple name) ອົງຕື້

pa3. To guide to take ພາ

paeng3. Expensive ແພງ

pa:k3 bua2. Onion ຜັກບົ່ວ

pa:k2 pohn2. To rest, to stay ພັກຜ່ອນ

pa:k3 sa:3 la:t2 Lettuce ຜັກສລັດ

pa:k3 tiam3. Garlic ຫົວຜັກທຽມ

pa:2 lat5 sa:2 wa:ng3. Royal Palace ພຣະຣາຊວັງ

pa:n3. Thousand ພັນ

pa:n3 la:2 nya3 Wife ພັນລະຍາ

pa3 sa4. Language ພາສາ

per:n2. He, she, they (formal) ເພິ່ນ

peua2. In order to, to, for ເພື່ອ

piang3 dtae2. Only ພຽງແຕ່

pi2 nohng5. Relative(s) ພີ່ນ້ອງ

pi:t3. Error, mistake ຜິດ

pi:2 ti3. Ceremonies ພິທີ

poh2. Father ພໍ່

poh:2. Because ເພາະ

po:p2. To meet ພົບ

puak^{5}. (plural prefix) ພວກ

puak^{5} kohy^{6}. We, our (common) ພວກຂ້ອຍ

pu^{6}. Person ຜູ້

pua^{4}. Husband ຜົວ

pu^{6} dai:^{1} pu^{6} neu:ng^{2}. Someone ຜູ້ໃດຜູ້ນຶ່ງ

pi^{6} diaw^{1}. Along, single ຜູ້ດຽວ

sa:^{2}. To wash (hair) ຊະ

sa:^{3} bai^{4} di^{1} . Hello, How are you, fine Good morning (or afternoon or evening) ສບາຍດີ

sa:^{3} bu^{1}. Soap ສະບູ

sa:^{3} dte:k^{3}. Steak (Fr.) ສະເຕັກ

sa:^{3} gohn^{2}. First(ly), before ສະກ່ອນ

sai^{5}. Left (direction) ຊ້າຍ

sai:^{4}. Where? ໃສ

sai:^{2}. In, into, to put on ໃສ່

sa:k^{2}. To wash (clothes) ຊັກ

saeng^{4}. Seng (boy's name) ແສງ

saep^{5}. Tasty, delicious ແຊບ

sa:^{3} la:t^{2} (pa:k^{3}). Salad (Fr.) ສລັດ(ຜັກ)

sam^{4}. Three ສາມ

sa^{4} mi^{3}. Husband ສາມີ

sa:m^{4} ka:n^{3}. Important ສຳຄັນ

sa:m^{4} la:p^{2}. For ສຳລັບ

sam^{4} loh^{5}. (Samloh) pedicab ສາມລໍ້

sam^{4} saen^{4} tai:^{3}. Samsenthai (ancient Lao King) ສາມແສນໄທ

sam^{4} si:p^{3}. Thirty ສາມສິບ

sa:n^{5}. Floor, stage ຊັ້ນ

sang^{5} Elephant ຊ້າງ

sang^{2} Craftsman ຊ່າງ

sa:n^{5} teu:ng^{2} Upstairs ຊັ້ນເທິງ

sa:n^{5} lu:m^{2}. Downstairs ຊັ້ນລຸ່ມ

sao^{3}. Twenty ຊາວ

sao:^{2} . To rent, to let ເຊົ່າ

sao:^{5}. Morning ເຊົ້າ

sa:^{3} pa^{3}. Assembly ສະພາ

sa:^{3} tan^{4} tut^{5}. Embassy ສຖານທູດ

se:n^{6}. Line road, long objects (classifier) ເສັ້ນ

sern^{3}. Please, to invite ເຊີນ

set^{6} ta^{4} ti:^{2} lat^{5}. Setthathirat (ancient Lao King) ເສດຖາທິຣາດ

seu^{2}. Name ຊື່

seu^{5}. To buy ຊື້

seu^{5} kohng^{4}. To shop ຊື້ຂອງ

seu:k^{3} sa^{4}. To study ສຶກສາ

seu^{2} seu^{2}. Only that, nothing else, straight ຊື່ໆ

si^{2}. Four ສີ່

si^{4}. Color ສີ

si:^{2}. Will ຊິ

sia^{3}. Veranda ເຊັຽ

siang^{3} kwang^{4} . Xieng Khouang (city name) ຊຽງຂວາງ

sin^{5}. Meat ຊີ້ນ

si^{3} ne^{3}(ma)^{3} Movie ຊີເນ(ມາ)

si^{2} nyaek^{5}. Crossroad ສີ່ແຍກ

si:p^{3}. Ten ສິບ

si^{4} tan^{4}. SithanNeua (Place name) ສີຖານເໜືອ

sohn^{4}. To teach ສອນ

sohng^{4}. Two ສອງ

sohy^{2}. To help ຊ່ອຍ

so:m^{6}. Sausage ສົ້ມ

so:ng^{2}. To send ສົ່ງ

suan^{4} , Garden ສວນ

suan^{2} ສ່ວນ 1. Part
2. For, as for

suan^{2} kohy. As for myself ສ່ວນຂ້ອຍ

suan^{2} lai^{4}. Mostly ສ່ວນຫຼາຍ

suay^{4}. Late ສວຍ

sung^{4}. High, tall ສູງ

ta^{6}. To wait ຖ້າ

ta^{2} deua^{2}. Thadeua (town name) ທ່າເດື່ອ